2 to 22 DAYS IN EUROPE

P9-DEA-725

THE ITINERARY PLANNER

1992 EDITION

RICK STEVES
EDITED BY GENE OPENSHAW

John Muir Publications
Santa Fe, New Mexico

Originally published as *22 Days in Europe*

JMP travel guidebooks by Rick Steves
Asia Through the Back Door (with John Gottberg)
Europe Through the Back Door
Europe 101: History, Art, and Culture for the Traveler
   (with Gene Openshaw)
Kidding Around Seattle
Mona Winks: Self-Guided Tours of Europe's Top Museums
   (with Gene Openshaw)
2 to 22 Days in Europe
2 to 22 Days in France (with Steve Smith)
2 to 22 Days in Germany, Austria, and Switzerland
2 to 22 Days in Great Britain
2 to 22 Days in Norway, Sweden, and Denmark
2 to 22 Days in Spain and Portugal

John Muir Publications, P.O. Box 613, Santa Fe, NM 87504

ISSN 1059-2946
ISBN 1-56261-030-9

Distributed to the book trade by
W. W. Norton & Company, Inc.
New York, New York

Maps: David C. Hoerlein
Typography: Copygraphics, Inc
Printer: Banta Company
Cover Photo: Rick Steves

CONTENTS

Europe

HOW TO USE THIS BOOK

This book is the tour guide in your pocket. It lets you be the boss by proposing a clear step-by-step plan for the best 22-day introduction to Europe. This guidebook helps you organize your time and offers hard opinions to give you maximum travel thrills per mile, minute, and dollar. It's for travelers who'd like the organization of a tour but the freedom of a do-it-yourself trip. You can follow it like the 22 Commandments, or use the information to create your own best itinerary.

Realistically, most travelers are interested in the predictable biggies—Rhine castles, Sistine Chapel, Eiffel Tower, and beer halls. This tour covers those, while mixing in a good dose of "back door intimacy"—forgotten Italian hill towns, mom and pop châteaux, idyllic Riviera harbors, and traffic-free Swiss Alp villages.

This *2 to 22 Days in Europe* plan is carefully shaped and balanced to avoid tourist burnout by including only the most exciting castles and intimate villages. I've been very selective. For example, there are dozens of great Italian hill towns. We'll zero in on just my favorite. The best is, of course, only my opinion. But after fifteen busy years of travel writing, lecturing, tour guiding and exploring Europe, I've developed a sixth sense of what tickles the traveler's fancy in Europe. I love this itinerary.

While the trip is designed as a car tour (3,000 miles), it also makes a great three-week train trip. Each day's journey is adapted for train travel with explanations, options, and appropriate train schedules.

22 Days in Europe originated (and is still used) as the handbook for those who join me each summer on my "Back Door Europe" Tours. And, since most large organized tours work to keep their masses ignorant while visiting many of the same places we'll cover, this book can serve as a self-defense manual for anyone taking a typical big bus tour who wants to maintain his or her independence and flexibility.

A three-week car rental (including gas and tolls split two ways) or a three-week, first-class Eurailpass costs around $500. It costs $600 to $900 to fly round-trip to Amsterdam from the U.S.A. For room, board, and sightseeing, figure about $50 a day for 22 days, totaling $1,100. This is a feasible budget if you know the tricks (which I teach in my book *Europe Through the Back Door*). Add $300 or $400 fun money, and you've got yourself a great European adventure for around $2,600. Do it!

Of course, connect-the-dots travel isn't perfect, just as color-by-numbers isn't great art. But this book is your friendly Frenchman, your German in a jam, your handbook. It's your well-thought-out and tested itinerary. I've done it—and refined it—twenty times on my own and with groups. Use it. Take advantage of it. But don't let it rule you.

The Layout

Read this book from cover to cover, then use it as a rack upon which to hang more ideas as your trip evolves. As you study and travel and plan and talk to people, you'll fill it with notes. It's your tool. The book is completely modular and adaptable to any European trip. You'll find 22 units—or days—each built with the same sections:

1. **Introductory overview** for the day.

2. **Suggested hour-by-hour schedule** for the day (using the 24-hour clock).

3. **Transportation plan** for drivers, plus an adapted plan with schedules for train travelers.

4. **Orientation**, tourist information.

5. **List of Sightseeing Highlights** (rated: ▲▲▲ Don't miss; ▲▲ Try hard to see; ▲ Worthwhile if you can make it; no pyramid—worth knowing about).

6. An easy-to-read **map** locating all recommended places.

7. **Eating** and **Sleeping:** how and where to find the best budget places, including addresses, phone numbers, prices, and my favorites.

8. **Itinerary Options** for those with more or less than the suggested time, or with particular interests. This itinerary is flexible!

There's also a cultural overview for each country. The back of the book includes the adapted 22-day train schedule, a weather chart, a calendar of local festivals, a tour telephone directory, and a complete youth hostel directory for the route. Use the Appendix.

This itinerary assumes you are a well-organized traveler who lays departure groundwork on arrival, reads a day ahead in the itinerary, uses the telephone routinely, keeps a list of things that should be taken care of, takes full advantage of the local tourist offices, and avoids problems whenever possible before they happen. If you expect to travel smart, you will. If you insist on being confused, your trip will be a mess. Do what you can to call ahead, or double-check hours and times when you arrive.

When to Go

The best months to travel are May, June, September, and October. Peak season (July and August) offers the sunniest weather, and the most exciting slate of activities—but the worst crowds. During this very crowded time, it's best to arrive early in the day or to call hotels in advance (call from one hotel to the next; your receptionist can help you). Refer to the Appendix weather chart.

Prices

I've priced things throughout this book in local currencies with rough exchange reminders at the beginning of each Eating and Sleeping section. These prices, as well as the hours, telephone numbers, and so on, are accurate as of late 1991. Things are always changing, and I have tossed timidity out the window knowing you'll understand that this book, like any guidebook, starts growing old even before it's printed. Approximate prices are given. While discounts are not listed, seniors (60 and over), students (with ISIC cards), and youths (under 18) often get substantial discounts. . . but only by asking.

Accommodations

European accommodations are a good value and, with
some know-how, easy to find. You have a wide range of
budget accommodations to choose from—youth hostels,
campgrounds, bed and breakfasts, and one- or two-star
hotels. I like places that are clean, small, central, with
firm beds, traditional, inexpensive, not in other guidebooks, and friendly. Most places listed are a good value,
having five of these seven virtues.

Hotels

Unless otherwise noted, hotel prices are for two people
in a double room with breakfast. Those listed in this
book will range from about $30 (very simple, toilet and
shower down the hall) to $100 (maximum plumbing and
more) for a double, with most clustering around $50. It's
higher in big cities and heavily touristed cities and less off
the beaten track. Three or four people can nearly always
save lots of money by requesting larger rooms. Traveling
alone can get expensive: the cost of a single room is often
only 20 percent less than a double.

It's helpful to understand each country's rating system.
For instance, the French rate their hotels from zero to
four stars, depending on the amenities offered. Trust me,
unless you require a masseuse for your poodle, you'll
never need more than the French equivalent of a one- or
two-star hotel. For anything above two stars, you're paying for things like the availability of room service, and
mini bars and TVs in your room. You'll save $10 to $20 if
you ask for a room without a shower and just use the
public shower down the hall. (Although in many cases
the rooms with the extra plumbing are larger and more
pleasant.) If you're on a tight budget, make it clear that
you don't want a bathroom. Europeans assume Americans can't live without one. A bathtub costs about $5
more than a shower. In France, double beds are cheaper
than twins. Unclassified hotels (no stars) can be great bar-
gains, though some seem to specialize in beds designed
for spineless humans (lay before you pay).

A very simple continental breakfast is almost always included. (In Europe, breakfasts, like towels and people, get smaller as you go south.) If you like juice and protein for breakfast, supply it yourself. I enjoy a box of juice in my hotel room and often supplement the skimpy breakfasts with a piece of fruit and a separately wrapped little piece of cheese. (A zip-lock baggie is handy for petite eaters to grab an extra breakfast roll and slice of cheese, when provided, for a fast and free light lunch.)

Rooms are safe. Still, zip cameras and money out of sight. More (or different) pillows and blankets are usually in the closet or available on request. Remember, in Europe, towels and linen aren't always replaced every day—drip-dry and conserve.

To reserve a hotel room from the U.S.A., write (simple English is usually fine) to the address listed and identify clearly the dates you intend to be there. (A two-night stay in August would be "2 nights, 16/8/92 to 18/8/92"— European hotel jargon uses your day of departure.) You will receive a letter back requesting one night's deposit. Send a $50 signed traveler's check or a bank draft in the local currency. More and more, travelers can reserve a room with a simple phone call, leaving a credit card number as a deposit. You can pay with your card or by cash when you arrive, and if you don't show up, you'll be billed for one night anyway. Ideally, the hotel receptionist will hold a room for you without a deposit if you promise to arrive by midafternoon and call to reconfirm two days before arrival. When you reserve or confirm through the TI (Tourist Information office) they often get a fee from you and a percentage from the hotel. Whenever possible, go direct.

You can do this tour without making long-distance hotel reservations. Even so, when you know where you'll be tomorrow night, life on the road is easier if you telephone ahead to reserve a bed. The most highly recommended hotels in this book get lots of likable and reliable 22 Days readers and will usually hold a room with a phone call until 6:00 p.m. with no deposit. They are usually accustomed to us English-speaking "monoglots."

Except in July or August, I would do this entire tour call-
ing listed places the morning of the day I plan to arrive.
Use the telephone! I've listed numbers with area codes.
See the Appendix for long-distance dialing instructions.

Bed and Breakfast

You can stay in private homes throughout Europe and
enjoy double the cultural intimacy for less cost than
hotels. You'll find them mainly in smaller towns and in
the countryside. In Germany, look for *Zimmer* signs. For
Italian *affitta camere* and French *chambre d'hôte* (CH),
ask at the local tourist office. Doubles with breakfast cost
$30 to $40. Breakfast is not always included. Ask. This is a
great way to get to know the locals. While your hosts will
rarely speak English (except in Switzerland and Holland),
they will almost always be enthusiastic and a delight to
share a home with.

Youth Hostels

For $6 to $15, you can stay at one of Europe's 2,000 youth
hostels. Remember to get a youth hostel card before you
go. Except in Bavaria, where you must be 27 years old or
under (unless you're a family with a family card traveling
with kids under 16), travelers of any age are welcome as
long as you don't mind dorm-style accommodations and
making lots of traveling friends. Cheap meals are sometimes available, and kitchen facilities are usually provided
for do-it-yourselfers. Expect crowds in the summer, snoring, and lots of youth groups giggling and making rude
noises while you try to sleep. Family rooms are sometimes available on request, but it's basically boys' dorms
and girls' dorms. Unfortunately, you usually can't check
in before 5:00 p.m. and must be out by 10:00 a.m. An
11:00 p.m. curfew is often enforced. More and more
hostels are getting their business act together, taking
credit card reservations over the phone, and leaving sign-
in forms on the door for each room available. In the
north, many hostels have a new telex reservation system

where you can reserve and pay for your next hostel from the one before. See the Appendix for a listing of the youth hostels along our route.

Camping

For $4 or $5 per person per night, you can camp your way through Europe. Camping is an international word, and you'll see signs everywhere. This tour works great for campers. In fact, almost every overnight stop has a campground within a reasonable walk or bus ride from the town center and train station. All you need is a tent and a sleeping bag and (since this book does not list campgrounds) a camping Europe guidebook or a directory of campgrounds. Europeans love to holiday camp. It's a social rather than a nature experience and a great way for traveling Americans to make local friends. Many campgrounds will have a small grocery store and washing machines, and some even come with discos and mini golf. Hot showers are better here than at many hotels. Camping is ideal for families traveling by car on a tight budget.

Eating European

Europeans, especially the Italians and the French, are masters at the art of fine living. That means eating, long and well. Two-hour lunches, three-hour dinners, and endless hours sitting in outdoor cafés are the norm. Americans eat on their way to an evening event and complain if the check is slow in coming. For Europeans, the meal is an end in itself and only rude waiters rush you.

Even those of us who liked dorm food will find that the local cafés, cuisine, and wines become a highlight of our European adventure. Trust me, this is sightseeing for your palate, and even if the rest of you is sleeping in cheap hotels, your taste buds will want an occasional first-class splurge. You can eat well without going broke. But be careful, you're just as likely to blow a small fortune on a mediocre meal as you are to dine wonderfully for $12.

Restaurants

When restaurant hunting, choose places filled with
locals, not the place with the big neon signs boasting,
"We Speak English and accept credit cards." Look for
menus posted outside; if you don't see one, move along.
Also look for set-price menus (called the *tourist menu*,
prix-fixe, or just *le menu*) that give you several choices
among several courses. Galloping gourmets, bring a
menu translator. (The *Marling Menu Master* is excellent.)
These days, tipping is included in the bill in most cafés
and restaurants. If it's not, the menu will tell you.

Picnic

So that I can afford the occasional splurge in a nice restaurant, I like to picnic. Besides the cost, picnicking is a great
way to sample local specialties. And, in the process of
assembling your meal, you get to plunge into local markets like a European.

On days you choose to picnic, gather supplies early.
You'll probably visit several small stores to assemble a
complete meal, and many close at noon. While it's fun to
visit the small specialty shops, local *supermarchés* give
you the same quality with less color, less cost, and more
efficiency.

Here's my picnic paraphernalia: a cardboard box for
my backseat pantry, plastic cups, paper towels, water bottle
(the standard, disposable, European half-liter plastic
mineral water bottle works fine), a damp cloth in a zip-
lock baggie, Swiss army knife, and a petite tablecloth. To
take care of juice once and for all, stow a rack of liter
boxes of orange juice in the trunk. (Look for "100%" on
the label or you'll get a sickly orange drink.)

Remember, picnics (especially French ones) can be an
adventure in high cuisine. Be daring, try the smelly
cheeses, midget pickles, ugly pâtés, sissy quiches, and
minuscule yogurts. Local shopkeepers are happy to sell
small quantities of produce and even slice and stuff a
sandwich for you. A typical picnic for two might be fresh
bread (half loaves on request), two tomatoes, three car-

rots, 100 grams of cheese, 100 grams of meat (100 grams = about a quarter pound, called an *etto* in Italy), two apples, a liter box of orange juice, and a yogurt. Total cost for two—$7 or $8.

When not in the picnicking mood, look for food stands selling take-out sandwiches and drinks, delis with stools or a table, a department store self-service, or simple little eateries for fast and easy, sit-down restaurant food. Many restaurants offer good value, 3- to 5-course "menus" at lunch only. The same menu often costs much more at dinner.

Border Crossings

Crossing borders in Europe is easy. Sometimes you won't even realize it's happened. When you do change countries, however, you change money, postage stamps, gas prices (Italy and France are most expensive), ways to flush a toilet, words for "hello," figurehead monarchs, and breakfast breads. Plan ahead for these changes (coins and stamps are worthless outside their home countries). I spend the last money of a country I'm leaving on gas, candy, tacky souvenirs, or a telephone call home just before crossing the border.

Language and Culture

You'll be dealing with an intensely diverse language and customs situation; work to adapt. The U.S.A. is huge but bound by a common language. Europe's cultural stew is wonderfully complex. We just assume Germany is "Germany"; but Germany is *Tyskland* to the Norwegians, *Allemagne* to the French, and *Deutschland* to the people who live there. While we think shower curtains are logical, many countries just cover the toilet paper and let the rest of the room shower with you. Europeans give their "ones" an upswing and cross their "sevens." If you don't adapt, your "seven" will be mistaken for a sloppy "one" and you'll miss your train (and perhaps be mad at the French for "refusing to speak English"). Fit in! If the beds are too short, the real problem is that you are too long.

Transportation
By Car or Train

This itinerary works both ways. The book is written directly to the driver, with notes throughout to train travelers and a carefully reworked plan in the Appendix for the most efficient 22-day train tour of Europe. Each mode of transportation has pros and cons. Cars are an expensive headache in big cities but give you more control for delving deep into the countryside. Groups of three or more go cheaper by car. If you're packing heavy (with kids), go by car. Trains are best for city-to-city travel and give you the convenience of doing long stretches overnight. By train I arrive relaxed and well-rested—not so by car.

The Eurailpass gives you several options: three weeks of unlimited first-class travel for $550, one month for $680, any 9 days out of 21 for $450, and any 14 days out of a month for $610 (overnight trips count as one day). You cannot buy one in Europe. (Get it through your travel agent, or see the special Eurail deal in my catalog in the back of the book.) This pass is probably the train traveler's best bet. Sample 1992 prices for second-class train tickets (first class is 50% more) are: Amsterdam-Frankfurt $67, Frankfurt-Munich $60, Munich-Venice $55, Venice-Rome $43, Rome-Interlaken $86, Interlaken-Paris $85, Paris-Amsterdam $57. In other words, individual second-class tickets for this 22-day trip would cost you about $100 less than three weeks of unlimited first-class travel on a Eurailpass. If you do this trip by train, study the 22-day itinerary adapted for train travelers in the Appendix (and notice how this trip can work with the cheaper 9 out of 21 days "flexipass"). My book, *Europe Through the Back Door*, has a handy and lengthy chapter on train travel skills.

Car Rental

Research car rental before you go. It's much cheaper to arrange car rentals in the United States, so check rates with your travel agent. Rent by the week with unlimited mileage. If you'll be renting for more than three weeks, ask your agent about leasing, which is a scheme to save on insurance and taxes. I normally rent the smallest, least expensive model. Explore your drop-off options (ideally, on this tour, drop it off on the way in to Paris—Colmar, Reims, Beaune, or Versailles).

Your car rental price includes minimal insurance with a very high deductible. A CDW (Collision Damage Waiver) insurance supplement covers you for this deductible. This provides great peace of mind but is a bad value when purchased from your car rental agency. But, since deductibles are horrendous, ranging from $1,000 to the entire value of the car, I usually spring for the CDW. Ask your travel agent about money-saving alternatives to this car rental agency rip-off. Unfortunately, many budget alternatives have a ceiling far below your rental company's deductible figure. The way I understand it, the roughly $10 a day you'll spend for CDW is where the car rental agency makes up for its highly competitive, unprofitably low, weekly rental rates.

Driving in Europe

All you need is your valid U.S. driver's license and a car. I've never needed an International driver's license. Gas is expensive—$2 to $4 per gallon. I use the freeways whenever possible. They are free in Holland, Germany, and Austria; you'll pay a one-time road fee of about $20 as you enter Switzerland; and the Italian *autostrada* and the French *autoroutes* are punctuated by toll booths. The alternative to these super freeways often is being marooned in rural traffic. The autobahn/-strada/-route usually saves enough time, gas, and nausea to justify its expense. Mix scenic country road rambling with high-speed autobahning, but don't forget that in Europe, the shortest distance between two points is the autobahn. You'll learn never to cruise in the passing lane. The gas and tolls for this trip, if you take all the autobahns, will cost around $400.

Parking is a headache in the larger cities. Ask for advice on safety at your hotel. You'll pay about $15 a day to park safely in big cities. You might want to keep a pile of coins in your ashtray for parking meters, public phones, wishing wells, and laundromat dryers.

Scheduling
Your overall itinerary strategy is a fun challenge. Read through this book and note the problem days when most museums are closed. (Mondays are bad in Amsterdam, Munich, Dachau, Florence, and Rome; Tuesday is bad in Paris.) Many museums and sights, especially large ones and those in Italy, stop admitting people 30 minutes to an hour before closing time.

Sundays have the same pros and cons as they do for travelers in the U.S.A. City traffic is light, and sightseeing attractions are generally open, but shops and banks are closed. Rowdy evenings are rare on Sundays. Saturdays in Europe are virtually weekdays with earlier closing hours. Hotels in tourist areas are most crowded on Fridays and Saturdays.

Plan ahead for banking, laundry, post office chores, and picnics. Mix intense and relaxed periods. Every trip needs at least a few slack days. I've built the itinerary to minimize one-night stands (only the Rhine, Italian hill towns, and Florence), which can be hectic and tiring.

To function smoothly in Europe, get comfortable with the 24-hour clock. I've used "military time" throughout this book. Everything is the same until noon. After noon, just subtract 12 and you'll get the p.m. time. (So 16:30 is 4:30 p.m.)

This itinerary is fast but feasible. It's designed for the American who puts up with the shortest vacation time in the rich world and wants to see everything . . . but doesn't want the "if it's Tuesday it must be Belgium" craziness. It can be done if all goes well, but all won't go well. A few slack days come in handy. Eurailers should streamline with overnight train rides (see adapted train itinerary in the Appendix). I've listed many more sights than any mortal tourist could possibly see in 22 days. They're rated so that you can make the difficult choices to shape your most comfortable, smooth, and rewarding trip.

Pace yourself. Assume you will return. Every traveler's touring tempo varies. Personalize this busy schedule, plug in rest days, and skip sights where and when you need to. Stretching this trip to 28 or 30 days would be luxurious. (Your boss will understand.)

Keeping Up with the News (If You Must)
To keep in touch with world and American news while traveling in Europe, read the *International Herald Tribune*, which comes out almost daily via satellite from many places in Europe. Every Tuesday, the European editions of *Time* and *Newsweek* hit the stands with articles of particular interest to European travelers.

Sports addicts can get their "fix" from *USA Today*. *The European* is trying to do for Europe what *USA Today* has done for/to the U.S.A. News in English will only be sold where there's enough demand—in big cities and tourist centers. If you are concerned about how some event might affect your safety as an American traveling abroad, call the U.S. consulate or embassy in the nearest big city for advice.

Receiving Mail in Europe
To pick up mail in Europe, reserve a few hotels along your route in advance and give their addresses to friends, or use American Express Mail Services. Most American Express offices in Europe will keep mail for one month. (Get their free listing of addresses.) This service is free to anyone using an AmExCo card or travelers checks (and available for a small fee to others). Allow 10 days for U.S. to Europe mail delivery. Federal Express makes two-day deliveries . . . for a price.

Terrorism
As those who enjoyed their European travels in 1991 can attest, media hype about terrorism has no business affecting your travel plans. Viewed emotionally, it may seem dangerous. But statistically, while terrorism is a risk, the streets of Europe are much safer than the streets of urban America (where 8,000 people are killed every year by

hand guns). Just keep the risk in perspective, and melt into Europe traveling like a temporary local. Terrorists don't bomb the kinds of hotels listed in this book—that's where they sleep.

Recommended Guidebooks

This small book is your itinerary handbook. While you could have a fine trip relying only on this book, I'd supplement it with a guidebook or two. Guidebooks are $15 tools for $2,500 trips. My favorites are the following.

General, low-budget, directory-type guidebook: *Let's Go: Europe* is ideal for low-budget student train travelers. Whether you're young or old, rich or poor, student or professor, going by car or train, it's the best directory-type guidebook for hard-core, go-local travelers. The nightlife and youth scene (which I have basically ignored) are best covered in *Let's Go*. If you like the *Let's Go* style, the individual books in that series (Italy and France) are the best anywhere. Arthur Frommer's individual country guidebooks (for Germany, France, and Italy) cater to a moderate budget. Frommer's *Europe on $40 a Day* is very good but covers only big cities. For this trip, rip out and bring along his chapters on Venice, Rome, Florence, and Paris.

Cultural and sightseeing guides: The tall, green Michelin guides (Germany, Austria, Italy, Switzerland, Paris) have nothing on room and board but lots on driving, the sights, customs, and culture. The little blue American Express Guides to Venice, Florence, Rome, and Paris are even handier.

Phrase books: Unless you speak German, Italian, and French, you'll need a phrase book. Berlitz puts out pocket guides to each of those languages, as well as a little book covering fourteen European languages more briefly (but adequately for me). Galloping gluttons enjoy Berlitz's pocket-sized 14-language *Menu Reader*. Frommer's *Fast n' Easy Phrase Book*, covering Europe's four major languages (German, Italian, French, and Spanish), fits our itinerary nicely. In many ways, a cheap, little English-

Italian (for example) dictionary is more practical than a phrase book.

Rick Steves's books: Finally, my books, *Europe Through the Back Door* and *Europe 101*, will give you practical skills to travel smartly and independently and information to really understand and enjoy your sightseeing. To keep this book pocket-sized, I've resisted the temptation to repeat the most applicable and important information already included in my other books; there is virtually no overlap.

Europe Through the Back Door (Santa Fe, N.M.: John Muir Publications, 1992) gives you the basic skills that make this demanding 22-day plan possible. Chapters cover choosing and using a travel agent, minimizing jet lag, packing light, driving or train travel, finding budget beds without reservations, changing money, theft and the tourist, hurdling the language barrier, health, travel photography, ugly-Americanism, laundry, itinerary strategies, and more. The book also includes special articles on my forty favorite "Back Doors," seven of which are included in this tour (hill towns, Cività di Bagnoregio, Cinque Terre, Romantic Road, Castle Day, Swiss Alps, and Alsace).

Europe 101: Art for Travelers (co-written with Gene Openshaw; Santa Fe, N.M.: John Muir Publications, 1990) gives you the story of Europe's people, history, and art. A little "101" background knowledge brings Europe's sights to life. You'll step into a Gothic cathedral, nudge your partner, and whisper excitedly, "Isn't this a great improvement over Romanesque?!"

Mona Winks: Self-guided Tours of Europe's Top Museums (co-written with Gene Openshaw; Santa Fe, N.M.: John Muir Publications, 1990) gives you self-guided tours through Europe's most exhausting and important museums, with one- to three-hour tours of the major museums and historic highlights in this 22-day plan including Amsterdam's Rijksmuseum and Van Gogh Museum; Venice's St. Mark's, the Doge's Palace, and Accademia Gallery; Florence's Uffizi Gallery, Bargello, Michelangelo's David, and a Renaissance walk through the town center; Rome's Colosseum, Forum, Pantheon, the Vatican Museum, and St. Peter's basilica; and Paris's Louvre, the exciting Orsay Museum, the Pompidou Modern Art Museum, and a tour of Europe's greatest palace, Versailles. If you're planning on touring these sights, *Mona* will be a valued friend.

Your bookstore should have these three books, or you can order directly from John Muir Publications using the order form in the back of this book.

For this trip, I'd buy (1) *Let's Go: Europe* (rip out appropriate chapters), (2) *Mona Winks* (take only applicable chapters), (3) a phrase book, and (4) Michelin's *Green Guide for Italy*. (Total cost: about $50.) Read *Europe Through the Back Door* and *Europe 101* at home before departing. Only the Michelin guides are readily available in Europe, often cheaper than in the U.S.A.

Maps
Don't skimp on maps. Train travelers do fine with Michelin's #970 Europe map or even just the free Eurailpass map and local tourist office freebies. But drivers need a good map for each leg of their journey. European gas stations and bookstores have good maps. Get the most sightseeing value out of your maps by studying the key.

This book's maps are concise and simple, designed and drawn by Dave Hoerlein (who travels this route each year as a tour guide) to make the text easier to follow, to help you locate recommended places, and to get to the tourist office where you'll find a more in-depth map (usually free) of the city or region.

Send Me a Postcard, Drop Me a Line
While I do what I can to keep this book accurate and up-to-date, Europe just won't sit still. If you enjoy a successful trip with the help of this book and would like to share your discoveries (and make my job a lot easier), please send in any tips, recommendations, criticisms, or corrections to 109 4th N., P.O. Box C-2009, Edmonds, WA 98020. To update this book before your trip or share tips,

tap into our free computer bulletin board travel information service (206-771-1902:1200 or 2400/8/N/1). All
correspondents will receive a two-year subscription to
our *Back Door Travel* quarterly newsletter (it's free anyway). Thanks, and happy travels!

Raise Your Dreams to Their Upright and Locked Position

My goal is to free you, not chain you. Please defend your
spontaneity as you would your mother. Use this book to
avoid time- and money-wasting mistakes, to get more
intimate with Europe by traveling as a temporary local
person, and as a starting point from which to shape your
best possible travel experience.

If you've read this far you're smart enough to do this
tour on your own. Be confident. Enjoy the hills as well as
the valleys. Judging from all the positive feedback and
happy postcards I get from travelers who used earlier editions of *2 to 22 Days in Europe*, it's safe to assume you're
on your way to a great European vacation—independent,
inexpensive, and with the finesse of an experienced
traveler. Europe, here you come.

BACK DOOR TRAVEL PHILOSOPHY
AS TAUGHT IN *EUROPE THROUGH THE BACK DOOR*

Travel is intensified living—maximum thrills per minute and one of the last great sources of legal adventure. Travel is freedom. It's recess, and we need it.

Experiencing the real Europe requires catching it by surprise, going casual. . ."Through the Back Door."

Affording travel is a matter of priorities. (Make do with the old car.) You can travel—simple, safe, and comfortable—anywhere in Europe for $50 a day plus transportation costs. In many ways, spending more money only builds a thicker wall between you and what you came to see. Europe is a cultural carnival, and time after time, you'll find that its best acts are free and the best seats are the cheap ones.

A tight budget forces you to travel close to the ground, meeting and communicating with the people, not relying on service with a purchased smile. Never sacrifice sleep, nutrition, safety, or cleanliness in the name of budget. Simply enjoy the local-style alternatives to expensive hotels and restaurants.

Extroverts have more fun. If your trip is low on magic moments, kick yourself and make things happen. If you don't enjoy a place, maybe you don't know enough about it. Seek the truth. Recognize tourist traps. Give a people the benefit of your open mind. See things as different but not better or worse. Any culture has much to share.

Of course, travel, like the world, is a series of hills and valleys. Be fanatically positive and militantly optimistic. If something's not to your liking, change your liking. Travel is addicting. It can make you a happier American, as well as a citizen of the world. Our Earth is home to six billion equally important people. It's humbling to travel and find that people don't envy Americans. They like us, but with all due respect, they wouldn't trade places.

Globe-trotting destroys ethnocentricity. It helps you understand and appreciate different cultures. Travel changes people. It broadens perspectives and teaches new ways to measure quality of life. Many travelers toss aside their hometown blinders. Their prized souvenirs are the strands of different cultures they decide to knit into their own character. The world is a cultural yarn shop. And Back Door travelers are weaving the ultimate tapestry. Come on, join in!

DAY 1 Arrive at Amsterdam's Schiphol Airport. Pick up your car or activate your Eurailpass. Set up in Haarlem, a cozy, small-town home base 20 minutes from Amsterdam. Everything's so Dutch!

DAY 2 A busy day of sightseeing in Amsterdam. Visit Anne Frank's house, take the canal orientation tour, have a canalside picnic lunch, and tour the Van Gogh Museum and the Rijksmuseum. Return to small-town Holland for an Indonesian "rice table" feast.

DAY 3 Wander through the local folk life at Arnhem's Dutch open-air folk museum, the best in the Low Countries. Drive through the eye of Germany's industrial storm, popping out on the romantic Rhine River. Check into a guest house on the Rhine. Dinner below a floodlit castle.

DAY 4 Crawl through Rheinfels, the Rhine's mightiest castle. Cruise the most exciting hour of the river, from St. Goar to Bacharach. Picnic in the park at Bacharach, with free time left to explore the old town. Autobahn to Germany's walled medieval wonder town, Rothenburg.

DAY 5 After an early morning walk around the old city wall, grab breakfast and catch an introductory walking tour. The rest of the day is free for sightseeing or shopping. (This is Germany's best shopping town.)

DAY 6 In the morning, explore the Romantic Road, Germany's medieval heartland. Tour the concentration camp at Dachau. After a late lunch in a Munich beer hall, take a quick walk through downtown Munich before driving farther south into Austria. Dinner in the Tirolean town of Reutte.

DAY 7 Castle Day! Beat the crowds to "Mad" King Ludwig's magnificent Neuschwanstein Castle. Visit the dazzling baroque Wies Church and explore busy Oberammergau before returning to your Austrian home base to climb to the ruined castles of Ehrenberg and ride a thrilling alpine luge. Your evening is free to find some Tirolean fun. There should be a whole lotta slap dancing and yodeling going on.

DAY 8 Morning free in Innsbruck's historic center with time to enjoy its great Tirolean folk museum. Then drive over the Alps to Italia! Orient yourself in Venice with a cruise down the Grand Canal and check into your very central hotel. After a typical Venetian dinner enjoy gelato, cappuccino, and the magic of St. Mark's Square at night.

DAY 9 Your morning tour includes the highlights of Venice: Doge's Palace, St. Mark's, the bell tower. Rest of the day is free for browsing, shopping, or art. Are you ready for the famous "Back Door Stand-Up-Progressive-Venetian-Pub-Crawl-Dinner?"

DAY 10 It's three hours to Florence, birthplace of the Renaissance. Spend the afternoon in Europe's art capital with time to enjoy Michelangelo's David, the Duomo, and the Uffizi Gallery. Evening in Florence's ramshackle, other-side-of-the-river neighborhood.

DAY 11 Morning free in Florence for more art, shopping, gelati. After a fat slice of pizza and a fruit cup, drive south to the tiny, time-passed village of Civitàdi Bagnoregio, near Orvieto. After setting up in Angelino's hotel, spend the late afternoon and early evening immersed in the traffic-free village of Civitàduring. Curl your toes around its Etruscan roots. Dinner at the village's only restaurant, or eat "bunny" at Angelino's. Drop into Angelino's gooey, wine- and laughter-stained cantina.

DAY 12 Morning free to tour Orvieto, spend more time exploring Civitàduring, or just relax at Angelino's before taking the brutal plunge into Rome. Drive your chariot into the city of Julius, Peter, and Benito; set up and enjoy a short siesta. Fill the late afternoon and the cool, early evening with the Caesar shuffle—a historic walk from the Colosseum, through the ancient Forum and over the Capitoline Hill.

Europe in 22 Days

DAY 13 The morning is busy with fascinating sights in the core of old Rome—including the incomparable Pantheon. After a self-service lunch and a necessary siesta, the afternoon is free, but you'll have no trouble filling it. For a colorful dinner, catch a taxi to Trastevere, Rome's wrong side of the Tiber River, a seedy, seamy land of laundry, card games, graffiti, and soccer in the streets. Tonight's walk takes you past Rome's top night spots: Piazza Navona (for Tartufo ice cream), the floodlit Trevi Fountain, and the Spanish Steps.

DAY 14 Learn something about eternity by spending the morning touring the huge Vatican Museum. Of course, your reward for surviving Rome is the artistic culmination of the Renaissance, Michelangelo's Sistine Chapel. Then, after a lunch and siesta break, tour St. Peter's, the greatest church on earth. Scale Michelangelo's 100-yard-tall dome. The early evening is for the "Dolce Vita Stroll" down the Via del Corso with Rome's beautiful people.

DAY 15 Drive north to Cinque Terre. Lunch under Pisa's tipsy tower. Then, up to La Spezia, where you'll leave your car and take the train into the Italian Riviera for this vacation from your vacation. Find a room in a pensione, hotel, or private home. Fresh seafood, local wine, and Mediterranean stars in your eyes.

DAY 16 All day free for hiking, exploring villages, swimming, relaxing on the beach: fun in the sun. You'll fall in love with this sunny, traffic-free alternative to the French Riviera. Evening is free—beware the romance on the breakwater.

DAY 17 Leave very early. Hug the Mediterranan to Genoa, then swing north past Milan into Switzerland, where you'll climb over Susten Pass and tumble into the lap of the Swiss Alps, the Bernese Oberland. After a stop in Interlaken, ride the gondola to the stop just this side of heaven, Gimmelwald. This traffic-free, alpine, fairy-tale village has one chalet-hotel, the Mittaghorn, and that's where you'll stay. Walter will have a hearty dinner waiting.

DAY 18 Hike day. You'll spend the day memorably above the clouds taking the lift to the tip of the Schilthorn for a 10,000-foot breakfast and possibly hiking down. Or sit in a meadow and be Heidi. Or shop and explore the town of Mürren. After dinner, rub your partner's feet with coffee schnapps and Swiss chocolate while the moon rises over the Jungfrau.

DAY 19 Ride the lift to Männlichen high in the Jungfrau region. Picnic under the staggering north face of the Eiger. Spend the afternoon driving out of Switzerland and into France. Evening in Colmar, Alsace, where you'll check into Bernard's Hôtel Le Rapp.

DAY 20 All day to explore historic Colmar and the Wine Road (*Route du Vin*) of the Alsace region. Lovely villages, wine-tasting tours, and some powerful art. Evening is free in cobbled Colmar. Don't miss this opportunity to enjoy the Alsatian cuisine—some of France's best.

DAY 21 Long drive to Paris with a midday stop for a picnic in Reims. Tour Reims's magnificent cathedral for a lesson in Gothic architecture. This is champagne country. The various champagne cellars give tours—free tasting, of course. After setting up in Paris, learn the subway system and orient yourself. Find an Eiffelian viewpoint and preview this grand city studded with famous and floodlit buildings.

DAY 22 This tour's finale is a very busy day—big surprise, huh? Catch the best of Paris beginning with a morning tour of the Latin Quarter, Notre-Dame, Île de la Cité, and the historic center of Paris. After a self-service lunch and a tour of the highlights of the Louvre, the late afternoon is free for more sights, shopping, or to walk the glamorous Champs-Élysées. Spend the evening up on Montmartre for a grand city view, people watching, crêpes, a visit to Sacré-Coeur church, and free time to enjoy the Bohemian artists' quarter.

Hopefully you'll spend another day in Paris and tour Versailles, Europe's greatest palace. There's so much to see—but this book is called *2 to 22 Days* and we've run out of time.

Basic Itinerary Options
Though the 22-day tour ends in Paris, you could continue on, flying home from another city. Paris, Amsterdam, and London are each fine return points. To return to Amsterdam from Paris is a seven-hour drive or a five-hour, $50 train ride.

If you have a few extra days, you can start and/or end this tour in London. After three nights and two days there, with possible day trips to Bath and Cambridge, catch the $50, eight- to ten-hour trip to Belgium or Holland. Boats go daily overnight from England to Hoek van Holland (near Delft) or Oostende (near the great town of Brugges). From Paris, it's an easy seven-hour trip to London and your return flight.

To add Greece, rearrange this 22-day tour starting in London, then proceed to Paris, Amsterdam, Germany, Switzerland, and Italy before catching the boat from Brindisi, Italy, to Patras, Greece (24-hour crossing, several each day, free with Eurail). See the Greek ruins, enjoy a vacation from your vacation in the sunny isles, and fly home from Athens. (An open-jaw ticket, flying you into London and home from Athens, is reasonable. This tour is ideal for a 21-day Eurailpass.)

Many cheap flights connect the U.S.A. and Frankfurt. You could easily start your tour there, picking up a rental car or catching a train at the Frankfurt airport's train station, going to Rothenburg (a great first-night-in-Europe place), and finishing three weeks later with a pleasant day on the Rhine, within two or three hours of the airport and your flight home. Don't sleep in Frankfurt; just train into its station and catch the easy shuttle train service from there to the airport.

To make the trip shorter (15 days) and easier—and less exciting—skip Italy by going from Austria directly to Switzerland. My five other 2 to 22 Days guidebooks, covering Great Britain, Spain/Portugal, Germany/Austria/Switzerland, France, and Norway/Sweden/Denmark, offer tempting ways to double—or triple—your vacation game plan.

DEPART U.S.A.

Call 72 hours before departure to confirm your ticket. (Those who don't can be bumped with no recourse if the flight is overbooked.) Call again before going to the airport to confirm that your departure time is as scheduled. Expect delays. Bring something to do—a book, a journal, nail clippers, some handwork—to make any waits easy on yourself. Once airborne, chant softly, "Tight knees, cold peas, I promise not to fuss. If I land safely, even delayed, this sure beats a bus." Repeat as needed.

To Minimize Jet Lag

• Leave well rested. Pretend you're leaving a day earlier than you really are. Be completely packed and ready to go so you can enjoy a peaceful last day. Jet lag can bring a budding cold into full bloom.
• During the flight, minimize stress to your system by eating lightly and avoiding alcohol, caffeine, and sugar. Every chance I get, I say, "Two orange juices, no ice please." Take walks.
• After boarding the plane, set your watch ahead to European time. Start adjusting mentally before you land.
• Sleep through the in-flight movie, or at least close your eyes and fake it.
• On the day you arrive, keep yourself awake until a reasonable local bedtime. Jet lag hates fresh air, bright light, and exercise (take a long evening city walk).
• You'll probably wake up wired but with the birds the next morning. Fighting it is futile. Enjoy a pinch-me-I'm-in-Europe sunrise walk.

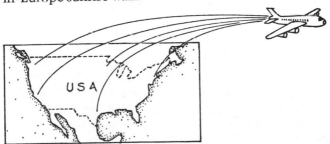

ARRIVE IN AMSTERDAM

When flying to Europe, because of flight time and the time difference, you usually land the next day. Amsterdam's Schiphol Airport, seven miles out of town (and below sea level), is efficient, English-speaking, and "user friendly." Its bank keeps long hours and offers fair rates. (Save time and avoid the bank line by changing money in the luggage pickup area while your bags are still coming.) Schiphol Airport has an information desk, baggage lockers, on-the-spot car rental agencies, an expensive room-finding service, and easy public transportation.

Bus or train cheaply into Amsterdam or Haarlem. Airport taxis are expensive. The airport has a train station of its own. (You can validate your Eurailpass and hit the rails immediately or, to stretch your train pass, buy the short ticket today and start the pass later.) Schiphol flight information, tel. 020/6010966, can give you your airline's Amsterdam number for reconfirmation before going home.

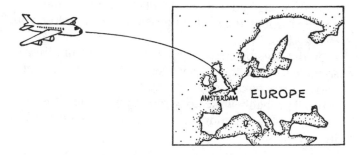

To central Amsterdam, catch a direct train (20 minutes, f5, leaving every 15 minutes); for Haarlem, take the train with a change at Amsterdam-Sloterdijk (45 minutes), or hop the slower (one hour) but direct bus #174 or #176 from the far side of the street, just behind the airport train station. For Delft and points south, use the train.

THE NETHERLANDS

- 13,000 square miles (Maryland's size).
- 14 million people (1,050 per square mile, 15 times the population density of the U.S.A.).
- 1 guilder = about U.S. $.50.

The Netherlands, Europe's most densely populated country, is also one of its wealthiest and best organized. Efficiency is a local custom. The average income is higher than America's. Forty percent of the labor force works with raw materials or in food processing, while only 8 percent are farmers. Seventy percent of the land is cultivated, and you'll travel through vast fields of barley, wheat, sugar beets, potatoes, and flowers.

Holland is the largest of twelve states that make up the Netherlands. Belgium, the Netherlands, and Luxembourg have united economically to form Benelux. Today you'll find no borders between these Low Countries—called that because they are. Half of the Netherlands is below sea level, on land that has been reclaimed from the sea. That's why the locals say, "God made the Earth, but the Dutch made Holland." Modern technology and plenty of Dutch elbow grease are turning more and more of the sea into fertile farmland. In fact, a new twelfth state—Flevoland, near Amsterdam—has just recently been drained, dried, and peopled.

The Dutch are friendly, generally speak very good English, and pride themselves on their frankness. Traditionally, Dutch cities have been open-minded, loose, and liberal (to attract sailors in the days of Henry Hudson), but they are now paying the price of this easygoing style. Amsterdam has become a bit seedy for many travelers' tastes. Enjoy more sedate Dutch evenings by sleeping in a small town nearby and side-tripping into the big city.

The Dutch guilder (f, for its older name, florin) is divided into 100 cents (c). There are about f2 in a U.S. dollar ($1 = f2). To find prices in dollars, simply divide the prices you see by 2 (e.g., f7.50 = $3.75). The colorful Dutch money has Braille markings.

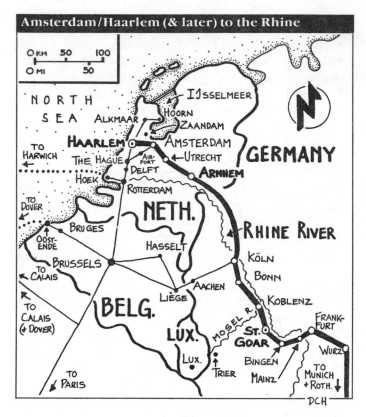

Amsterdam/Haarlem (& later) to the Rhine

The country is so small, level, and well covered by trains and buses that transportation is a snap. Major cities are connected by speedy trains that come and go every 10 or 15 minutes. Connections are excellent, and you'll never wait more than a few minutes. Buses will take you where trains don't, and bicycles will take you where buses don't. Bus stations, train stations, and bike rental places usually cluster.

The Netherlands is a bicyclist's delight. The Dutch average four bikes per family and have put a small bike road with its own traffic lights beside every big auto route. You can rent bikes at most train stations and drop them off at most other stations.

Shops and banks stay open from 9:00 to 17:00. The industrious Dutch know no siesta.

The best "Dutch" food is Indonesian (from the former colony). Find any *Indisch* restaurant and experience a *rijstafel* (rice table), which may have as many as thirty exciting dishes. *Nasi rames* is a cheaper mini version of a rijstafel. Local taste treats are cheese, pancakes (*pannekoeken*), Dutch gin (*jenever*, pronounced like "your neighbor"), light pilsner beer, and "syrup waffles." Yogurt in Holland (and throughout Northern Europe) is delicious and drinkable right out of its plastic container. *Broodjes* are sandwiches of fresh bread and delicious cheese—cheap at snack bars, delis, and "broodje" restaurants. For cheap fast food, try a Middle Eastern *shwarma*, roasted lamb in pita bread. Breakfasts are big by continental standards. Lunch and dinner are served at U.S.A. times.

Experiences you owe your tongue in Holland: a raw herring (outdoor herring stands are all over), a slow coffee in a "brown café," an old jenever (smooth, local gin) with a new friend, and a rijstafel.

Haarlem—Small-Town Home Base near Amsterdam

Cute, cozy yet real, handy to the airport, and just 20 minutes by train from downtown Amsterdam (f8 round-trip, trains go every 10 minutes), Haarlem is a fine home base, giving you small-town, overnight warmth with easy access to wild and crazy Amsterdam.

Haarlem is the hometown of Frans Hals and Corrie Ten Boom. The excellent Frans Hals museum, with several of his greatest paintings, is open Monday to Saturday 11:00 to 17:00, Sunday 13:00 to 17:00. While the Ten Boom clock shop closed in 1991, the Ten Boom House (*The Hiding Place*) at 19 Barteljorisstraat, is open for tours, probably Monday to Saturday, 10:00 to 16:30. Haarlem's Grote Kerk (church) houses Holland's greatest church pipe organ (regular free concerts, summer Tuesdays at 20:15, some Thursdays at 15:00, the TI has a schedule of concerts). The church is open and worth a look if only to see its Oz-like organ (Monday-Saturday 10:00-16:00).

Most of all, Haarlem is a busy Dutch market town buzzing with shoppers biking home with bouquets of flowers. Enjoy Saturday and Monday market days when the square

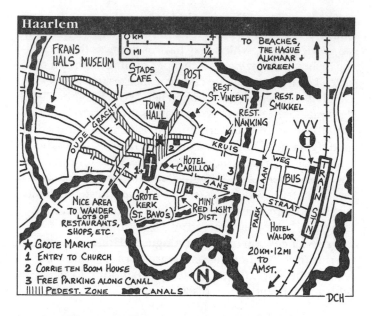

Haarlem

FRANS HALS MUSEUM

STADS CAFÉ

POST

TOWN HALL

REST. ST. VINCENT

REST. NANKING

REST. DE SMIKKEL

TO BEACHES, THE HAGUE ALKMAAR & OVEREEN

VVV

OUDE GRACHT

KRUIS

WEG

HOTEL CARILLON

JANS

STRAAT

BUS

PARK LAAN

TRAIN STN

GROTE KERK (ST. BAVO'S)

"MINI" RED LIGHT DIST.

HOTEL WALDOR

20 KM · 12 MI TO AMST.

NICE AREA TO WANDER LOTS OF RESTAURANTS, SHOPS, ETC.

★ GROTE MARKT
1 ENTRY TO CHURCH
2 CORRIE TEN BOOM HOUSE
3 FREE PARKING ALONG CANAL
||||| PEDEST. ZONE   CANALS

N

DCH

bustles like a Brueghel painting with cheese, fish, flowers, and lots of people. You'll feel comfortable here. Buy some flowers to brighten your hotel room. (Bike rental shops, f8/day, at the train station and at Koningstraat 36, near the market square.)

For the cutest little red-light district anywhere, wander around the church in the Begijnhof (two blocks northeast of the church, off Lange Begijnestraat, f50, no senior or student discounts). Don't miss the mall marked by the green neon sign, t'Poortje.

For evening fun, the bars around the Grote Kerk and along Lange Veerstraat are colorful, lively, and full of music. Don't be shocked if locals drop into a bar, plunk down f25 for a little baggie of marijuana, and casually roll a joint. (If you don't like the smell of pot, avoid cafés with plants in the windows.) Holland is an easygoing, love-yourself-as-you-love-jenever kind of place.

For simpler fun, grab two Dutch quarters and a friend and step into the tiny disco-for-two under the church across from the Hotel Carillon. (It looks like a space-age Sani-can.) The door closes and it's just the two of you, a mirror, lights, and piped-in music. There's even a little toilet if you need one. You can stay up to 15 minutes, but save the last dance for me. (Open 24 hours daily.)

Sleeping in Haarlem (f1 = about U.S. $.50)

The helpful Haarlem tourist office ("VVV" at the train station, open Monday to Saturday 9:00 to 17:30, tel. 023/319059) can nearly always find you a f26 bed in a nearby private home for a f7 per person fee. Haarlem is most crowded in April, May, and August, but hotels happily hold a room for a phone call, and you should have no trouble landing one. If this is your first night in Europe, make a telephone reservation from home. Nearly every Dutch person you'll encounter speaks English.

Hotel Carillon (f46 for tiny loft singles, f75-f100 for basic doubles, Grote Markt 27, Haarlem, tel. 023/31 05 91, fax 023/31 49 09) is right on the town square. Rooms have lace windows and are reached by ste-e-e-p stairs. Frans, who runs the place, with the help of Fritz, John, and Darina, his friendly crew, will hold a room with no deposit until 20:00, if you telephone him. Hotel Carillon's location is ideal, and its lounge/bar/breakfast room couldn't be more atmospheric. Even though its well-worn rooms are a cut below its competitors, I stay here. Street-front rooms have great town square views and lots of street noise.

The rollicking **Stads Café** (f45 singles, f70-f85 doubles, f115 triples, without breakfast, Zijlstraat 56-58, two blocks off the marketplace, tel. 023/32 52 02) has big, bright, and cheery rooms with TVs and solid modern wooden furniture. This place's restaurant hops at night (see below), but the rooms are in the back and very quiet.

Hotel Waldor (f75-f110 doubles, Jansweg 40 Hoek Parklaan, tel. 023/31 26 22), in a creaky, classy old building, has decent rooms behind dingy hallways. It's just two blocks from the station, five minutes from the town square. The owner, Louis, plans some serious expansion and renovation in the future.

Hotel Amadeus (f110 doubles, Grote Markt 10, 2011 RD Haarlem, tel. 023/32 45 30, fax 023/32 23 28, accepts

VISA card numbers to secure reservations) has 15 small, bright rooms, all with simple modern furnishing and private showers. Some have square views and TVs. While this place is ideally located in a characteristic building on the market square opposite Hotel Carillon, it is quiet and has easier stairs and an elevator. The lush old lobby is on the second floor in a "pianola bar."

Just outside town: the **Hotel Fehres** (f75-f85 doubles, 299 Zijlweg, tel. 023/27 73 68) is in a garden-filled, residential setting, a 25-minute walk from Haarlem or a 5-minute walk from the Overveen station, one stop west of Haarlem with twice-an-hour train connections to Amsterdam. Friendly Mrs. Fehres pampers her guests.

Jugendherberg Jan Gijzen, the youth hostel at Jan Gijzenpad 3 (tel. 023/37 37 93), is about two miles from the station (bus 2 or 6) and charges f20 with breakfast, f5.50 extra for sheets, plus f5 for nonmembers. You will probably have 20 roommates. Call first. Closed November through February.

Parking in Haarlem is free and fairly safe all day wherever you can find unmetered and unmarked places, such as along the canal (Nieuwe Gracht) and along parts of Parklaan. Otherwise, there are several large reasonable garages.

Those returning to Haarlem before flying home should reserve and pay for their last night's hotel room now.

Eating in Haarlem

Enjoy a memorable Indonesian rijstafel feast at the friendly **Nanking Chinese-Indonesian Restaurant** (Kruisstraat 16, tel. 023/32 07 06). Couples eat plenty, hearty, and cheaper by ordering a bowl of soup (Nanking soup of the day, f7, is good) and splitting a f22 Indonesian rice table for one. Say "hi" to gracious Ai Ping, and don't let her railroad you into a Chinese (her heritage) dinner. For more expensive and impressive, less personable, but entirely Indonesian meals, try **Mooi Java** (across from the station) or **De Lachende Javaan** ("The Laughing Javaan") near the market square at Frankestraat 25.

For a Dutch specialty, how about pancakes for dinner at the **Pannekoekhuis "De Smikkel"** (Kruisweg 57, two blocks in front of the station, closes at 20:00 and on Mondays)? Dinner and dessert pancakes cost f10 each (there's a f2.50 cover charge, so splitting pancakes is okay).

For a motivating "bread line" experience with basic/bland food, well-worn company, and the cheapest price in town (f8), eat at **Eethuis St. Vincent** (on Nieuwe Groenmarket, open Monday-Friday 12:00-13:30 and 17:00-19:00).

For good food, classy atmosphere, and f30 dinners, try the **Bastiaan** (Lange Veerstr. 8), **De Drie Konijntjes** ("The Three Rabbits," 4 Warmoesstr.), the **Hotel Carillon,** or, for red meat, **Wilma and Albert's**, near the church.

Eko Eet Cafe (f16 menu, Zijlstraat 39, near the Nieuwe Greenmarket) is the place for a cheery and tasty vegetarian meal in Haarlem.

The **Stads Café** (Zijlstraat 56-58, tel. 023/32 52 02, just off the square) offers a three-ring circus of reasonable food (downstairs, something from the menu or the f19 buffet rijstafel; upstairs, the f19 cheese or meat fondue buffets). A new favorite is their "meat on a hot rock sizzling at your table" meal. This place, with its stained glass, candle-lit, honky tonk atmosphere, salad bar, and nightly piano music, knows how to have fun being a restaurant.

All restaurants listed are within a few blocks of the Grote Markt (Market Square).

Delft

Delft, peaceful as a Vermeer painting (he was born there) and lovely as its porcelain, is another safe, pleasant, and very comfortable place to overcome jet lag and break into Holland and Europe. Delft is 60 minutes by train south of Amsterdam. Trains (f15, f26 round-trip) depart every half hour.

While Delft lacks major sights, it's a typically Dutch town with a special soul. You'll enjoy it best just wandering around, watching people, munching local syrup-waffles, or gazing from the canal bridges into the water

and seeing the ripples wrinkle your face. The town bustles during its Saturday morning antique market. Its
colorful Thursday food market attracts many traditional
villagers. (Tourist Information, tel. 015/12 61 00.)

The town is a museum in itself, but if you want something with a turnstile, it has an impressive army museum,
and you can tour the Royal Porcelain Works (daily 9:00-
17:00, Sunday 10:00-16:00, tel. 015/56 02 34) to watch
the famous seventeenth-century blue Delftware go from
clay to art.

Reservations are unnecessary in Delft. Just drop in or
call from the airport. Delft has several simple hotels on its
market square, the best being **Hotel Monopole** (f65
doubles, 48A Markt, Delft, tel. 015/12 30 59). Luke, who
runs the place, serves 56 varieties of pancakes. **Hotel
Central** (f140+ doubles, Wijnhaven 6, 2611 CR, Delft,
tel. 015/12 34 42, located between the station and the
square) is good but expensive.

The **Peking** Chinese-Indonesian restaurant (two
minutes off the square, Brabantse Turfmarkt 78, tel.
015/14 11 00) serves a grand but reasonable rijstafel feast
(Again, one is plenty for two.)

Edam
For the ultimate in cuteness and peace, make tiny Edam
your home base. It's 20 minutes by bus from Amsterdam.
Hotel De Fortuna (f70-f150 doubles, Spuistraat 1, 1135
AV Edam, tel. 02993/71671, fax 71469) is an eccentric
canalside mix of flowers, cats of leisure, caged birds, duck
noises, giant spiderwebs, and Wurlitzer glissandos, offering steep stairs and low-ceilinged rooms in several
ancient buildings in the old center of Edam. The TI (tel.
02993/71727) has a list of cheaper rooms in private
homes. **Tai Wah** has good reasonable takeout (and eat in
the De Fortuna garden) or eat-in Indonesian food at Lin-
gerzijde 62.

Don't miss the Edam Museum, a small, quirky house
offering a fun peek into a 400-year-old home and a floating cellar. Wednesday is the town's market day, and in July
and August (10:00-12:30, Wednesday) it includes a traditional cheese market.

AMSTERDAM

Amsterdam is a progressive way of life housed in the closest thing to a seventeenth-century city Europe has to offer. It's a city built on good living, cozy cafés, great art, street-corner jazz, stately history, and a spirit of live and let live (with more canals than Venice). While Amsterdam has grown a bit seedy for many people, it's a great and historic city and an experiment in freedom, worth a full day of sightseeing on even the busiest itinerary.

Suggested Schedule	
9:00	Anne Frank House, Westerkerk.
10:00	Palace, Dam Square, walk to Spui on Kalverstraat, Amsterdam's bustling, pedestrian-only shopping street. Visit the Begijnhof.
12:00	Lunch: picnic or Amsterdam University cafeteria.
13:00-17:00	Museums. The Rijksmuseum, Van Gogh Museum, and Stedelijk Museum (modern art) are side by side.
17:00	Walk through Leidseplein (nightclub center) to Muntplein (flower market along canal) to Spui. Catch the hour-long canal boat tour.
19:00	Walk past the Dam Square, the red-light district and sailors' quarters, and back to the central station, returning to your small-town home base for a gastronomic trip to Indonesia.

Orientation

The central train station is your starting point (tourist information, bike rental, and trolleys and buses fanning out to all points). Damrak is the main street axis connecting the station with the Dam Square (people-watching and hangout center) and the Royal Palace. From this spine the city spreads out like a fan, with ninety islands, hundreds of bridges, and a series of concentric canals laid out in the seventeenth century, Holland's Golden Age. The city's major sights are within walking distance of the Dam Square.

"Amsterdam in a day," if not thorough, is very exciting. Plan your time carefully and enjoy a big Dutch breakfast. And remember, in Amsterdam, every Monday is "Black Monday": museums are closed and shops are only open in the afternoon. *Gracht* means canal, *plein* is square, and most canals are lined by streets with the same name.

Tourist Information
Amsterdam has a hardworking but inefficient information office across the street from the station (VVV is the Dutch sign for TI, daily 9:00-23:00, tel. 020/626 6444). The painfully slow-moving lines are often 30 minutes long. Most people are waiting there just to pick up the information brocures and get a room.

Avoid this line by going straight to the VVV cash window (where everyone ends up anyway to pay for their maps, etc.). Consider buying: the Falk map of the city (f3), *What's On* (f2.50, bimonthly entertainment calender listing all the museum hours and much more), the walking tour booklet for the historic center (f2). *Use It*, the free youth tourist magazine for Amsterdam, filled with good budget tips, is more helpful than the f3.50 *Amsterdam, City of Many Faces* (simple map, listing of all the hotels, and more general Amsterdam info) VVV publication.

And there's no reason you need the TI to book you a room. The phones work logically, everyone speaks English, and the listings you have in this book are a better value than the potluck booking the TI will charge you for. If you have a quick question, telephone it in, or drop by the less crowded TI at Leidseplein.

The uncrowded and helpful transit information office (GVB) is next to the TI (in front of the station). Their free *Tourist Guide to Public Transport* includes a transit map and explains your ticket options and how to get to all the sights by tram.

The cheapest tickets are "strip cards." Any downtown ride costs two strips (good for an hour of transfers). A card with fifteen strips costs f10 at the GVB, the post office, or tobacco shops. These strips are good on buses all over Holland (e.g., 6 strips for Haarlem to the airport), and you can share them with your partner. You can also just pay f2 per ride as you board. Day cards give you unlimited transportation for a 24-hour period from 06:00 to 06:00 for f10. If you get lost, 10 of the city's 17 trams

take you back to the central train station. The longest
walk a tourist would make is 45 minutes from the station
to the Rijksmuseum. On foot, watch out for more than
just cars. The Amsterdam train station information center
also requires a long wait. Try to save time by taking care
of business in a small town station or travel agency.

All Amsterdam telephone numbers now have 7 digits. If
you come across an old 6-digit number, add a 6 to the
beginning. Telephone cards (f5, f10, or f25) are sold at the
TI, tobacco shops, post office, and train stations. Telephone code: 020.

Sightseeing Highlights—Amsterdam

▲▲▲Rijksmuseum—Start your visit with a free, short
slide show on Dutch art (every 20 minutes all day). Focus
on the Dutch Masters: Rembrandt, Hals, Vermeer, and
Steen. Buy the cheap museum map and plan your attack.

I'd recommend following the museum's chronological
layout to see painting evolve from narrative religious art
to religious art starring the Dutch love of good living and
eating to the Golden Age when secular art dominates.
With no local church or royalty to commission big can-
vases in the Protestant Dutch republic, artists specialized
in portraits of the wealthy city class (Hals), pretty still lifes
(Claesz), and nonpreachy slice-of-life art (Steen). The
museum has four quietly wonderful Vermeers. And, of
course, Rembrandt is the main draw. Study the *Night
Watch* history room before you see the real thing. Other
works by Rembrandt show his excellence as a portraitist
for hire (*De Staalmeesters*) and offer some powerful psy-
chological studies (*St. Peter's Denial*—with Jesus in the
dark background).

The bookshop has good posters, prints, slides, and
handy theme charts to the museum, if you always wondered about the role of cats, for example, in Dutch art.
(f6.50, Tuesday-Saturday 10:00-17:00, Sunday 13:00-17:00,
decent cafeteria, tram 1, 2, 5, 16, 24, 25). For a "brown
bar" atmosphere to digest all this art, the nearby Park
Café (Stadhouderskade 25) is just right.

▲▲▲**Van Gogh Museum**—Next to the Rijksmuseum, this outstanding and user-friendly museum is a stroll through a beautifully displayed garden of van Gogh's work and life. Don't miss it. Security here is very tight after a recent break-in and theft. (f10, 10:00-17:00, Sunday 13:00-17:00. Poster collectors, buy your cardboard tube here.)

Stedelijk Modern Art Museum—Next to the Van Gogh Museum, this place is fun, far out, and refreshing, especially *The Beanery* by Kienholz. (f7, daily 11:00-17:00.)

▲▲**Anne Frank House**—A fascinating look at the hideaway where young Anne hid when the Nazis occupied the Netherlands. Pick up the English pamphlet at the door, and don't miss the thought-provoking neo-Nazi exhibit in the last room. Fascism smolders on. (Monday-Saturday 9:00-17:00, Sunday 10:00-17:00, summer until 19:00, 263 Prinsengracht.)

Westerkerk—Near Anne Frank's house, this landmark church, with Amsterdam's tallest steeple, is worth climbing for the view. (Be careful: on a hot day Amsterdam's rooftops sprout nude sun worshipers.) Erratic hours, usually mid-May through mid-September 10:00-16:00, closed Sunday; tower open June through September, Tuesday, Wednesday, Friday, and Saturday 14:00-17:00.

Royal Palace Interior—It's right on the Dam Square, built when Amsterdam was feeling its global oats, and worth a look (open July and August, 12:30-16:00).

▲▲**Canal Boat Tour**—These long, low, tourist-laden boats leave constantly from several docks around the town for a good, if uninspiring, 60-minute quadra-lingual introduction to the city. The only one with a live guide is very central at the corner of Spui and Rokin, about 5 minutes from the Dam Square. No fishing, but bring your camera for this relaxing orientation.

There is also a "Canal Bus" with an all-day ticket that shuttles tourists from sight to sight. And the Touristtram gives you a 70-minute swing through the town's visual highlights with no stops (f10, from the City Hall). For information on the Yellow Bike Tour (3.5 hours, f28) and walking tours (3 hours, f20), call 620 6940.

▲**Begijnhof**—A tiny, idyllic courtyard in the city center
where the charm of old Amsterdam can still be felt.
Notice house #34, a 500-year-old wooden structure (rare
since repeated fires taught city fathers brick was wiser).
Peek into the hidden Catholic Church opposite the
church where the pilgrims worshiped while waiting for
their voyage to the New World. It's on Begijnensteeg
Lane, just off Kalverstraat between 130 and 132. The fine
Amsterdam historical museum (with a good-value restaurant) is next door at 92 (daily 11:00-17:00).
Rembrandt's House—Interesting for his fans. Lots of
sketches. (Jodenbreestraat 4; Monday-Saturday 10:00-
17:00, Sunday 13:00-17:00.)
▲**Tropenmuseum (Tropical Museum)**—As close to
the Third World as you'll get without lots of vaccinations,
this imaginative museum offers wonderful re-creations of
tropical life scenes and explanations of Third World
problems. (Open Monday-Friday 10:00-17:00, Saturday
and Sunday 12:00-17:00; 2 Linnaeusstr., tram 9.)
Netherlands Maritime (Scheepvaart) Museum—
This is fascinating if you're into *scheepvaarts*. (Open
10:00-17:00, Sunday 13:00-17:00, closed Monday, English
explanations; 1 Kattenburgerplein, bus 22 or 28.)
▲**Herrengracht Canal Mansion, the Willet Holt-
huysen Museum**—This 1687 patrician house offers a
fine look at the old rich of Amsterdam, with a good
15-minute English introduction film and a seventeenth-
century garden in back for a pleasant picnic. (Daily
11:00-17:00; Herrengracht 605, tram 4 or 9.)
Shopping—Amsterdam brings out the browser even in
those who were not born to shop. Shopping highlights
include *Waterlooplein* (flea market), various flower markets (along Singel Canal near the mint tower, or *Muntto-
ren*), diamond dealers (free tours), and Kalverstraat, the
best walking/shopping street (parallel to Damrak).
▲**Red-Light District**—Europe's most high-profile
ladies of the night shiver and shimmy in display case windows between the station and the Oudekerk along Voorburgwal. It's dangerous late at night but a fascinating walk

any time after noon. Only Amsterdam has two sex museums—one in the red-light district (lousy) and one on Damrak (cheaper and better). Both are open late, graphic, with something to offend almost everyone, but heck, it's historic (and safe), and there are descriptions in English.

▲**Rent a Bike**—Two wheels are twice as good as four for getting around Amsterdam (the TI has a suggested city bike tour pamphlet and a great regional bike map, f5). In one day, I biked through the red-light district, to Our Lord in the Attic (a fascinating hidden church at O.Z. Voorburgwal 40), to Herrengracht Mansion (at Herrengracht 605), to Albert Cuypstraat Market (colorful daily street market), to a diamond-polishing exhibit behind the Rijksmuseum, through Vondelpark (Amsterdam's "Central Park," good for people watching and self-service cafeteria lunch), to the Jordaan district, to Anne Frank's, to Westerkerk (climbed tower), to the Royal Palace, and down Damrak back to the station where I stumbled bow-legged onto the train. You can rent bikes for about f7 per day (with a hefty f200 deposit) at the central train station (long hours, entrance to the left as you leave the station, tel. 624 8391).

Vondelpark—Amsterdam's huge and lively city park gives the best look at today's Dutch youth, especially on a sunny summer weekend.

Sleeping in Amsterdam
Beds Downtown: Amsterdam has plenty of cheap beds in informal private hostels, formal youth hostels, student hotels, and its giant "sleep-in." (The latest specifics are in *Use It.*) The VVV (tourist office) across from the station can, for a f2 fee, find you a room in the price range of your choice.

The **Christian Youth Hostel Eben Haezer** (f14 per bed including sheets and breakfast, maximum age is 35, near Anne Frank's house, Bloemstr. 179, tel. 624 4717) is scruffy with 20-bed women's dorms and a 40-bed men's dorm but friendly, well run, and your best rock-bottom budget bet. They serve cheap, hot meals, run a snack bar, and offer lockers to all. English is the first language here; they'll happily hold a room for a phone call (ideally 3-7 days in advance).

Amsterdam's two IYHF youth hostels are **Vondelpark** (Amsterdam's top hostel, lots of school groups, right on the park at Zandpad 5, f22 with breakfast, tel. 683 1744) and **Stadsdoelen YH** (just past the Dam Square, at Kloveniersburgwal 97, f22 with breakfast, tel. 624 6832, mid-March through October).

Boatel Cruises Amstel (f30 to f41 per person in doubles and quads, many with TVs and private showers, including breakfast, Ruyterkade 5, tel. 626 4247, fax 639 1952) is the last surviving Amsterdam boatel (floating hotel), and it looks like it's permanently moored. Located on the harborfront 50 yards behind the station and kept shipshape by a captain who runs the place like it's at sea, this is a great value.

Hotel Toren (f160-f230 doubles, 164 Keizersgracht, tel. 622 6352, fax 626 9705) is a historic canalside mansion with an elegant but cluttered lobby and well-furnished rooms, all with private showers. This splurge is classy, quiet, and very central (near Anne Frank's house).

Hotels in the Leidseplein Area: The area around Amsterdam's museum square (Museumplein) and the rip-roaring nightlife center (Leidseplein) is colorful, comfortable, convenient, and affordable. The following hotels are easy to reach from the central station (tram 1, 2, or 5) and within easy walking distance of the Rijksmuseum.

Kooyk Hotel (f100 doubles, Leidsekade 82, 1017 PM Amsterdam, tel. 020/623 0295) is a homey place with 19 bright and cheery rooms. Each room has a W.C. and is simply but thoughtfully appointed. Showers are down the hall.

Hotel Maas (f175 doubles with shower, Leidsekade 91, tel. 020/623 3868, fax 622 2613) has an elevator and a phone, TV, coffee pot, and modern shower in each room. It's a big, well-run, classy, quiet, and hotelesque place that manages to keep a small feel.

Quentin Hotel (f70-f95 doubles without breakfast, showers down the hall, Leidsekade 89, tel. 020/626 2187) is an artsy and classy place with an elitist air.

Eating in Amsterdam

Dutch food is fairly basic. Picnics are cheap and easy. *Eet-cafes* are local cafés serving cheap broodjes, soup, eggs, and so on. Cafeterias and automatic food shops are also good bets for budget eaters. For a good Indonesian f23 rijstafel in a pleasant flowery locale, try **Kow Loon** (498 Singel, one block from the mint tower, tel. 625 3264) or **Speciaal** in the Jordaan area (f40 rijstaffel, 142 Nwe. Leliestraat, open from 17:30).

For a budget cafeteria meal at the city university, find the **Atrium** (Oude Zijds Achterburgwal 237, about 4 blocks west of the Beginhof), which serves f7 meals Monday through Friday from 12:00 to 14:00 and 17:00 to 19:00.

For pancakes and smoky but family atmosphere, try the **Pancake Bakery** (f12 pancakes, even an Indonesian pancake for those who want two experiences in one, near Anne Frank's house, Prinsengracht 191, tel. 625 1333). For pizza, **Pizza Pepino** (Leidsekruisstraat 32, behind the incredibly colorful Bulldog Bar) is happy and very Italian.

Drop by a bar for a jenever (Dutch gin), the closest thing to an atomic bomb in a shot glass. While cheese gets harder and sharper with age, jenever grows smooth and soft. Old jenever is best.

Drugs: Amsterdam is Europe's counterculture mecca. While hard drugs are definitely out, marijuana causes about as much excitement as a bottle of beer. Many bars feature a "pot man" with an extensive menu and f25 bags of whatever in the corner (walk east from the Dam Square on Damstraat for a few blocks). **The Bulldog** on Leidse-plein is an interesting bar.

Side Trips

Many day tours into small-town Holland are easy from Amsterdam. Buses go to quaint, nearby villages from the station. The famous towns (such as Volendam, Marken Island, and Edam) are very touristy but still fun.

Alkmaar is Holland's cheese capital—especially fun (and touristy) during its weekly cheese market, Fridays from 10:00 to noon.

Zaandijk has the great Zaanse Schans, a seventeenth-century Dutch village turned open-air folk museum where you can see and learn about everything from cheesemaking to wooden shoe carving. Take an inspiring climb to the top of a whirring windmill (get a group of people together and ask for a short tour); you can even buy a small jar of fresh, windmill-ground mustard for your next picnic. Zaandijk is your easiest one-stop look at traditional Dutch culture and the Netherlands' best collection of windmills. (Free, open daily, April-October, 9:00-17:00, closed off-season, ten miles north of Amsterdam, 15 minutes by train: take the Alkmaar-bound train to Station Koog-Zaandijk and walk—past a fragrant chocolate factory—for ten minutes.) Skip Zaandijk if you'll be visiting the even better folk museum at Arnhem tomorrow.

The energetic can enjoy a rented bicycle tour of the countryside. A free ferry departs from behind the Amsterdam station across the canal. In five minutes Amsterdam will be gone, and you'll be rolling through your very own Dutch painting. Local entrepreneurs arrange great cheap bike tours from Amsterdam, or you can pick up the TI's bike map and pedal alone.

Other easy day trips from Amsterdam are Rotterdam (world's largest port, bombed flat in World War II, towering Euro-mast, harbor tour, great pedestrian zone, TI tel. 010/413 6006, easy train connections to Amsterdam) and The Hague (TI tel. 070/354 6200, tram 8 to the Peace Palace, tram 8 to the beach resort of Scheveningen, tram 9 to the mini-Holland amusement park of Madurodam).

For a quick and easy look at a dike, and a shell-lover's Shangri-la, visit the beach resort of Zandvoort, just 10 minutes by car or train west of Haarlem (from Haarlem, follow road signs to Bloomendal). To the south, between posts 68 and 70, the beach bathers are working on all-around tans.

The Aalsmeer Flower Auction is your best look at the huge Dutch flower industry. About half of all the flowers exported from Holland are auctioned off here in six huge halls. Visitors are welcome to wander on elevated walkways, through what claims to be the biggest building on earth, over literally trainloads of fresh-cut flowers. (Monday through Friday 7:30-11:00, the earlier the better, f4, bus 171 from Amsterdam's station to Hortensieplein in Aalsmeer, then bus 40 to "bloemveiling." Or take bus #140 from Haarlem.) This is very close to the airport and a handy last fling before catching a morning flight. If you're traveling in April or May, you can see millions of these flowers still alive at the Keukenhof Garden near Haarlem.

FROM HOLLAND TO THE RHINE

In the morning, explore traditional Dutch culture in a huge and creative open-air folk museum. Climb a windmill. Study a thatch. Then hit the road or rails to Germany's romantic Rhineland in the most direct way.

Suggested Schedule	
8:00	Drive from Haarlem to Arnhem.
9:30	Tour Arnhem's open-air folk museum.
12:00	Pancake lunch.
14:00	Drive to St. Goar or Bacharach on the Rhine. Consider an hour stop in Boppard, a tour of Rheinfels Castle, or a cruise from St. Goar to Bacharach today.
19:00	Dinner at hotel and evening free in St. Goar or Bacharach.

Transportation: Haarlem to the Rhine (250 miles)
By car from Haarlem, skirt Amsterdam to the south on E9 following signs to Utrecht, then E12 east to Arnhem. Take the second Apeldoorn exit (after the Oosterbeek exit, just before Arnhem, you'll see the white Openlucht Museum sign). From there, signs will direct you to the nearby Openlucht Museum.

From the museum, wind through a complicated route to return to the freeway (ask at the parking lot for help). Follow A12 freeway signs to Zutphen/Oberhausen. Zutphen is the Dutch border town (good TI and two banks, with rates only a few percent worse than in town). Crossing into Germany, follow the autobahn signs for Oberhausen, then Köln, then Koblenz for two hours through the eye of Germany's industrial storm, the tangled urban mess around Düsseldorf and Essen. Past Köln get on E5, then cross the Rhine on Highway 48 toward Koblenz. Take the first Koblenz exit to cross the Mosel River into town (from the bridge, you can see the Mosel River on your right and the Deutches Ecke where the Rhine and Mosel merge on your left).

Pass through boring Koblenz quickly, following signs to road 9 (to Boppard and Mainz) along the Rhine's west bank. As you leave Koblenz, you'll see the huge brewery of Königsbacher and the yellow castle of Stoltzenfels. Boppard, St. Goar, and Bacharach are just down the road.

Trains make the 70-minute trip from Amsterdam to Arnhem twice an hour. At Arnhem station, take bus 3 or 13 (fastest) to the Openlucht Museum. If you'd prefer a direct Amsterdam-Rhine train, you can skip Arnhem, leave Amsterdam early, and stop off in historic Köln (described tomorrow). There are plenty of small milk-run trains to take you from Koblenz to Boppard, St. Goar, and Bacharach.

Sightseeing Highlights

▲▲▲ **Arnhem's Open-Air Dutch Folk Museum**—An hour east of Amsterdam in the sleek city of Arnhem is Holland's first, biggest, and best folk museum. You'll enjoy a huge park of windmills, old farms, traditional crafts in action, and a pleasant education-by-immersion in Dutch culture. The f10 English guidebook gives a fascinating rundown on each historic building. (Open daily 9:00-17:00, Saturday and Sunday from 10:00, f10 entry, tel. 085/57 61 11, fax 085/57 63 47. Interesting papermaking exhibit. Free guided tours for groups with three weeks written notice.)

Enjoy a rustic lunch at the Pancake House (De Hanekamp Inn, 74 on museum maps). The *veluwa* (meaning "swamp") pancake is a meal in itself for f10.

▲▲ **Kröller-Müller Museum, Hoge Veluwe National Park**—Also near Arnhem is the Hoge Veluwe National Park, Holland's largest (13,000 acres), which is famous for its Kröller-Müller Museum. This huge and impressive modern art collection, including 276 works by Vincent van Gogh, is set deep in the natural Dutch wilderness. The park has lots more to offer, including hundreds of white-painted bikes you're free to use to make your explorations more fun. Pick up more information at the Amsterdam or Arnhem Tourist Office (VVV), tel. 085/42 03 30, bus #12 connects the train station with the park and museum in the summer.

GERMANY (DEUTSCHLAND)

• United Germany is 136,000 square miles (the size of Montana).
• Population is 77 million (about 650 people per square mile, declining slowly).
• The West was 95,000 square miles (like Wyoming), with a population of 61 million.
• The East was 41,000 square miles (like Virginia), with a population of 16 million.
• One deutsche mark (DM) = about U.S.$.60 (about 1.7 DM = U.S.$1).

Deutschland is energetic, efficient, organized, and Europe's economic muscle man. Eighty-five percent of its people live in cities, and average earnings are among the highest on earth. Ninety-seven percent of the workers get a one-month paid vacation, so that during the other eleven months, they can create a gross national product of about one-third that of the United States and growing. Germany has risen from the ashes of World War II to become the world's fifth biggest industrial power, ranking fourth in steel output and nuclear power and third in automobile production. Its bustling new cities are designed to make people feel like they belong. It shines culturally, beating out all but two countries in production of books, Nobel laureates, and professors. And think of the Olympic gold medals coming their way next time around.

While its East-West division lasted about forty years, historically, Germany has been and continues to be divided North and South. Northern Germany was barbarian, is Protestant, and assaults life aggressively; southern Germany was Roman, is Catholic, and enjoys a more relaxed tempo of life. The southern German, or Bavarian,

dialect is to High (northern) German what the dialect of Alabama or Georgia is to the northern United States. The American image of Germany is Bavaria (probably because that was "our" sector immediately after the war) where the countryside is most traditional. This historic north-south division is less pronounced these days as Germany becomes a more mobile society. Of course, the big chore facing Germany today is integrating the rotten and wilted economy of what was East Germany into the sleek and efficient powerhouse economy of the West.

Germany's most interesting tourist route today—
Rhine, Romantic Road, Bavaria—was yesterday's most
important trade route, along which Germany's most
prosperous and important medieval cities were located.
Germany as a nation is just 120 years old. In 1850, there
were thirty-five independent countries in what is now
one Germany. In medieval times, there were over 300,
each with its own weights, measures, coinage, king, and
lotto. Many were surrounded by what we'd call "iron curtains." This helps explain the many diverse customs
found in such a compact land.

Germans eat lunch from 11:30 to 14:30 and dinner
between 18:00 and 21:00. Each region has its own gastro-
nomic twist, so order local house specials whenever possible. Pork, fish, and venison are good, and don't miss the
bratwurst and sauerkraut. Potatoes are the standard
vegetable. Great beers and white wines abound. Try the
small local brands. Go with whatever beer is on tap.
Gummi Bears are a local gumdrop candy with a cult following (beware of imitations—you must see the word
"Gummi"), and Nutella is a chocolate nut spread specialty that may change your life.

Banks are generally open from 8:00 to 12:00 and 14:00
to 16:00, other offices from 8:00 to 16:00. August is a
holiday month for workers, but that doesn't really affect
us tourists (unless you're on the road on the 15th, when
half of Germany is going over the Alps one way and half
returning the other).

Rhineland Sightseeing
See tomorrow.

Sleeping on the Rhine
St. Goar
Rhine Zimmer and Gasthäuser (rooms in private homes
and guest houses) abound, offering beds for 25-30 DM
per person. For cheaper beds, there are several exceptional Rhine-area youth hostels. And each town has a
helpful TI eager to set you up. Finding a room should be

easy any time of year. St. Goar and Bacharach are the best towns for an overnight stop. They are about ten minutes apart, and each is served by the same milk-run trains and boats and is connected by a fine riverside bike path. Bacharach is a little less touristy. St. Goar has the famous castle.

Hotel Landsknecht (90 DM doubles, one mile north of town, 5401 St. Goar, tel. 06741/2011, fax 06741/7499) is newly renovated and the best splurge for drivers with bucks. Klaus Nickenig and family run this classy place, which has a great Rhine terrace and top-notch dining.

In town, and easier for those without wheels, is **Hotel Montag** (80 DM doubles, Heerstrasse 128, just across the street from the world's largest free-hanging cuckoo clock, tel. 06741/1629). Mannfred Montag and his family speak English and run a good crafts shop (especially for steins) adjacent. Even though Montag gets a lot of bus tours, it is friendly and laid back.

Hotel Hauser (88 DM doubles with shower and Rhine view balconies, Heerstrasse 77, tel. 06741/333) is older, with more frayed edges and antlers, and as central as can be. It has bright rooms but dingy halls.

Hotel Traube (72 DM doubles, all with showers, breakfast, and a great Rhine view, Heerstrasse 75, 5401 St. Goar, tel. 06741/7511) goes beyond antlers. The dining room is fluttering with stuffed birds of prey. The carpets are depressing, and the rooms are plain, but the location, across the street from the boat dock, is great. Just down the street, the **Jägerhaus** (70 DM doubles with shower, Heerstrasse 61, tel. 06741/1665) doesn't appreciate one-night stays but will work in a pinch.

St. Goar's best Zimmer are the homes of **Frau Kurz** (54 DM doubles, 30 DM single, Ulmenhof 11, 5401 St. Goar/Rhein, tel. 06741/459, 2 minutes walk above the station) and similarly priced **Frau Wolters** (Schlossberg 24, tel. 06741/1695, on the road to the castle). Both charge less for longer stays and are cozier and more comfortable than hotels, with homey TV rooms and great river and castle views.

The very Germanly run **St. Goar hostel** (Bismarck-weg 17, tel. 06741/388 in morning and after 17:00), the big, beige building under the castle, is a good value, with cheap dorm beds, a few smaller rooms, and hearty dinners.

Bacharach

Overlooking Bacharach is **Jugendherberge Stahleck**, Germany's most impregnable youth hostel. This twelfth-century castle on the hilltop with a royal Rhine view (closed from 9:00-15:00, IYHF members of all ages wel-come, 17 DM dorm beds, 4 DM for sheets, normally places available but call and leave your name, tel. 06743/1266, English spoken) is a gem but very much a youth hostel—with barrackslike dorms crowded with metal bunkbeds, showers in the basement, and often filled with school groups. It's a 10-minute climb on the trail from the town church, or you can drive up. It's energetically run by Evelyn and Bernhard Falke, who serve up hearty and very cheap meals.

Hotel Kranenturm (70 DM doubles, with a discount for staying several nights, Langstrasse 30, tel. 06743/1308) gives you the feeling of a castle without the hostel-ity or the climb. This is my choice for the best combination of comfort and hotel privacy with Zimmer warmth, central location, and medieval atmosphere. Run by hardworking Kurt and Fatima Engel, this is actually part of the medi-eval fortification. Its former *kranen* (crane) towers are now round rooms. Centuries ago when the riverbank was higher, cranes on this tower loaded barrels of wine onto Rhine boats. Hotel Kranenturm is located virtually on the train tracks but a combination of medieval sturdiness and triple-pane windows makes sleep no problem. The cur-rent of materialism has no eyes, and the Kranenturm really stretches it to get toilets and showers in each room Kurt is a great cook, and his Kranenturm ice cream spe-cial may ruin you (8.50 DM, one is enough for two).

Frau Amann (44-50 DM doubles, Oberstrasse 13, in the old center on a side lane a few yards off the main street, tel. 06743/1271) rents four rooms in her quiet, homey, and traditional place. Guests get a cushy living room and a self-serve kitchen and the free use of bikes. You'll laugh right through the language barrier with this lovely woman. Zimmer normally discount their price if you're staying longer.

Annelie and Hans Dettmar (50-56 doubles, Oberstr. 8, on the main drag in the center, tel. 06743/2661 or 2979) are a young couple who rent six rooms (one is a huge family-of-four room, several have kitchenettes) in a modern house above their crafts shop. They speak English well and rent bikes for 8 DM per day.

Frau Erna Liefchied (50 DM doubles, Blucherstr. 39, 6533 Bacharach, tel. 06743/1510, speaks German fluently) shares her ancient, higgledy-piggledy, half-timbered house next to the medieval town gate three blocks away from the river with travelers. The rooms are very comfortable.

For inexpensive and atmospheric dining in Bacharach, try the **Hotel Kranenturm**, **Altes Haus** (15-25 DM dinners in the oldest building in town) or the less expensive but still atmospheric **Weinstuben Münze**, across the street.

THE RHINE TO ROTHENBURG

Spend today exploring the Rhine's mightiest castle, cruising down its most legend-soaked stretch, and autobahning to Rothenburg, Germany's best-preserved medieval town.

Suggested Schedule	
8:15	Bank and browse in St. Goar.
9:00	Tour Rheinfels Castle, explore St. Goar.
11:55	Catch the Rhine steamer, cruise and picnic to Bacharach.
13:00	Drive to Rothenburg, with possible stop for the Würzburg palace.
17:00	Find hotel and get set up. Free evening in Rothenburg.

Transportation on the Rhine
While the Rhine flows hundreds of miles from Switzerland to Holland, the chunk from Mainz to Koblenz is by far the most interesting. This stretch, studded with the crenellated cream of Germany's castles, is busy with boats, trains, and highway traffic. It's easy to explore. While many do the whole trip by boat, I'd tour the area by train or car and cruise just the most scenic hour, from St. Goar to Bacharach. Sit on the top deck with your handy Rhine map-guide and enjoy the parade of castles, towns, boats, and vineyards.

There are several boat companies, but most travelers sail on the bigger, more expensive, but more romantic Köln-Düsseldorf line (free with Eurail, tel. 0261/1030). Boats run daily in both directions (the "fast" boat doesn't go on Monday) from May through September with fewer boats off-season. Complete, up-to-date, and more complicated schedules are posted at any station, Rhineland hotel, or TI.

Rhine Steamer Schedule (Köln-Düsseldorf Line)				
Daily/dates	Koblenz	Boppard	St. Goar	Bacharach	Bingen
May-Sept	—	9:00	10:15	11:20	12:55
Apr-Oct	9:00	10:40	11:55	12:55	14:20
May-Sept	11:00	12:40	13:55	14:55	16:20
Apr-Oct	14:00	15:40	16:55	17:55	19:20
fast, May-Oct	11:05	11:30	11:50	12:08	12:28
July-Aug	12:30	14:10	15:25	16:25	17:50
May-Oct	12:20	11:20	10:35	9:55	9:10
July-Aug	15:50	14:40	13:35	12:45	12:00
fast, May-Oct	16:17	15:55	—	—	15:05
Apr-Sept	20:00	18:50	18:00	17:20	16:35

Cost: Koblenz-Bingen 50 DM, St. Goar-Bacharach 12 DM, free with Eurail, groups of 15 get a 20% discount.

In St. Goar, the Köln-Düsseldorfer dock is at the far end of Main Street. If you rush the castle, you can catch the 10:15 boat and picnic in Bacharach. Or take it easy and picnic on the 11:55 boat. Purchase tickets at the dock 5 minutes before departure. The boat is never full. (Confirm times at your hotel the night before.)

The smaller Bingen-Rüdesheimer line (tel. 06721/14140, Eurail not valid, tickets at St. Goar TI) is 25 percent cheaper than K-D with three 2-hour St. Goar-Bacharach round-trips daily in summer (departing St. Goar at 11:00, 14:15, and 16:10; departing Bacharach at 10:10, 12:30, 15:00; 9 DM one way, 11 DM round-trip).

If you're driving, the boat ride can present a problem. Your choices: (1) skip the boat; (2) take a round-trip Bingen-Rüdesheimer ride from St. Goar; (3) draw pretzels and let the loser of your group drive to Bacharach, prepare the picnic, and meet the boat; (4) take the boat to Bacharach and return by train, spending your waiting time exploring that old half-timbered town; (5) bring a bike on the boat (free) and bike back, or; (6) decide it's an insurmountable problem, get depressed, and stay in the hotel all day.

Taking the boat one-way and returning by train works well. Milk-run Rhine valley trains leave major towns

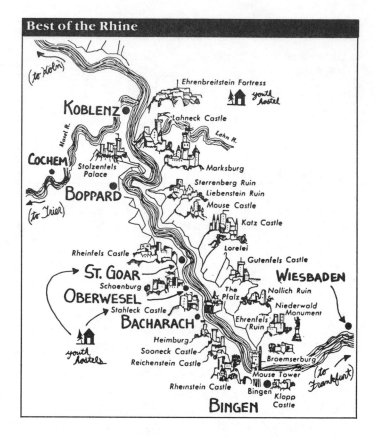

Best of the Rhine

almost hourly, and rides are very quick (St. Goar-
Bacharach 12 min., Bacharach-Mainz 30 min., Mainz-
Frankfurt 30 min.).

There's a lovely riverside bike path from St. Goar to
Bacharach, and you can rent bikes at the St. Goar TI or at
several Bacharach Zimmer. Those with more time and
energy can sail to Bingen and bike back, visiting Rheinstein and Reichenstein castles, and maybe even taking a
ferry across the river to Kaub. While there are no bridges
between Koblenz and Mainz, several small ferries do the
job constantly and cheaply.

For train travelers, if you're rushed, the speediest
schedule is to tour Rheinfels castle from 9:00 to 10:00,
cruise from St. Goar to Bacharach from 10:15 to 11:20,

picnic in Bacharach, and catch the early afternoon train to Frankfurt and on to Rothenburg.

Sightseeing Highlights—The Romantic Rhine (working south from Koblenz to Bingen)
▲▲▲ **Der Romantische Rhine Blitz Zug Fahrt**—A fast tour of the best of the Rhine by train (or car), traveling north to south, from Koblenz to Mainz.

One of Europe's great train thrills is zipping down the Rhine. Here's a quick-and-easy, from-the-train-window tour (works for car, boat, or bike also) that skips the syrupy myths and the life story of Dieter von Katzeneinbogen that fill normal Rhine guides.

The stretch from St. Goar to Bacharach is best by boat, but you could argue it's the same river by 50 mph train. For more information than necessary, buy the handy *Rhine Guide from Mainz to Cologne* (5 DM book with fold-out map, at most shops). Sit on the left (river) side of the train going south from Koblenz. While nearly all the castles listed are viewed from this side, clear a path to the right window for the times I yell "crossover."

I put up the large black-and-white kilometer markers along the riverbank years ago just to help with this tour. They tell the distance from the Rhinefalls, where the Rhine leaves Switzerland and becomes navigable. Now the boats have learned to accept these as navigational aids as well.

We're tackling just 36 miles of the 820-mile-long Rhine. Ever since Roman times, when this was the empire's northern boundary, the Rhine has been one of the world's busiest shipping rivers. You'll see a steady flow of barges with 1,000- to 2,000-ton loads. Along both banks are tour buses carrying 48 people, very busy train tracks, and highways.

Many of the castles you see today were robber baron castles, put there by petty rulers (remember, there were 300 independent little countries in medieval Germany) to levy tolls on all the passing river traffic. There were ten customs stops between Koblenz and Mainz alone. (No wonder merchants were proponents of the creation of larger nation-states.)

A robber baron would put his castle on, or even in, the river and stop each ship, often with the help of chains, and get his toll. Other castles were built to control and protect settlements. Some were the residences of kings. As times changed, so did the life-styles of the rich and feudal. Many castles were abandoned for comfortable mansions in the towns.

Most of the Rhine castles were originally built by petty princes in the eleventh, twelfth, and thirteenth centuries. Since the pope successfully asserted his power over the German emperor in 1076, local princes ran wild over the rule of their emperor. The castles saw military action in the 1300s and 1400s, as emperors began trying to reassert control over Germany's 300 silly kingdoms and tossing out the robber baron rascals.

The castles were also involved in the Reformation wars, which saw Europe's Catholic and "protesting" dynasties fight it out using a fragmented Germany as their battleground. These wars, known as the "Hundred Years" war, the "Thirty Years" war, or even the first "World War" (since so many countries participated), devastated Germany for 100 years until 1648.

The French destroyed most of the castles prophylactically (Louis XIV in the 1680s, the Revolutionary Army in the 1790s, and Napoleon in 1806). They were often rebuilt in neo-Gothic style in the Romantic age of the late 1800s; today they are enjoyed as restaurants, hotels, youth hostels, and museums.

The Rhine's Most Romantic 62 Kilometers (keyed to riverbank km markings)

km 590—Koblenz: This Rhine tour starts at Koblenz city with Ehrenbreitstein castle fortress across the river (described below).

km 585—Burg Lahneck (above the modern autobahn bridge over the Lahn river) was built in 1240 to defend local silver mines, then ruined by the French in 1688, and rebuilt in the 1850s in neo-Gothic style. Burg Lahneck faces the yellow Schloss Stolzenfels (out of view above the train, worth touring, a 10-minute climb from the tiny car park, closed Monday).

km 580—Marksburg (with the three modern chimneys behind it) is the best-looking of all the Rhine castles and the only surviving medieval castle on the Rhine. Because of its commanding position, it was never attacked. It was once a state prison. Now the bars help keep in English-speaking visitors suffering through the mandatory German language tours of its fascinating interior.

km 570—Boppard: After a broad horseshoe bend in the river you come to Boppard, a Roman town with some impressive remains of its fourth-century walls. Notice the Roman tower just before the Boppard station and the substantial chunk of Roman wall just after (stop-worthy, see below).

km 567—The "Hostile Brothers" castles (with the white square tower): Take the wall between Berg Ster-renberg and Burg Liebenstein (actually designed to improve the defenses of both castles), add two greedy and jealous brothers, a fair maiden, and create your own legend. The castles are restaurants today.

km 559—Burg Maus: This castle got its name because the next castle was owned by the Katzenelnbogen fam-ily. In the 1300s, it was considered a state-of-the-art for-tification. In 1806, Napoleon had it blown up with state-of-the-art explosives. It was rebuilt true to its original plans around 1900.

km 556—Burg Katz: From the town of St. Goar you'll see Burg Katz (Katzenelnbogen) across the river. Look back on your side of the river to see the mighty Rheinfels Castle over St. Goar. Be quick, there's a tunnel, and it's gone.

Together, Burg Katz (b. 1371) and Rheinfels had a clear view up and down the river and effectively controlled traffic. There was absolutely no duty-free shopping on the medieval Rhine. Katz got Napoleoned in 1806 and was rebuilt around 1900; today, it's a convalescent home

St. Goar (a recommended stop, see below) was named for a sixth-century hometown monk. It originated in

Celtic times (really old) as a place where sailors would stop, catch their breath, send home a postcard, and give thanks after surviving the seductive and treacherous Loreley crossing (see km 554).

Burg Rheinfels (b. 1245) withstood a siege of 28,000 French troops in 1692, but was creamed by the same country in 1797. It was huge, the biggest on the Rhine, then used as a quarry. Today it's a hollow but interesting museum (your best single hands-on castle experience on the river, see below).

km 554—The Loreley: Steep a big slate rock in centuries of legend and it becomes a tourist attraction—the ultimate Rhinestone. The Loreley (with two flags on top, name painted near shoreline) rises 450 feet over the narrowest and deepest point of the Rhine. The fine echoes were thought to be ghostly voices in the old days, fertilizing the legendary soil.

Because of the reefs just upstream (called the "Seven Maidens") many ships never made it to St. Goar. Sailors (after days at river) blamed their misfortune on a *wunderbar* Fräulein whose long blond hair almost covered her body. Heinrich Heine's *Song of Loreley* (read the Cliff Notes version on local postcards) tells the story of how a count, after his son was killed because of this siren, sent his men to kill or capture her. When the soldiers cornered the nymph in her cave, she called on Father Rhine for help. Huge waves, the likes of which you'll never see today, rose out of the river and carried her to safety. And she has never been seen since.

But, alas, when the moon shines brightly and the tour buses are parked, a soft, playful Rhine whine can still be heard from the Loreley. As you pass, listen carefully (sailors . . . sailors . . . over my bounding waves). You'll be saved by two tunnels and then, unless the river's high, see the killer reefs (km 552).

km 550—Obersesel (cross to other side of train), a Celtic town in 400 B.C., then a Roman military station, has some of the best Roman wall and tower remains on the Rhine. Its Schönburg castle is a youth hostel today. Okay, back to the river side.

km 546—Burg Gutenfels (white-painted hotel sign) and the ship-shaped **Pfalz Castle** (built in the river in the 1300s) worked very effectively to tax medieval river traffic. The town of Kaub grew rich as Pfalz raised its chains when boats came and lowered them only when the merchants had paid their duty. Those who didn't spent time touring its fascinating prison with a floor that went up and down with the river level. In 1504, a pope called for the destruction of Pfalz, but a six-week siege failed. Pfalz is tourable, accessible by ferry from the other side.

km 543—Bacharach (cross to other side of train) is a great stop (see below) with fourteenth-century fortifications preserved throughout the town. One of the old towers is my favorite Rhine hotel. The train screams within ten yards of Hotel Kranenturm (blink and you'll miss it). Bacharach prospered from its wood and wine trade. The thirteenth-century Burg Stahleck above the town is now a youth hostel.

km 540—Lorch is a pathetic stub of a castle. Notice the small car ferry, one of several between Koblenz and Mainz, where there are no bridges.

km 538—Castle Sooneck (cross to other side of train), built in the eleventh century, was twice destroyed by people sick and tired of robber barons. On the same side (at km 534) you'll see Burg Reichenstein and (at km 533) Burg Rheinstein, which was one of the first to be rebuilt in the Romantic era (both are tourable and connected by a pleasant trail, info at TI).

km 530—Ehrenfels Castle: Opposite the Bingerbrück station you'll see the ghostly Ehrenfels Castle (clobbered by the Swedish in 1636 and by the French in 1689). Since it had no view of the river traffic to the north, it built the cute little *Mäuseturm* (Mouse Tower) on an island (the yellow tower you'll see near the station today). Rebuilt in the 1800s in neo-Gothic style, today it's used as a Rhine navigation signal station.

km 528—Niederwald Monument: Across from the Bingen station on a hilltop is the 120-foot-high Niederwald monument, a memorial built with 32 tons of bronze in 1877 to commemorate "the reestablishment of the German Empire." A lift takes tourists to this statue from the famous and extremely touristy wine town of Rüdesheim. At this point, your train or car leaves the Rhine and your blitz tour is over.

Recommended stops along the Rhine Gorge
Koblenz—Not a nice city—it was really hit hard in World War II—but it has a certain magnetism due to its place as the historic *Deutsches-Eck* (German Corner), the tip of land where the Mosel joins the Rhine. Koblenz has Roman origins. (Its name is Latin for "confluence.") Walk through the park, noticing the blackened base of what was once a huge memorial to the Kaiser. Across the river, the yellow Ehrenbreitstein fortress is now a youth hostel with all the comfort of a World War I trench. It's a long hike from the station to the Koblenz boat dock.
▲**Boppard**—This is a more substantial town than St. Goar or Bacharach. Park near the center (or at the DB train station and walk). Just above the market square are the remains of a Roman wall. Below the square is a fascinating church. Notice the carved Romanesque crazies at the doorway. Inside, to the right of the entrance, you'll see Christian symbols from Roman times. Also notice the painted arches and vaults; originally, most Romanesque churches were painted this way. Down by the river notice the high water (*Hochwasser*) marks on the arches from various flood years.
▲**St. Goar**—A pleasant town, established as a place where sailors who survived the Loreley could stop and thank the gods, St. Goar has good shops (steins and cuckoo clocks, of course), a waterfront park, and a helpful TI. It's worth a stop for its Rheinfels Castle. The small supermarket on Main Street is fine for picnic fixin's. The friendly Montag family in the shop under the Hotel Montag has Koblenz to Mainz Rhine guidebooks, fine steins, and copies of my Germany, Austria, Switzerland guidebook. And across the street, that must be the biggest cuckoo clock in the world.

The St. Goar Tourist Office (8:00-12:30, 14:00-17:00, Saturday 9:30-12:00, closed Sunday, tel. 06741/383) now functions as the town's train station (free left luggage service, 5 DM per half day bike rentals). They have information on which local wineries do tours and tastings in English for individuals.

▲▲**Rheinfels Castle**—This mightiest of Rhine castles is an intriguing ruin today. Follow the castle map with English instructions (.50 DM from the ticket window). If you follow the castle's perimeter, circling counterclockwise, and downward, you'll find a few of the several miles of spooky tunnels. Explore. Bring your flashlight (and bayonet). These tunnels were used to lure and entomb enemy troops. You'll be walking over the buried remains (from 1626) of 300 unfortunate Spanish soldiers. Be sure to see the reconstruction of the castle in the museum showing how much bigger it was before Louis XIV destroyed it. And climb to the summit for the Rhine view (3 DM, daily 9:00-18:00, in October until 17:00, off-season Saturday and Sunday only, free English tours at 11:00 and 16:00, ten minutes steep hike up from St. Goar).

▲▲**Bacharach**—Just a very pleasant old town that misses most of the tourist glitz. Next to the K-D dock is a great park for a picnic. The friendly TI is helpful (open Monday-Friday 9:00-12:00 and 14:00-15:00, tel. 06743/1297, follow signs through a courtyard, up the stairs, and down the squeaky hall). Some of the Rhine's best wine is from this town. Those in search of a stein should stop by the huge Jost beerstein "factory outlet" just a block north of the church.

Mainz, Wiesbaden, Rüdesheim, and Frankfurt—These towns are all too big, too famous, and not worth your time. Mainz's Gutenberg Museum is also a disappointment.

Side Trips (if you have more time in the Rhine area)
▲▲**Mosel Valley**—The Mosel is what many visitors hoped the Rhine would be—peaceful, sleepy, romantic, with fine wine, plenty of castles, hospitable little towns,

and lots of Zimmer. Boat, train, and car traffic here is a trickle compared to the roaring Rhine. While the Mosel moseys from France to Koblenz, where it dumps into the Rhine, the most scenic piece of the valley lies between the towns of Bernkastel-Kues and Cochem. I'd savor only this section.

The town of **Zell** is best for an overnight stop. It's peaceful, with a fine riverside promenade, a pedestrian bridge over the river, plenty of Zimmer, colorful shops, restaurants, and *Weinstuben*.

Beilstein, farther downstream, is the quaintest of all Mosel towns. Check out its narrow lanes, ancient wine cellar, resident (and very territorial) swans, and ruined castle.

Cochem, with its majestic castle and picturesque medieval streets, is the touristy hub of this part of the river. Even with the tourist crowds, it's worth a stop. The Cochem castle is spectacular—even if it is the work of over-imaginative nineteenth-century restorers (mid-March-October, 9:00-17:00, tours on the hour, 3 DM). Consider a boat ride from Cochem to Beilstein (1 hour) or to Zell (3 hours).

▲▲▲**Burg Eltz**—My favorite castle in all of Europe is set in a mysterious forest, left intact for 700 years, and furnished throughout as it was 500 years ago. Even with its German-only tours, it's a must. By train or from the boat dock, it's a steep one hour climb from Moselkern station, midway between Cochem and Koblenz (April-October, Monday-Saturday, 9:00-17:30, Sunday 10:00-17:30, tel. 02672/1300, 7 DM).

▲▲**Bonn**—Bonn was chosen for its sleepy, cultured, and peaceful nature as a good place to plant Germany's first post-Hitler government. Now that Germany is one again, Berlin will retake its position as capital of Germany. Apart from the tremendous cost of switching the seat of government, over 100,000 jobs are involved, and lots of Bonn families will have some difficult decisions to make.

Today Bonn is sleek, modern, and, by big-city standards, remarkably pleasant and easygoing. Stop here not only to see Beethoven's house (10:00-17:00, Sunday 10:00-13:00, 5 DM) but to come up for a smoggy breath of the real world before diving into the misty, romantic Rhine.

The excellent TI is directly in front of the station (8:00-21:00, Sunday 9:30-12:30, tel. 0228/77 34 66, free room-finding service). A good value is the Hotel Eschweiler (95-130 doubles, Bonngasse 7, 5300 Bonn 1, tel. 0228/63 17 60 or 63 17 69, fax 69 49 04). It's plain but perfectly located just off the market square, on a pedestrian street next to Beethoven's place (ten-minute walk from the station—don't drive). The Bonn youth hostel (cheap, way out of town in the woods on Venusberg, bus 621, tel. 28 12 00) is clean and modern.

▲▲**Köln (Cologne)**—This big, no-nonsense city, Germany's fourth largest, has a compact and fascinating center. Since the Rhine was the northern boundary of the Roman Empire, Köln, like most of these towns, goes back 2,000 years. It was an important cultural and religious center throughout the Middle Ages. Even after World War II bombs destroyed 95 percent of it, Cologne remains, after a remarkable recovery, a cultural and commercial center as well as a fun, colorful, and pleasant-smelling city.

Its *Dom*, or cathedral, is far and away Germany's most exciting Gothic church (100 yards from the station, open 7:00-19:00, free tours in German only). Next to the Dom is the outstanding Römisch-Germanisches Museum, Germany's best Roman museum (Tuesday-Sunday 10:00-17:00, Wednesday and Thursday until 20:00; you can view its prize piece, a fine mosaic floor, free from the front window). Sadly, the displays are in German only. The Wallraf-Richartz Museum has a fine new home next to the Roman museum and the cathedral. It has a great collection of paintings by the European masters with a modern and pop art bonus (Friday-Sunday 10:00-18:00, Tuesday-Thursday 10:00-20:00, closed Monday, tel. 0221/221 2379). The helpful TI is near the station, opposite the Dom's main entry (tel. 0221/221 3345, daily 8:00-22:30, closes early in winter).

Transportation: Rhineland to Rothenburg (180 miles)

From Bacharach to Mainz by car (or hourly train), you'll see a few more castles. After that you can hit the autobahn, skirting Frankfurt and setting *das Auto-pilot* on Würzburg. You'll pass U.S. military bases, Europe's busiest airport, lots of trucks, World War II road vehicles, and World War III sky vehicles.

It's a 75-mile straight shot to Würzburg; just follow the blue (for autobahn) signs. The Spessart rest stop at Rohrbrunn (tel. 06094/220, open 10:00-13:00 and 14:00-19:00) has a tourist information office, where friendly Herr Ohm can telephone Rothenburg (and speak German) for you. Pick up a tourist booklet called *Let's Go Bavaria*, brochures on Würzburg, Rothenburg, and the Romantic Road, and a Munich map, all free and in English.

Leave the freeway at the Würzburg/Stuttgart/Ulm road 19 exit and follow 19 south to just before Bad Mergentheim, where a particularly scenic slice of the Romantic Road will lead you directly into Rothenburg. If you're plugging in a stop at Würzburg, take the later Heidingsfeld-Würzburg exit and follow the signs to Stadmitte, then to Residenz (*wo ist . . . ?* means "where is?"). Signs will direct you from downtown Würzburg scenically south (direction Stuttgart/Ulm) on road 19 to Rothenburg.

Train travelers will have missed the Romantic Road bus, so they'll have to go straight to Rothenburg with a possible stop in Würzburg. (The Residenz is a 15-minute walk from the station). The three-hour train ride from Frankfurt to Rothenburg goes Frankfurt Central–Würzburg–Steinach–Rothenburg, with trains departing almost hourly. The tiny Steinach-Rothenburg train often leaves from the "B" section of track, away from the middle of the station, shortly after the Würzburg train arrives. Don't miss it. Time killed in Steinach is already dead.

The Romantic Road bus tour leaves from the Europa bus stop next to the Frankfurt station (south side, daily 8:15 departure, mid-March to October) and at the Würzburg station (daily 9:00, mid-May to September, never full).

Sightseeing Highlights between Frankfurt and Rothenburg

Frankfurt—Probably a nice place to live, but I wouldn't want to visit. Don't visit Frankfurt unless you're stranded at the airport before flying home. If that happens, pick up a city map at the tourist information office (TI) in the station (long hours, tel. 069/212 8849), walk down sleazy Kaiserstrasse past Goethe's house (great man, mediocre sight) to Römerberg, Frankfurt's lively market square. A string of museums is just across the river along Schaumainkai (all open Tuesday-Saturday, 10:00-17:00). Try to avoid driving or sleeping in Frankfurt. Pleasant Rhine towns are just a quick drive or train ride away.

If you must spend the night in Frankfurt, you can sleep near the station at Pension Lohmann (70 DM, Stuttgarterstr. 31, tel. 069/23 25 34), at Hotel Goldener Stern (70-90 DM, Karlsruherstr. 8, tel. 069/23 33 09) or at the youth hostel (cheap, bus 46 from station to Frankenstein Place, Deutschherrnufer 12, tel. 069/61 90 58).

Romantic Road (Romantische Strasse)—The best way to connect Frankfurt with Munich or Füssen is via the popular Romantic Road. This path winds you past the most beautiful towns and scenery of Germany's medieval heartland. Any tourist office can give you a brochure listing the many interesting baroque palaces, lovely carved altarpieces, and walled medieval cities you'll pass along the way. From Frankfurt or Würzburg in the north to Munich or Füssen in the south, the route includes these highlights:

▲▲**Würzburg**—A historic city, though freshly rebuilt since World War II, Würzburg is worth a stop to see its impressive Prince Bishop's Residenz, bubbly baroque chapel (*Hofkirche*), and sculpted gardens. This is a Franconian Versailles with grand stairways, 3-D art, and a tennis court-sized fresco by Tiepolo. Tag along with a tour if you can find one in English, or buy the fine little guidebook. Open daily 9:00-17:00 April-September (closed Mondays) and 10:00-15:30 October-March. Last entry one-half hour before closing, admission 3.50 DM.

Germany's Romantic Road

Easy parking right there, or a 15-minute walk from the station. (TI tel. 0931/37436)

▲**Weikersheim**—Palace with fine baroque gardens (luxurious picnic spot), folk museum, and picturesque town square.

▲**Herrgottskapelle**—Tilman Riemenschneider's greatest carved altarpiece in a peaceful church (one mile from Creglingen). The fast and fun Fingerhut (thimble) museum is just across the street. Both sights are open until 18:00.

▲▲▲**Rothenburg o.d. Tauber**—See tomorrow's plan.

▲ **Dinkelsbühl**—Rothenburg's little sister (see Day 3).

▲▲**Wieskirche**—Germany's most glorious baroque-rococo church. In a sweet meadow. Newly restored. Heavenly (see Day 7).

▲▲▲ **Neuschwanstein**—"Mad" King Ludwig's Disney-esque castle (see Day 7).

The drive gives you a good look at rural Germany. My favorite sections are from Weikersheim to Rothenburg and from Landsberg to Füssen. By car, simply follow the green Romantische Strasse signs.

By train . . . take the bus. The Europa Bus Company makes this trip twice a day in each direction (Frankfurt-Munich mid-March through Oct., Würzburg-Füssen mid-May through Sept.) The 11-hour ride costs about $60 but is free with a Eurailpass. Each bus has a guide who hands out brochures and narrates the journey in English, with stops in the towns of Rothenburg (two hours) and Dinkelsbühl (45 minutes) and briefly at a few other attractions. There is no quicker or easier way to travel across Germany and get such a hearty dose of its countryside.

Bus reservations are free but rarely necessary (except possibly on a summer weekend; call 069/790 3240 three days in advance). You can stop over where you like. Study the timetable to see how you can start and end in different towns and switch buses if you like along the way. To catch the Frankfurt departure, there is a ridiculously early (around 5:30) train from the Rhine villages or a later train that arrives a few minutes after the bus is scheduled to depart. The bus company says it will hold the bus for that train if you call in a reservation and make this request.

Romantic Road bus schedule				
Frankfurt	8:15	—	19:55	—
Würzburg	10:15	9:00	18:10	19:20
Rothenburg	11:35	12:00	15:15	15:35
Dinkelsbühl	14:45	14:30	12:35	13:10
Augsburg	17:40	16:55	10:20	11:00
Munich	18:55	—	9:00	—
Füssen	—	19:35	—	8:15

ROTHENBURG OB DER TAUBER

Today we enjoy Germany's most exciting medieval town. Rothenburg is well worth two nights and a whole day. In the Middle Ages, when Frankfurt and Munich were hick towns, Rothenburg was Germany's second-largest free imperial city with a whopping population of 6,000. Now it's the best-preserved medieval walled town, enjoying tremendous tourist popularity without losing its charm.

Suggested Schedule	
7:00	Walk the wall.
8:30	Breakfast.
9:00	Stop at the TI to confirm plans. Climb the tower, visit the city museum and the Medieval Crime and Punishment Museum. Buy a picnic.
12:00	Picnic in the castle garden, rest.
13:30	City walking tour.
16:00	More museums, shop or walk through the countryside. Sleep Rothenburg.

Orientation—Rothenburg

Think of the Rothenburg town map as a human head. Its nose—the castle garden—sticks out to the left, and the neck is the skinny lower part, with the youth hostel and my favorite hotels.

Rothenburg's heyday was from A.D. 1150 to 1400 when it was the crossing point of two major trade routes: Tashkent-Paris and Hamburg-Venice. Most of the buildings you'll see were built by 1400. The city started around the long-gone castle (built 1142, destroyed in 1356). You can see the shadow of the first town wall, which defines the oldest part of Rothenburg in today's street plan. A few gates from this wall survive. The richest, and therefore biggest, houses were in this central part. The commoners built higgledy-piggledy (read picturesquely) farther from

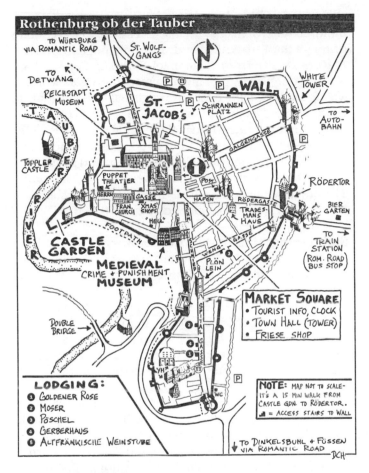

Rothenburg ob der Tauber

TO WÜRZBURG VIA ROMANTIC ROAD

ST. WOLF-GANGS

N

WHITE TOWER

WALL

TO DETWANG

REICHSTADT MUSEUM

ST. JACOB'S

SCHRANNEN PLATZ

GALGENGASSE

TO AUTO-BAHN

TOPPLER CASTLE

PUPPET THEATER

HERRN GASSE

FRAN. CHURCH

XMAS SHOPS

HELL

POST

HAFEN

RÖDERGASSE

TRADES-MANS HAUS

RÖDERTOR

BIER GARTEN

TO TRAIN STATION (ROM. ROAD BUS STOP)

CASTLE GARDEN

FOOTPATH

MEDIEVAL CRIME & PUNISHMENT MUSEUM

PLÖN LEIN

DOUBLE BRIDGE

SPITAL GASSE

YH

WC

MARKET SQUARE
• TOURIST INFO, CLOCK
• TOWN HALL (TOWER)
• FRIESE SHOP

LODGING:
❶ GOLDENER ROSE
❷ MOSER
❸ PÖSCHEL
❹ GERBERHAUS
❺ ALTFRÄNKISCHE WEINSTUBE

NOTE: MAP NOT TO SCALE—IT'S A 15 MIN WALK FROM CASTLE GDN. TO RÖDERTOR.
▣ = ACCESS STAIRS TO WALL

↓ TO DINKELSBUHL & FÜSSEN VIA ROMANTIC ROAD

—DCH—

the center near the present walls. Today, the great trade is tourism, and two-thirds of the town's people are employed serving you.

Too often, Rothenburg brings out the shopper in visitors before they've had a chance to appreciate the historic city. True, this is a great place to do your German shopping, but first see the town. The TI on the market square has guided tours in English (daily in summer at 13:30 from the Market Square, 5 DM including church and altar). If none are scheduled, you can hire a private guide. For 60 DM, a local historian—who's usually an intriguing

character as well—will bring the ramparts alive. Eight
hundred years of history are packed between the cobbles
(through the TI, or call Mannfred Baumann, tel. 09861/
4146, or Frau Gertrud Wagner, tel. 09861/2288).

Start your visit by picking up a map, the *Sights Worth
Seeing and Knowing* brochure (a virtual walking guide to
the town, read it all), and information at the TI on the
main square (Monday-Friday 9:00-12:00 and 14:00-18:00,
Saturday 9:00-12:00 and 14:00-16:00, closed Sunday, tel.
09861/40492). Confirm sightseeing plans and ask about
the daily 13:30 walking tour and evening entertainment.
The best town map is available free at the Friese shop,
two doors from the TI. Telephone code: 09861.

Sightseeing Highlights—Rothenburg

▲▲ **Walk the Wall**—Just over a mile around, with great
views, and providing a good orientation, this walk can be
done by those under 6 feet tall in less than an hour and
requires no special sense of balance. Photographers will
go through lots of film, especially before breakfast or at
sunset when the lighting is best and the crowds are least.
The best fortifications are in the Spitaltor (south end).
Walk from there counterclockwise to the forehead.
Climb the Rödertor en route.

▲ **Rödertor**—The wall tower nearest the train station is
the only one you can climb. It is worth the hike up for the
view and a fascinating rundown on the bombing of
Rothenburg in the last weeks of World War II (the northeast corner of the city was destroyed, photos, English
translation, 1 DM, 9:00-17:00).

▲▲ **Climb Town Hall Tower**—The best view of
Rothenburg and the surrounding countryside and a
close-up look at an old tiled roof from the inside (open
9:30-12:30 and 13:00-16:00, weekends 13:00-16:00) is
yours for a rigorous (214 steps, 180 feet) but interesting
climb and 1 DM. Ladies, beware, some men find the view
best from the bottom of the ladder just before the top.

▲▲ **Herrengasse and the Castle Garden**—Any town's
Herrengasse, where the richest patricians and merchants
(the *Herren*) lived, is your chance to see its finest old

mansions. Wander from the market square down Herrengasse (past the old Rothenburg official measurement
rods, on the city hall wall), drop into the lavish front
rooms of a ritzy hotel or two, and continue down
through the old gate (notice the tiny, after-curfew door in
the big door and the hole from which hot tar was poured
onto attackers) into the garden that used to be the castle.
(Great Tauber Riviera views at twilight.)

▲▲▲ **Medieval Crime and Punishment Museum**—
The best of its kind, full of fascinating old legal bits and
Kriminal pieces, instruments of punishment and torture,
even a special cage—complete with a metal gag—for
nags. Exhibits in English. Open daily 9:30-18:00, 14:00-
16:00 in winter, 4 DM, fun cards and posters. Goofy
photo opportunity in the stocks outside.

▲▲ **St. Jacob's Church**—Here you'll find a glorious
500-year-old wooden altarpiece by Tilman Riemenschneider, located up the stairs and behind the organ.
Riemenschneider was the Michelangelo of German
wood-carvers. This is the one required art treasure in
town. Open daily 9:00-17:30, Sunday 10:30-17:30, 2 DM.

Meistertrunk Show—Be on the main square at 11:00,
12:00, 13:00, 14:00, 15:00, 20:00, 21:00, or 22:00 for the
ritual gathering of the tourists to see the less-than-
breathtaking reenactment of the Meistertrunk story.

In 1631, the Catholic army took the Protestant town
and was about to do its rape, pillage, and plunder thing
when the mayor said, "Hey, if I can drink this entire
3-liter tankard of wine in one gulp, will you leave us
alone?" The invading commander, sensing he was dealing with an unbalanced people, said, "Sure." Mayor
Nusch drank the whole thing and the town was saved.
(I've often wondered how the mayor celebrated . . .)

Hint: for the best show, don't watch the clock; watch
the open-mouthed tourists gasp as the old windows flip
open. At the late shows, the square flickers with flash
attachments.

Historical Vaults—Under the town hall tower is a city
history museum, which gives a good look at medieval
Rothenburg and a good-enough replica of the famous

Meistertrunk tankard (well described in English, 9:00-
18:00, 10:00-17:00 off-season, 2 DM).
**Museum of the Imperial City (Reichsstadt
Museum)**—This stuffier museum, housed in the former
Dominican Convent gives a more in-depth look at old
Rothenburg with some fine art and the supposed Meistertrunk tankard, labeled *Kürfurstenhumpen* (open daily
10:00-17:00, 13:00-16:00 in winter, 3 DM).
St. Wolfgang's Church—This fortified Gothic church
is built into the medieval wall at Klingentor (near the
"forehead"). Explore its dungeonlike passages below, and
check out the shepherd's dance exhibit to see where they
hot-oiled the enemy back in the good old days.
Alt Rothenburger Handwerferhaus—This 700-year-
old tradesman's house shows the typical living situation
of Rothenburg in its heyday (Alter Stadtgraben 26, near
the Markus Tower, daily 9:00-18:00, 3 DM).
▲**Walk in the Countryside**—Just below the *Burggar-
ten* (castle garden) in the Tauber Valley is the cute, skinny,
600-year-old castle/summer home of Mayor Toppler
(open summers only, 13:00-17:00). It's furnished inti-
mately and well worth a look. Notice the photo of
bombed-out 1945 Rothenburg on the top floor. Then
walk on past the covered bridge and huge trout to the
peaceful village of Detwang. Detwang is actually older
than Rothenburg, with another great Riemenschneider
altarpiece in its church (the second oldest in Franconia,
from 968).
A Franconian Bike Ride—For a fun, breezy look at the
countryside around Rothenburg, rent a bike from the
train station, 10 DM per day (5 DM with a train pass or
ticket), open 5:00-18:30. For a pleasant half-day pedal,
bike south down to Detwang via Topplerschloss and
Fuchesmill (an old water mill across the street). Then go
north along the level bike path to Tauberscheckenbach,
then uphill about 20 minutes to Adelshofen and south
back to Rothenburg.
Swimming—Rothenburg has a fine modern recreation
center with an indoor/outdoor pool and a sauna, a few

minutes walk down the Dinkelsbühl Road (past the bottom of the neck, tel. 09861/4565 for hours).
Franconian Open-Air Museum—Twenty minutes drive from Rothenburg in the undiscovered "Rothenburgy" town of Bad Windsheim is a small, open-air folk museum that, compared with others in Europe, isn't much. But it's trying very hard and gives you the best look around at traditional rural Franconia.

Shopping

Rothenburg is one of Germany's best shopping towns. Do it here, mail it home, and get it out of your hair. Lovely prints, carvings, wine glasses, Christmas tree ornaments, and beer steins are popular.

The Kathe Wohlfahrt Christmas trinkets phenomenon is spreading across the half-timbered reaches of Europe. In Rothenburg, tourists flock to the Kathe Wohlfahrt Kris Kringle Market and the Christmas Village (on either side of Herrengasse, just off the main square) eagerly buying into a 20-year-old tradition. This is a Christmas wonderland, replete with enough twinkling lights to require a special electric hookup, instant Christmas spirit mood music (best appreciated on a hot day in July), and American and Japanese tourists filling little woven shopping baskets with 5 to 10 DM goodies to hang on their trees. (Okay, I admit it, my Christmas tree dangles with a few KW ornaments.)

The Friese shop (just off Market Square, west of the tourist office on the corner across from the public W.C.) offers a charming contrast. It's very friendly and gives shoppers with this book tremendous service: a 10 percent discount, 14 percent tax deducted if you have it mailed, and a free Rothenburg map. Anneliese, who runs the place with her sons, Frankie and Berni, charges only her cost to ship things, changes money at the best rates in town with no extra charge, and lets tired travelers leave their bags in her back room for free.

For good prints and paintings, visit friendly Wilma Diener's shop at Untere Schmiedgasse 2. For less coziness

but a free shot of schnapps, visit the larger Ernst Geissen-
dörfer print shop, located where the main square hits
Schmiedgasse.

Those who prefer to eat their souvenirs shop the *Bäck-
erei* (bakeries). Their succulent pastries, pies, and cakes
are pleasantly distracting. Skip the good-looking but bad-
tasting "Rothenburger schnee balls."

Evening Fun and Beer Drinking
The best beer garden for balmy summer evenings is just
outside the wall at the Rödertor (red gate). If this is dead,
as it often is, go a few doors farther out to the alley (left)
just before the Sparekasse for two popular bars and the
hottest disco in town.

For a rare chance to mix it up with locals who aren't
selling anything, bring your favorite slang and tongue-
twisters to the English conversation club (Wednesdays,
20:00) at Mario's Altefränkische Weinstube. This dark and
smoky pub is an atmospheric hangout any night but
Tuesday when it's closed (Klosterhof 7, off Klingengasse,
behind St. Jacob's church, tel. 09861/6404).

Sleeping in Rothenburg (about 1.7 DM = U.S.$1)
Rothenburg is crowded with visitors, including probably
Europe's greatest single concentration of Japanese
tourists, but when the sun sets, most go home to big-city,
high-rise hotels, and room-finding is easy. The first five
listings are at the south end of town, a 7-minute (without
shopping) walk downhill from the marketplace (which
has a tourist office with room-finding service). Walk
downhill on Schmiedgasse (*Gasse* means lane) until it
becomes Spitalgasse (hospital lane).

I stay in **Hotel Goldener Rose** (59 DM doubles without shower, classy 75 DM doubles in the annex behind
the garden, Spitalgasse 28, 8803 Rothenburg, tel. 09861/
4638), where scurrying Karin serves breakfast and stately
Henni causes many monoglots to dream in fluent
Deutsche. The hotel has only one shower for two floors
of rooms and the street side can be noisy, but the rooms

are clean and airy, and you're surrounded by cobbles, flowers, and red-tiled roofs. The Favetta family also serves good, reasonably priced meals. Remember to keep your key to get in after they close (side gate in alley).

For the best, real, with-a-local-family, comfortable, and homey experience, stay with **Herr und Frau Moser** (28 DM per person, one double and one triple, Spitalgasse 12, tel. 09861/5971). This charming retired couple speak little English but try very hard. Talk in slow, clear, simple English.

Pension Pöschel (60 DM doubles and 30 DM singles, Wenggasse 22, tel. 09861/3430) is also friendly with bright rooms a little closer to the Marketplace. Just across the street, the **Gastehaus Raidel** (58 DM doubles, Wenggasse 3, tel. 3115), with bright rooms but cramped facilities down the hall, works in a pinch (it's run by grim people who make me sing the Adams Family theme song).

Hotel Gerberhaus (80-130 DM doubles, all with private showers, Spitalgasse 25, 8803 Rothenburg, tel. 09861/3055, fax 09861/86555), a new hotel in a 500-year-old building, mixes modern comforts into bright and airy rooms while keeping the traditional flavor.

Rothenburg's fine youth hostel, the **Rossmühle** (16 DM beds, 4 DM sheets, 7 DM dinners, tel. 09861/4510, reception open 7:00-9:00, 17:00-19:00, 20:00-22:00, will hold rooms until 18:00 if you call, lock-up at 23:30) has about three double bunks per room and is often filled with school groups. This droopy-eyed building is the old town horse mill (used when the town was under siege and the river-powered mill was inaccessible). They also run the simpler and 4 DM cheaper **Spitalhof** hostel, next door. Remember, this is Bavaria, which has a 27-years age limit for hosteling, except for families traveling with children under 16.

Gasthof Marktplatz (55 DM doubles overlooking the town square and 80 DM doubles with showers, tel. 09861/6722) has simple rooms and a cozy atmosphere and is right on the town square. Its cheap rooms are the

only rooms listed in this book that have access to absolutely no shower, just a sink in the room.

Bohemians with bucks enjoy the **Hotel Altfränkische
Weinstube Am Klosterhof** (85-100 DM, all with
showers, Klosterhof 7, tel. 09861/6404), located just off
Klingengasse behind St. Jacob's church. A young couple,
Mario and Erika, run this dark, smoky pub in a 600-year-
old building. Upstairs they rent *gemütliche* rooms with
an upscale Monty Python atmosphere, TVs, modern
showers, open-beam ceilings, and *Himmelbette* (cano-
pied four-posters that are called "heaven beds"). Their
pub is a candlelit classic, serving hot food until 22:00,
closing at 01:00. You're welcome to drop by on Wednesday evenings (20:00) for the English Conversation Club.

If money doesn't matter, the **Burg Hotel** (200 DM doubles, Klostergasse 1, on the wall near the castle garden,
tel. 09861/5037), with elegance almost unimaginable in a
medieval building with a Tauber valley view and a high-
heeled receptionist, offers a good way to spend it.

To get away from the tourism, stay in a nearby village
Zimmer. The clean, quiet, and comfortable old **Gasthof
Zum Schwarzen Lamm** in the village of Detwang just
below Rothenburg (about 80 DM per double, tel. 09861/
6727) serves good food, as does the popular and very
local-style **Eulenstube** next door. **Gastehaus Alte
Schveinerei** (8801 Bettwar, tel. 09861/1541) offers good
food and quiet, comfy, reasonable rooms, a little farther
down the road in Bettwar.

(Reminder: Throughout this book, hotel prices, unless
otherwise indicated, are for double rooms with breakfast. More expensive listings are generally with a private
shower.)

Eating in Rothenburg
It can be tough to find a reasonable meal (or a place serving late) in the town center. Galgengasse (Gallows Street)
has two cheap and popular standbys: **Pizzeria Roma** (19
Galgengasse, 11:30-24:00) serves 10 DM pizzas and normal schnitzel fare. **Gasthof zum Ochen** (26 Galgengasse,

11:30-13:30, 18:00-20:00, closed Thursday) offers decent
10 DM meals. **Zum Schmolzer** (corner of Stollengasse
and Rosengasse) is a local favorite for its cheap beer and
good food. If you need a break from schnitzel, the **Hong
Kong China Restaurant**, outside the town near the
train tracks (1 Bensenstr., tel. 09861/7377) serves good
Chinese food.

Itinerary Options

This "two nights and a full day" plan assumes you have a
car. Eurailers taking the Romantic Road bus tour must
leave around 13:30, so you'll have to decide between half
a day or a day and a half here. For sightseeing, half a day is
enough. For a rest, a day and a half sounds better.

Countless renowned travelers have searched for the
elusive "untouristy Rothenburg." There are many con-
tenders (Michelstadt, Miltenberg, Bamberg, Bad Windsheim, Dinkelsbühl, and others I decided to forget), but
none holds a candle to the king of medieval German cuteness. Even with crowds, overpriced souvenirs, Japanese-
speaking night watchmen, and yes, even with schnee
balls, Rothenburg is best. Save time and mileage and be
satisfied with the winner.

ROMANTIC ROAD TO THE TIROL

This day has many facets and many miles. From the cutesy Romantic Road, make a powerful pilgrimage to the concentration camp at Dachau. Then, change moods with a beer hall lunch in Germany's most livable city, Munich, before rejoining the Romantic Road on its southernmost leg to Füssen. Settle down across the border in the Austrian town of Reutte.

Suggested Schedule	
7:00	Early departure, drive south on Romantic Road.
9:30	Tour Dachau, museum, and grounds.
11:00	Drive into Munich for a beer hall lunch and a look at the town center.
15:00	Drive to Reutte.
19:00	Dinner.
20:30	Tirolean folk evening (if possible).

Transportation: Rothenburg to Reutte, Austria (200 miles)

Get an early start to enjoy the quaint hills and rolling villages of this romantic region. (To make more time in Munich, I'd skip breakfast and leave by 7:00. Squeezing Munich into today's plan rushes things, but I think it's worthwhile.) Germany's major medieval trade route is today's top tourist trip. Drive through cute Dinkelsbühl (cheaper souvenirs than Rothenburg) and continue south. After crossing the baby Danube River (Donau in German), you'll reach Augsburg where the autobahn zips you into Munich (München). Signs direct you off the freeway to Dachau. Then signs to KZ Gedenkstätte lead you to the memorial's parking lot.

From Dachau, Dachauerstrasse leads you right into Munich. This is big-city driving at its worst, so check your insurance, fasten your seat belt, and remind yourself that Germany is now our ally. You'll see the cobweb-style Olympic Village with its huge TV tower on the left. An easy option for drivers is to park there and ride the subway (U-bahn) to Marienplatz (downtown). Or, work your way right to the center of things, setting your sights on the twin domes of the Frauenkirche—the symbol of Munich—and parking between that landmark church and the Bahnhof (train station). Your goal is to park as close to the center as possible, explore it for a few hours, and head south following the autobahn signs to Innsbruck, then Landsberg, Lindau, and Füssen. On weekdays, leave by 16:00 to avoid the nightly traffic jam. (To skip Munich and the big-city driving, from Dachau cross back over the autobahn following signs to Fürstenfeld, then Inning, then Landsberg, and on to Füssen.)

Leave the Munich-Lindau autobahn at Landsberg and wind south again on the Romantic Road, to Füssen. Just before Füssen, you'll see hang gliders circling like colorful vultures and, in the distance, the white, shimmering dream castle, Neuschwanstein. Follow the little road to the left to drive under it. If the weather's good, stop for a photo. Füssen is just down the road. Reutte is just over the Austrian border from here.

Train travelers catch the Romantic Road bus tour from the Rothenburg train station; two buses come through in the early afternoon. You can catch one bus into Munich (arrives at 18:55) or the other direct to Füssen (arrives at 19:35, long after the last bus to Reutte). Ask about exact times in Rothenburg at the train station or tourist office. Be early! If you stake out a seat when the bus arrives, you'll have a better chance of being on it when it leaves two hours later. Without a car, Dachau is best done from Munich (get the flier explaining public transportation from Munich to Dachau at the TI in the station).

Today and tomorrow, we'll cross the German-Austrian border several times. Our plan calls for sleeping tonight and tomorrow night just a few miles south of Germany in the Austrian town of Reutte and making a loop tomorrow from Austria back through Germany, returning to our Austrian home base.

Sightseeing Highlights

▲ **Dinkelsbühl**—Just a small Rothenburg without the
mobs but cute enough to merit a short stop. Kinderzeche
children's festival turns Dinkelsbühl wonderfully on end
each mid-July. (TI tel. 09851/3031.) Park near the church
in the center, buy a picnic, and just browse. You'll find an
interesting local museum, a well-preserved medieval wall
with twenty towers, gates, and a moat.

▲▲ **Dachau**—Dachau was the first Nazi concentration
camp (1933). Today it's the most accessible camp to
travelers and a very effective voice from our recent but
grisly past, warning and pleading, "Never Again," the
memorial's theme. This is a valuable experience and,
when approached thoughtfully, well worth the drive. In
fact, it may change your life. See it. Feel it. Read and think
about it. After this most powerful sightseeing experience,
many people gain more respect for history and the
dangers of not keeping tabs on your government.

On arrival, pick up the mini-guide and notice when the
next documentary film in English will be shown (20
minutes, normally at 11:30 and 15:30). The museum and
the 25-minute movie are exceptional. Notice the expres-
sionist, Fascist-inspired art near the theater. Outside, be
sure to tour the reconstructed barracks and the memorial
shrines at the far end. (Near the theater are English books,

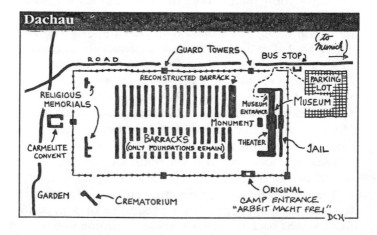

slides, and a good W.C. The camp is open 9:00-17:00, closed Monday.)

Munich

Munich is big—Germany's third-largest city, after Berlin and Hamburg—and growing fast, but its excellent tourist information office and sleek subway system make life easy for the five million visitors who come to town each year. On this plan we make time only for a quick intro-duction to Munich. But if you have extra time, Munich is worth it.

Take full advantage of the TI office in the train station (open 8:00-22:00 daily, tel. 089/239 1256 or 239 1257, opposite track 11). The industrious and hardworking EurAid office (half way to the Bahnhof Mission, down track 11, daily May through early October 7:30-11:30 and 13:00-18:00, closes at 16:30 in May) is an American whirl-pool of travel information designed for Eurailers and budget travelers. They know your train travel and accom-modations questions and have answers, in clear American English. They also do Dachau and King Ludwig tours, both a bit frustrating for those without cars. Pick up their free newsletter.

At the other end of the station, near track 30 is Radius Touristik (open daily, 8:30-18:30, May through mid-October, tel. 089/59 61 13, run by an Englishman, Patrick Holder), which rents three-speed bikes (4 DM/hour, 20 DM/day) and organizes introduction walks of the old city. Munich—level, compact, with plenty of bike paths—is for bikers.

You'll find Munich's architecture a bit sterile, as most of its historic center has been rebuilt since the World War II bombings. Its hotels are expensive, but after that, food, fun, and transportation are cheap. Most Munich sights are closed on Mondays. Telephone code: 089.

Sightseeing Highlights—Munich
▲▲ **Marienplatz and the Pedestrian Zone**—This is the glory of Munich: great buildings bombed flat and rebuilt, the ornate facades of the new and old City Halls

(Neues, built in neo-Gothic style in 1867, and the Altes Rathaus), outdoor cafés, and people bustling and lingering like the birds and breeze they share this square with. From here the pedestrian mall (Kaufingerstrasse and Neuhauserstrasse) leads you through a great shopping area, past plenty of entertaining street singers, the twin-towering Frauenkirche (with its 350-foot-high view point, built in 1470, rebuilt after World War II, closed through 1994 for more work), and several fountains, to Karlstor and the train station.

▲▲**Residenz**—For a good dose of imperial Bavarian grandeur, tour the palace of the Wittelsbach family. For 600 years, the Wittelsbachs ruled Bavaria from here. Don't miss the Schatzkammer (treasury), containing a thousand years of Wittelsbach knickknacks, which, like the palace, is open Tuesday to Saturday 10:00 to 16:30, Sunday 10:00 to 13:00, 3.50 DM. Take U-3, or 6, to Odeonsplatz, or walk from Marienplatz. (Nymphenburg Palace, the Wittelsbach summer palace, is great but only mediocre if you've already seen the Residenz.)

▲▲▲**Alte Pinakothek**—Bavaria's best collection of art is stored in a pleasing easy-to-handle museum, strong on Italian and northern European artists, Dürer and Rubens. Open 9:15 to 16:30, closed Monday, open 19:00 to 21:00 on Tuesday and Thursday. Take U-8 to Königsplatz or tram 18, 4 DM, free on Sunday.

▲▲▲**Deutsches Museum**—This German answer to our Smithsonian Institution has everything of scientific and technical interest, from astronomy to zymurgy, but can be disappointing due to its overwhelming size and lack of English descriptions. Open 9:00-17:00, 8 DM admission. S-Bahn to Isartorplatz or tram 18. Despite its reputation, unless you are (or wish you were) an engineer, two hours is enough time here.

Organized bus tours of the city and nearby countryside—Panorama Tours (at the station, tel. 089/59 15 04) offers all-day tours of Neuschwanstein and Linderhof (65 DM) and one-hour city orientation tours (at 10:00, 11:30, and 14:30, 13 DM).

Oktoberfest—When King Ludwig I had a marriage party in 1810 it was such a success that they made it an annual bash. These days the Oktoberfest starts on the third Saturday each September, with an opening parade of over 6,000 participants, and fills 6 or 8 huge beer tents with about 6,000 people each. Sixteen days and a million gallons of beer later, they roast the last ox.

While you can always find a festival in Munich's beer halls, the entire city celebrates each fall with this mother of all keggers. It's crowded, but if you arrive in the morning (except Friday or Saturday), the TI will be able to find you a room.

Sleeping in Munich

The area immediately south of the station is full of budget hotels (that's 80 DM doubles in Munich) but has gotten quite seedy. My listings are in more polite neighborhoods, nearly all within a five-or ten-minute walk of the station and handy to the center.

Jugendhotel Marienherberge (29 DM singles, 25 DM in 2- to 6-bed rooms, close to the station at Goethestrasse 9, tel. 089/55 58 91) is a very pleasant, friendly convent accepting young women only (loosely enforced 18- to 25-years age limit). If you qualify, sleep here.

YMCA (CVJM), open to people of all ages and most sexes (84 DM doubles, very central, just two blocks south of the station at Landwehrstrasse 13, tel. 089/55 59 41), has modern and simple rooms. Reservations are necessary. Cheap dinners are served from 18:00 to 21:00, Tuesday through Saturday.

Hotel Pension Erika (70-90 DM doubles, Landwehrstrasse 8, 8 Munich 2, tel. 089/55 43 27) is as bright as dingy yellow can be. Its cheap doubles are a great value.

Hotel Pension Utzelmann (85-135 DM doubles, 45 DM singles, 140 DM quad, Pettenkoferstrasse 6, 8000 Munich 2, tel. 089/59 48 89 or 59 62 28) is the best value of all. Most of the rooms are huge, especially the curiously cheap room 6. Each room is richly furnished with homey, lace tablecloth finishing touches. It's in an extremely decent neighborhood a ten-minute walk from the station, a block off Sendlinger Tor. Easy parking.

Hotel Uhland (130-210 doubles, with a huge breakfast, 1 Uhlandstrasse, near the Theresienwiese Oktoberfest grounds, a ten-minute walk from the station, tel. 089/53 92 77, fax 089/53 11 14), a mansion with sliding glass doors and a garden, is a worthwhile splurge.

Pension Diana (90 DM doubles, Altheimer Eck 15, 8000 Munich 2, tel. 089/260 3107) is on the third floor (no elevator) with 15 bright and airy doubles, an environment perfect for retired and married nuns. It's in the old center, a block off the pedestrian mall.

Pension Linder (85-95 DM doubles, Dultstrasse 1-Sendlinger Strasse, Munich 2, tel. 089/26 34 13) is clean, quiet, modern, and very concrete. The most central of my listings, it's across the street from the city museum, a few blocks from Marienplatz.

Eating in Munich
Munich's most memorable budget food is in the beer halls. There are many to choose from, but I'm stuck on the **Mathäuser Bierstadt** (tel. 089/59 28 96) at Bayerstrasse 5, halfway between the Hauptbahnhof (main train station) and Karlstor. The music-every-night atmosphere is thick; the fat and shiny leather band has church mice standing up and conducting three-quarter time with a breadstick. Meals are inexpensive (for a light 8.50 DM meal, I like #94 on the menu, Schweinswurst and Kraut), huge liter beers called *ein Mass* (or "ein pitcher" in English) are 8.50 DM, white radishes are salted and cut in delicate spirals, and huge surly beermaids pull mustard packets from their cavernous cleavages. Notice the vomitoriums in the W.C.

The most famous beer hall, the **Hofbräuhaus** (Platzl 9, near Marienplatz, tel. 089/22 16 76), is much more touristy. But do check it out; it's fun to see 200 Japanese drinking beer in a German beer hall. Also memorable, tasty, and rowdy is the **Weisses Bräuhaus** at Tal 10, between Marienplatz and Isartor. Hitler met with fellow Fascists here in 1920, when his Nazi party was in an embryonic state.

Neuschwanstein
See tomorrow.

Füssen
Important as the southern terminus of the trade route now known by today's tourists as the Romantic Road, Füssen is romantically situated under a renovated castle on the lively Lech River.

Unfortunately, it's entirely overrun by tourists—of the worst kind. Traffic in the summer is exasperating, but by bike or on foot it's not bad. The train station (where the Romantic Road bus tour leaves each morning at 8:15 and arrives each evening at 19:35, June through September) is a few minutes walk from the TI, good rooms, the hostel, and the town center, a cobbled shopping mall.

Halfway between Füssen and the border (as you drive) is the Lechfall, a thunderous look at the river with a handy potty stop.

Reutte
Reutte (pronounced ROY-teh, rolled r), population 5,000, is a relaxed town, far from the international tourist crowd but popular with Germans and Austrians for its climate. Doctors recommend its "grade 1" air.

You won't find Reutte in any American guidebook. Its charms are subtle. It never was rich or important; the carvings on the buildings are all painted on. Its castle is ruined, its churches are full, its men yodel for each other on birthdays, and its energy lately is spent soaking its German-speaking guests in gemütlichkeit.

Because most guests stay for a week, the town's attractions are more time-consuming than thrilling. The mountain lift swoops you high above the tree line to an alpine flower park with special slow-down-and-smell-the-many-local-varieties paths. The town Heimatmuseum (10:00-12:00, 14:00-17:00, closed Monday, in the Green

House on Untermarkt, around the corner from Hotel Golden Hirsch) offers a quick look at the local folk culture and the story of the castle, but so do the walls and mantles of most of the hotels.

Reutte has an Olympic-size swimming pool open from 10:00-21:00, which might be a good way to cool off after your castle hikes (off-season, 14:00-21:00, closed Monday, 55 AS).

For a major thrill on a sunny day, drop by the tiny airport in Hofen across the river and fly. For 30 minutes, a small single-prop plane (three people for 30 minutes, 1,200 AS, 60 minutes for 1,900 AS) can buzz the Zugspitze and Ludwig's castles and give you a bird's-eye peek at Reutte's Ehrenberg ruins. (That's about the cost of three lift tickets up the Zugspitze, and a lot easier.) Or, for something more angelic, how about *Segelfliegen*. For 240 AS, you get 30 minutes in a glider for two (you and the pilot). Just watching the tow rope launch the graceful glider like a giant, slow-motion rubber band gun is thrilling (May-October, 11:00-19:00, in good weather, tel. 05672/3207).

Sleeping in Reutte ($1 = about 12 AS, 1 AS = about U.S. $.08)

In July, August, and September, Munich and Bavaria are packed with tourists. Austria's Tirol is easier and cheaper. I like Reutte, just over the border, for its lack of crowds, its easygoing locals' contagious love of life, for the Austrian ambience, and out of habit.

The Reutte tourist office (one block in front of the station, or Bahnhof, open weekdays 8:00-12:00 and 13:00-18:00, Saturday 8:00-12:00 and, from mid-July to mid-August on Saturday and Sunday afternoons from 16:00-18:00, tel. 05672/2336, or, direct from Germany, 0043 5672/2336) is very helpful. Go over your sightseeing plans, ask about a folk evening, pick up a city map, ask about discounts with the hotel guest cards. Reutte has no laundromat (handy one in Venice).

Youth Hostels: Reutte has plenty of reasonable hotels and Zimmer and two excellent little youth hostels. If

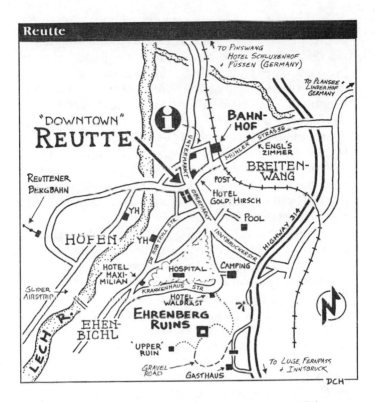

you've never hosteled and are curious, try one of these. The downtown youth hostel is clean, rarely full, serves no meals but has a fine members' kitchen, and accepts nonmembers (70 AS per bed, a pleasant 10-minute walk from the town center, follow the Jugendherberge signs to the Kindergarten sign, 6600 Reutte, Prof. Dengelstr. 20, Tirol, open mid-June to late August, tel. 05672/3039).

The **Jugendgastehaus Graben** (110 AS with breakfast, A-6600 Reutte-Höfen, Postfach 3, Graben 1, cross the river and follow the road left, toward the castle, about a mile from the station, tel. 05672/2644) accepts nonmembers, has 2 to 12 beds per room, and includes breakfast, shower, and sheets. Frau Reyman, who keeps the place traditional, homey, clean, and friendly, serves a great dinner. No curfew, open all year, bus connections to Neuschwanstein Castle.

Zimmer: The tourist office has a list of over 50 private homes that rent out generally elegant rooms with facilities down the hall, a pleasant communal living room, and breakfast. They charge about 160 AS a night, cheaper for longer stays, and will happily hold a room for you if you telephone. The TI can call and set you up just about any day of the year for free.

Edwin and Waltraud Engl's Zimmer (130 AS with breakfast, Mühler Strasse 23, tel. 05672/2326.) is my favorite; only one room for 2 or 3, elegant TV/living/breakfast room, friendly; they speak only a little English but will hold a room if you phone. And it's just 2 blocks behind the Reutte train station.

Also near the station, in a quiet residential street in the adjacent village of **Breitenwang** are the private rooms in the homes of **Maria Auer** (several very comfortable rooms at Kaiser Lothar Strasse 25, tel. 05672/29195) and **Walter Hosp** (Kaiser Lothar Strasse 29, tel. 05672/5377). Farther out, in the neighboring village of **Ehenbichl**, just behind the recommended Hotel Maximilian, is the comfortable home of **Armella Brutscher** (Unterried 24, tel. 05672/4294).

Hotels: Reutte is very popular with Austrians and Germans who come here year after year for a one-or two-week vacation. The hotels are big, elegant, and full of beautifully carved furnishings and creative ways to spend so much time in one spot. They serve great food and send their children away to hotel management schools. Breakfast is included, and showers are in the room. Your choices are: right in Reutte, out of town in a nearby village, in a quiet meadow with the cows, or in the forest under the castle. (To call Reutte from Germany, dial 0043-5672 and the four-digit number.)

Hotel Goldener Hirsch (660 AS doubles, 6600 Reutte-Tirol, tel. 05672/2508 and ask for Helmut or Monika, fax 05672/250 8100), a grand old hotel renovated with a mod Tirolean Jugendstil flair with sliding doors, mini-bars, TVs with cable in the rooms, and one lonely set of antlers, is located right downtown (two blocks from the station). They can help with cheaper rooms if they are full or too expensive. The Goldener Hirsch has a fine and reasonable restaurant (not serving on Monday).

Hotel Maximilian, just down the river a mile or so, in the village of Ehenbichl (700 AS doubles, A-6600 Ehenbichl-Reutte, tel. 05672/2585, fax 05672/25 85 54), is the best splurge. Its modern, 700 AS doubles include use of bicycles, sauna, Ping-Pong, a children's playroom, and the friendly service of the Koch family. Daughter Gabi speaks fine English. There always seems to be a special event here and if you're lucky, you'll hear the Koch family make music, an "edelweiss" experience. American guests are made to feel right at home. The Kochs can usually pick you up at the station.

Hotel Schluxen gets the "remote old hotel in an idyllic setting" award (540 AS, modern, rustic doubles with the best breakfast in town, Family Gstir, A-6600 Pinswang-Reutte, follow the tiny road after the border just before the bridge, sign to Oberpinswang, tel. 05677/8452). This newly refurbished old lodge, filled with locals, is just off the main road near the village of Pinswang, north of Reutte. This is a great place for kids—yours and the Gstir grandchildren. From Schluxen, it's an hour's hike over the mountain to Ludwig's Neuschwanstein castle. Consider parking here, having lunch (50-100 AS) on a sunny day filled with the sound of cowbells, and hiking (or biking, they rent bikes) to Ludwig's castle.

Gasthof-Pension Waldrast (500-600 AS per double, 6600 Ehenbichl, on Ehrenbergstrasse, a half-mile south of town, past the campground, just under the castle, tel. 05672/2443) separates a forest and a meadow and is warmly run by the Huter family. The big rooms are like living rooms, many with a fine castle view. This is a good coffee stop if hiking into town from the Ehrenberg ruins.

Eating in Reutte

Each of the hotels takes great pleasure in serving fine Austrian food at reasonable prices. Rather than go to a cheap restaurant, I'd order low on their menu. For cheap food, the **Prima** self-serve cafeteria (Mühler Strasse 20, near the station, 9:00-19:00 Monday-Friday) and the **Metzgerei Storf Imbiss** (better, but open Monday-Friday 8:30-15:00 only, above the deli across from the Heimatmuseum on Untermarkt Street) are the best in town.

Sleeping in Füssen, Germany (1.7 DM = about U.S.$1)

Füssen, two miles from Mad Ludwig's castles, is a cobbled, crenellated, riverside oom-pah treat, but very touristy. It has just about as many rooms as tourists, though, and a helpful tourist office with a free room-finding service, just two blocks past the train station (look for Kurverwaltung, open 8:00-12:00, 14:00-19:00, Saturday 10:00-12:00, 14:00-16:00, Sunday 10:00-12:00, shorter hours from October-June, tel. 08362/7077). I prefer Reutte, but without your own car this is a handier home base (unless you've got 35 DM for a taxi from the Füssen station to Reutte).

All places listed here are an easy walk from the train station and the town center. And they assured me they are used to travelers getting in at about 20:00 off the Romantic Road bus and will hold rooms for a promise on the phone.

The excellent Germanly run **Füssen youth hostel** (4- to 8-bed rooms, 17 DM for B&B, 7 DM for dinner, 3 DM for sheets, 27 is the maximum age, laundry and kitchen facilities, Mariahilferstr. 5, tel. 08362/7754) is a ten-minute walk from town; backtrack from the station. You might rent a bike at the station to get there quick and easy.

Zimmer: Haus Peters (60 DM doubles with shower and breakfast, Augustenstr. 5½, 8958 Füssen, tel. 08362/7171) is Füssen's best value. This elegant home just a block from the station (toward town, second left) has 5 rooms, including a great 100 DM four-bed family loft room. The Peters are friendly, speak English, and know what travelers like; there is a peaceful garden, a self-serve kitchen, at a good price. The funky old **Pension Garni Elisabeth** (70 DM doubles, plus 5 DM for showers, Augustenstr. 10, tel. 6275) is in a garden just across the street.

Hotels: Bräustuberl (76 DM doubles, Rupprechtstr. 5, just a block from the station, tel. 7843) has clean, bright rooms in a rather musty old beer hall-type place filled with locals who know a good-value meal.

Hotel Gasthaus zum Hechten is less colorful but right in the old town pedestrian zone (75-90 DM doubles, Ritterstr. 6, tel. 7906).

Gasthof Krone is a rare bit of pre-glitz Füssen, also in the pedestrian zone (bright, cheery, simple doubles for 70 DM, shower down the hall, Schrannengasse 17, tel. 7824).

The biggest and most respected hotel in town is the **Hotel Hirsch** (160 DM doubles, Augsburger Tor Platz 2, tel. 08362/5080), which goes way beyond the call of hotel duty but charges for it. Still, those with money enjoy spending it here.

Inexpensive farmhouse Zimmer abound in the Bavarian countryside around Neuschwanstein and are a great value. Look for *Zimmer Frei* signs. The going rate is about 60 DM per double including breakfast. You'll see plenty of green vacancy signs.

AUSTRIA (ÖSTERREICH—THE KINGDOM OF THE EAST)

• 32,000 square miles (the size of South Carolina, or two Switzerlands).
• 7.6 million people (235 people per square mile and holding, 85% Catholic).
• 1 AS = about US$.08, about 12 AS = U.S.$1.

During the grand old Habsburg days, Austria was Europe's most powerful empire. Its royalty built a giant kingdom of more than 50 million people by making love, not war (having lots of children and marrying them into the other royal houses of Europe).

Today, this small, landlocked country does more to cling to its elegant past than any other in Europe. The waltz is still the rage, and Austrians are very sociable. More so than anywhere else, it's important to greet people you pass on the streets or meet in shops. The Austrian's version of "Hi" is a cheerful *Grüss Gott* (May God greet you). You'll get the correct pronunciation after the first volley—listen and copy.

The Austrian schilling (S or AS) is divided into 100 Groschen (g). There are about 12 AS in a U.S. dollar, so each schilling is worth about 8 cents. Divide prices by ten and cut off a fifth to get approximate costs in dollars (e.g., 420 AS is 42 minus 8, or about $34). About 6.9 AS = DM 1 (merchants and waiters near the border accept DM and usually give you a reasonable 6.8 AS).

While they speak German, accept German currency (at least in Salzburg, Innsbruck, and Reutte), and talked about unity with Germany long before Hitler ever said "Anschluss," the Austrians cherish their distinct cultural and historical traditions. They are not Germans. Austria is mellow and relaxed compared to Deutschland. *Gemütlichkeit* is the local word for this special Austrian cozy-and-easy approach to life. It's good living—whether engulfed in mountain beauty or bathed in lavish high culture. The people stroll as if every day were Sunday, topping things off with a visit to a coffee or pastry shop.

It must be nice to be past your prime—no longer troubled by being powerful, able to kick back and be as happy as St. Francis's birds in the clean, untroubled mountain air. While Austrians make less money than their neighbors, they enjoy a short workweek and a long life span. Austria was a neutral country throughout the cold war. It is now free to get closer to Europe's economic community.

Austrians eat on about the same schedule we do. Treats include *Wiener Schnitzel* (breaded veal cutlet), *Knödel* (dumplings), *Apfelstrudel*, and fancy desserts. Don't miss the *Sachertorte*, a great chocolate cake from Vienna. White wines, *Heurigen* (new wine), and coffee are delicious and popular. Service is included in restaurant bills.

Shops are open from 8:00 to 17:00 or 18:00. Banks keep roughly the same hours but usually close for lunch

BAVARIA AND CASTLE DAY

Today you'll circle through the nutcracker and castle corner of Bavaria. After touring Europe's most ornate castle, King Ludwig's fantasy called Neuschwanstein, visit Germany's most ornate church, a newly restored rococo riot. Then choose between a quick look at Oberammergau, Bavaria's wood-carving capital and home of the famous Passion Play, or a tour of another of Ludwig's extravagant castles—the more livable Linderhof Palace. The thrill for the day is a luge ride—take a ski lift up and zoom down the mountain sitting on an oversized skateboard! And on the way home, hike up to the evocative Ehrenberg ruins, above your hometown of Reutte.

Suggested Schedule by Car (home base in Reutte)	
7:30	Breakfast.
8:00	Leave Reutte.
8:30	Neuschwanstein, tour Ludwig's castle.
11:30	Lakeside picnic under the castle.
12:15	Drive to Wies Church (20-minute stop) and on to Oberammergau.
13:45	Tour Oberammergau and theater town or Linderhof castle.
15:15	Drive back into Austria via Garmisch and the Zugspitze.
16:30	Sommerrodelbahn (luge) ride in Lermoos.
18:00	Hike to ruined castle.
19:30	Dinner in Reutte.
20:30	Tirolean folk evening (if not last night).

Suggested Schedule by Train (home base in Füssen)	
7:30	Breakfast
8:00	Bus or bike to Neuschwanstein, tour Ludwig's castle (one or both)
11:00	Lakeside picnic under the castle.
12:00	Bike (along lake, tiny road over border) or bus (via Füssen) to Reutte.
14:00	Hike up the Ehrenburg ruins. Bike or bus back to Füssen.

Bavaria and Tirol—The Castle Loop

Transportation—A Circle of 60 Miles

This day is designed for drivers (instructions are worked into the sightseeing descriptions). More than a day's worth of travel fun is laid out in a circular drive starting in Reutte.

Without your own wheels, it won't all be possible. Local bus service is inexpensive but spotty for sightseeing. Buses from the Füssen station to Neuschwanstein run hourly. Füssen-to-Wies Church buses go twice a day. Oberammergau-to-Linderhof buses run fairly regularly. Hitchhiking is possible, but hitting everything is highly improbable. Without a car, I'd sleep in Füssen or Reutte and skip the Wies Church and Oberammergau (or head-quarter in Munich and take an all-day bus tour). There are four Reutte-to-Füssen buses a day, the last at about 18:00. This is great biking country. Most train stations (including Reutte and Füssen) and many hotels rent bikes.

Sightseeing Highlights—Castle Day Circle
▲▲▲Neuschwanstein and Hohenschwangau Castles (Königsschlösser)—The fairy-tale castle, Neuschwanstein, looks like the home of the knights of the Round Table, but it's actually not much older than the Eiffel Tower. It was built to suit the whims of Bavaria's King Ludwig II and is a textbook example of the romanticism that was popular in nineteenth-century Europe.

It's best to see Neuschwanstein, Germany's most popular castle, early in the morning before the hordes hit. The castle is open every morning at 9:00; by 10:00, it's packed. Rushed English tours leave regularly telling the sad story of Bavaria's "mad" king. (Men, check out the views from the castle urinals.)

After the tour, climb up to Mary's Bridge to marvel at Ludwig's castle just as he did. This bridge was quite an engineering accomplishment a hundred years ago. From the bridge, the frisky enjoy hiking even higher to the Beware—Danger of Death signs and an even more glorious castle view. For the most interesting (but 15 minutes longer) descent, follow signs to the Pöllat Gorge.

The big, yellow Hohenschwangau Castle nearby was Ludwig's boyhood home. It is a more lived-in and historic castle and actually gives a much better glimpse of Ludwig's life. (Both castles cost 8 DM and are open daily 9:00-17:30, 10:00-16:00 November-March, tel. 08362/ 81035.)

The "village" at the foot of the castles was created for and lives off the hungry, shopping tourists who come in droves to Europe's "Disney" castle. The big yellow Bräustüberl restaurant by the lakeside parking lot is cheapest, with food that tastes that way. Next door is a little family-run, open-daily grocery store with the makings for a skimpy picnic and a microwave fast-food machine.

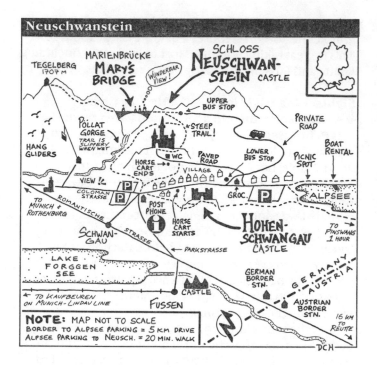

Picnic in the lakeside park or in one of the old-fashioned, rent-by-the-hour rowboats. At the intersection is the bus stop, the post/telephone office, and a helpful TI.

Park, if possible, at the closest lot (the lakeside Schloss Parkplatz am Alpsee; they all cost 4 DM). As you'll notice, it's a steep hike to the castle. Horse carriages (slower than walking) and buses (5 DM round-trip) shuttle you most of the way up but still leave you with a fair hike. Your work continues inside the castle as your tour takes you up and down over 300 stairs. Füssen-Hohenschwangau buses go twice an hour. These castles are called *Königsschlösser* in German.

To give your castle experience a romantic twist, hike or bike over from Hotel Schluxen in Austria. The mostly paved lane crosses a lonely German/Austrian border fence. It's an hour's hike with bus connections back to Füssen and Reutte or a great circular bike trip.

▲**Tegelberg Gondola**—Just north of Neuschwanstein, you'll see hang gliders hovering like vultures. They jumped from the top of the Tegelberg gondola. For 22 DM, you can ride high above the castle to that peak's 5,500-foot summit and back down (last lift at 17:00). On a clear day, you get great views of the Alps and Bavaria and the vicarious thrill of watching hang gliders and para-sailers leap into airborne ecstasy. From there, it's a fine two-hour hike down to Ludwig's castle.

▲▲**The Wies Church**—Germany's greatest rococo-style church, Wieskirche, is newly restored. Glorious no longer describes it. Flames of decoration, overripe but bright, bursting with beauty, Camcorders panning heavenward, this church is a droplet of heaven, a curly curlicue, the final flowering of the baroque movement. The ceiling depicts the Last Judgment. Walk down the sides to get close to the altar and the wooden statue of Christ, which supposedly wept and still attracts countless pilgrims. Take a commune-with-nature-and-smell-the-farm detour back through the meadow to the car park.

If you can't visit Wies, other churches that came out of a spray can from heaven are Oberammergau's church, Munich's Asam Church, the Würzburg Residenz chapel, or the splendid (free and nearby) Ettal Monastery. (Wies is 30 minutes down the road from Neuschwanstein. Drive north, turn right at Steingaden, and follow the signs. The northbound Romantic Road bus tour stops here for 15 minutes.)

The Echelsbacher Bridge, arching 250 feet over the Pöllat Gorge (b. 1929), is on the way between Wies and Oberammergau, where you hit road 23. Drivers should let their passengers walk across and meet them at the other side. Any kayakers? Notice the painting of the tradi-tional village wood-carver, who used to walk from town to town with his art on his back, on the first big house on the Oberammergau side (a shop called Almdorf Ammer-tal, with a huge selection of overpriced carvings and commission-hungry tour guides).

▲**Oberammergau**—The Shirley Temple of Bavarian villages and exploited to the hilt by the tourist trade, Oberammergau has a resilient charm. It's worth a wander. Browse through the wood-carvers' shops—small art galleries filled with very expensive whittled works—or the local Heimat (folk art) museum. (TI tel. 08822/1021, closed Saturday afternoon and Sunday.)

Visit the church, a poor cousin of the one at Wies. This church looks richer than it is. Tap on the "marble" columns. Wander through the graveyard. Ponder the death that two wars dealt Germany. Behind the church are the photos of three Schneller brothers, all killed within two years in World War II.

Once a decade, Oberammergau performs the Passion Play (next show in the year 2000). Five thousand people a day for 100 summer days attend the all-day dramatic story of Christ's Crucifixion. Until 2000, you'll have to settle for reading the book and taking the theater's 45-minute tours (cheap, in English, regular departures from 10:00-12:00 and 13:30-16:00) or seeing Nicodemus tooling around town in his VW.

Gasthaus zum Stern (70-80 DM doubles, Dorfstrasse 33, 8103 Oberammergau, tel. 08822/867) is friendly, serves good food, and for this tourist town, is a fine value (closed Wednesdays and November, will hold a room with a phone call, English spoken). Oberammergau's modern youth hostel (tel. 08822/4114) is on the river, a short walk from the center.

Driving into town, cross the bridge, take the second right, following *Polizei* signs, and park by the huge gray Passionsspielhaus. Leaving town, head out past the church, and turn toward Ettal on road 23. You're 20 miles from Reutte.

▲▲**Linderhof Castle**—This was King Ludwig's "home," his most intimate castle. It's small and comfortably exquisite—good enough for a minor god. Set in the woods, 15 minutes from Oberammergau, surrounded by fountains and sculpted, Italian-style gardens, it's the only palace I've toured that actually had me feeling envious. Don't miss the grotto. (April-September, 9:00-17:00, off-season 9:00–16:00, July and August until 17:30, fountains often erupt at 17:00, English tours constantly. Plan for lots of crowds, lots of walking, and a two-hour stop. Several buses a day from Oberammergau, included on Eurailpass. Tel. 08822/512, 7 DM.)

▲▲**Sommerrodlebahn (the Luge)**—From Oberammergau, you can drive through Garmisch, past Germany's highest mountain, the Zugspitze, into Austria via Lermoos. Or you can take the small, scenic shortcut to Reutte past Ludwig's Linderhof and along the windsurfer-strewn Plansee.

The Innsbruck-Lermoos-Reutte road passes the ruined castles of Ehrenberg (just outside Reutte) and two rare and exciting luge courses. In the summer, this ski slope is used as a luge course, or Sommerrodelbahn. This is one of Europe's great $5 thrills: take the lift up, grab a sledlike go-cart, and luge down. The concrete bobsled course banks on the corners, and even a novice can go very, very fast. Most are cautious on their first run and speed demons on their second. (Recently, a woman showed me her journal illustrated with a dried five-inch-long luge scab. Her husband disobeyed the only essential rule of luging—"keep both hands on your stick.") No one emerges from the course without a windblown hairdo and a smile-creased face. Both places charge a steep 60 AS per run, with discount cards for 5 or 10 trips, and run from about mid-May through September from 9:00 or 10:00 until about 17:00. Closed in wet weather.

The small and steep luge: The first course (a 100-meter drop over an 800-meter course) is 6 kilometers beyond Reutte's castle ruins; look for a chair lift on the right and exit on the tiny road at the yellow Riesenrutschbahn sign (tel. 05674/5350).

The longest luge: The Biberwihr Sommerrodelbahn, fifteen minutes farther toward Innsbruck, just past Lermoos in Biberwihr (the first exit after a long tunnel), is a better luge, the longest in Austria—1,300 meters. It opens at 9:00—a good tomorrow-morning alternative if today is wet.

(Just before this luge, behind the Sport und Trachten-stüberl shop is a wooden church dome with a striking Zugspitze backdrop. If you have sunshine and a camera, don't miss it.)

▲▲**Reutte's Ehrenberg Ruins**—The brooding ruins of Ehrenberg, just outside Reutte on the road to Lermoos, await survivors of the luge. These thirteenth-century rock piles are a great contrast to Ludwig's "modern" castles. Park in the lot at the base of the hill and hike up; it's a 20-minute walk to the small (*kleine*) castle for a great view from your own private ruins. Imagine how proud Count Meinrad II of Tirol (who built the castle in 1290) would be to know that his castle repelled 16,000 Swedish soldiers in the defense of Catholicism in 1632.

You'll find more medieval mystique atop the taller neighboring hill in the big (*grosse*) ruins. You can't see anything from below and almost nothing when you get there, but these bigger, more desolate and overgrown ruins are a little more romantic (and a lot harder to get to).

The easiest way down is via the small road from the gully between the two castles. The car park is just off the Lermoos-Reutte road with a café/guest house. Reutte is a pleasant 90-minute walk. Back in town, most hotels have sketches of the intact castle.

▲▲**Tirolean Folk Evening**—Ask in your hotel if there's a Tirolean folk evening tonight. About two evenings a week in the summer, Reutte or a nearby town puts on an evening of yodeling, slap-dancing, and Tirolean frolic—always worth the small charge and a few kilometers drive. Off-season, you'll have to do your own yodeling.

▲**Fallersheim**—A special treat for those who may have been Kit Carson in a previous life, this extremely remote log cabin village is a 4,000-foot-high, flower-speckled world of serene slopes and cowbells. Thunderstorms roll down the valley like it's God's bowling alley, but the pint-sized church on the high ground, blissfully simple after so much baroque, seems to promise this huddle of houses will survive and the river and breeze will just keep flowing. The couples sitting on benches are mostly Austrian vacationers who've rented cabins here. Many of them, appreciating the remoteness of Fallershein, are having affairs.

For a rugged chunk of local Alpine peace, spend a night in the local Matratzenlager Almwirtschaft Fallershein, run by friendly Kerle Erwin (80 AS per person with breakfast, open, weather permitting, May-November, 27 very cheap beds in a very simple loft dorm, meager plumbing, good inexpensive meals, 6671 Weissenbach 119a, b/Reutte, tel. 05678/5142) who rarely answers the telephone and when she does, she speaks no English. Crowded only on weekends. Fallershein is at the end of a miserable two-kilometer, fit-for-jeep-or-rental-car-only, gravel road that looks more closed than it is, near Namlos on the Berwang road southwest of Reutte. To avoid cow damage, park 300 meters below the village at the tiny lot before the bridge.

Itinerary Options

This is an awkward day for train travelers who may prefer spending this time in Munich and in Salzburg (two hours apart by hourly train). Salzburg holds its own against "castle day" and is better than Innsbruck. Consider a side trip to Salzburg from Munich and the night train from Munich to Venice.

OVER THE ALPS TO VENICE

Innsbruck, western Austria's major city and just a quick, scenic drive or train ride from Reutte, is a good place to spend the morning. Stroll through the traffic-free town center and have a picnic lunch. Then it's on to Italia. Italy is a whole new world—sunshine, cappuccino, gelato, and *la dolce vita*!

Suggested Schedule	
8:00	Drive from Reutte to Innsbruck.
10:00	Sightsee in downtown Innsbruck or tour Reifenstein Castle, lunch.
12:30	Drive from Innsbruck (or Reifenstein) to Venice.
17:30	Take Boat 34 down the Grand Canal to San Marco. Find your hotel.

Transportation: Reutte to Venice (270 miles)

From Reutte, the scenic highway takes you past ruined castles, through the resort of Lermoos, with spectacular views of the Zugspitze (Germany's tallest peak, about 10,000 feet), two luge courses (the longest, behind you on the left immediately after the tunnel), over scenic Fernpass (at 4,000 feet, the lowest pass from Bavaria into the Inn Valley, called Via Claudia Augusta when Emperor Claudius built the first road here in A.D. 46), past count-less little wooden huts (I can't get a straight answer: are they cow shower stalls, cheap ski resorts, fertility sheds, or migrant cow huts?), and into the valley of the Inn River. To get into Innsbruck, take the Innsbruck West exit. To leave, follow signs to Brenner Pass and Italy. On the hill just south of Innsbruck, you'll see the Olympic ski jump; to visit it (free and easy), follow Bergisel signs.

The dramatic Brenner Pass freeway sweeps you quickly and effortlessly over the Alps. The freeway's famous Europa Bridge comes with a $10 toll but saves you

enough gas, time, and nausea to be worthwhile. (Good
W.C. and picnic spot at the bridge. Fill your tank; gas is
more expensive in Italy.)

Italy is about 30 minutes south of Innsbruck. At the
border, drivers can stop by the ENIT (local automobile
club) office—you'll see the sign. They sell Italy's famous
discount gas coupons, but these coupons are no longer
available to non-Europeans at the border. They're barely
worth the trouble anyway.

In four hours, the autostrada zips you through a castle-
studded valley past impressive mountains, around Romeo
and Juliet's hometown of Verona, past a little-known
dinosaur park, and on into Venice. For the rest of this tour
you'll be paying tolls for your freeway driving.

At Venice, the freeway ends like Medusa's head. Follow
the green lights directing you to a parking lot with space.
Piazza Roma has the most convenient high-rise garages;
the first one is city owned and cheaper, the second ridiculously expensive. From there, you can catch the boat
of your choice deep into Europe's most enchanting city.

By train, it's 2.5 hours from Reutte to Innsbruck and six
hours from there to Venice. I'd take the overnight train
from Munich or Innsbruck direct to Venice. The train
drops you right on the Grand Canal. The station banks
and information services are normally slow and
crowded. The Bank of San Marco, just down the street
(left out of the station), normally has good rates and no
extra fee. In front of the station is the boat dock where
the floating "city buses" (*vaporetti*) stop. Or it's an easy
30-minute browse to San Marco if you decide to walk.

Sightseeing Highlights
▲**Innsbruck**—The building with the Golden Roof (Gol-
denes Dachl), built with 2,657 gilded copper tiles in 1496
by Emperor Maximilian as an impressive viewing spot for
his medieval spectacles, is in the historic center of town.
On this square you'll see the tourist information booth
with handy town maps, the newly restored, baroque-

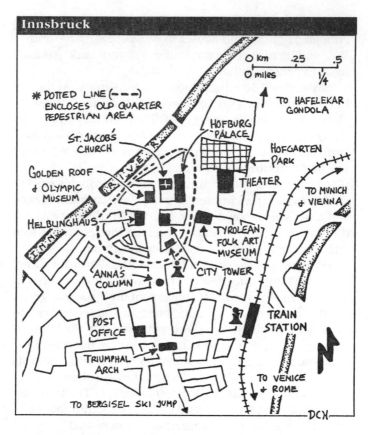

Innsbruck

* DOTTED LINE (- - -) ENCLOSES OLD QUARTER PEDESTRIAN AREA

style Helblinghaus, the city tower (climb it for a great view), and the new Olympics museum (behind the Golden Roof, 22 AS, 9:30-17:30 daily) with exciting action videos for winter sports lovers.

Nearby are the pastel yellow palace (Hofburg) and church (Hofkirche) and the unique Tiroler Volkskunst Museum. This museum (25 AS, open 9:00-17:00 daily, closed Sunday afternoons) is the best look anywhere at traditional Tirolean life-styles. Fascinating exhibits range from wedding dresses and babies' cribs to nativity scenes. Use the helpful English guidebook.

A very popular mountain sports center and home of the 1964 and 1976 Winter Olympics, Innsbruck is surrounded by 150 mountain lifts, 1,250 miles of trails, and

250 hikers' huts. If it's sunny, consider taking the Hafelekar lift right out of the city to the mountaintops above.

The quickest way to "see" Innsbruck is to make a short stop at the Olympic ski jump (Bergisel) just off the road as you head south. Climb to the Olympic rings eternal flame holder, find Dorothy Hamill on the list of gold medalists, and enjoy the commanding view.

▲ **Hall**—Just a couple of miles south of Innsbruck is the smaller, less touristy, and more enjoyable village of Hall (next freeway exit). Its market square, church, mint, and salt mine museum are all interesting. Gasthof Badl (430-560 AS doubles, at the freeway exit, tel. 05223/6784, fax 05223/67843) is a fine and friendly old hotel.

▲▲ **Reifenstein Castle**—For one of Europe's most intimate looks at medieval castle life, let the lady of Reifenstein (Frau Blanc) show you around her wonderfully preserved castle. She leads tours on the hour in Italian and German. She's friendly, speaks Italian and German, and will squeeze in what English she can.

Just inside Italy, leave the autostrada at Vipiteno/Sterzing (the town, like many in this area, has both a German and an Italian name), follow signs right toward Bolzano, then over the freeway to the base of the castle's rock. It's the castle on the west. Telephone 0472/76 58 79 (from Austria: 040/472/76 58 79) in advance to confirm your tour. The pleasant mini-park beside the drawbridge is a good spot for a picnic. (Pack out your litter.) Tours normally at 9:30, 10:30, 14:00, 15:00, and 16:00.

ITALY

- 116,000 square miles (the size of Arizona).
- 56,000,000 people (477 people per square mile).
- 1,300 lire = US$1. 1,000 lire = about U.S.$.75.

Ah, Italy! It has Europe's richest, craziest culture. If I have to choose just one, Italy is my favorite. If you take it on its own terms and accept the package deal, Italy is wonderful. Some people, often with considerable effort, manage to hate it. Italy bubbles with emotion, corruption, stray

hairs, inflation, traffic jams, body odor, strikes, rallies,
holidays, crowded squalor, and irate ranters shaking their
fists at each other one minute and walking arm in arm the
next. Have a talk with yourself before you cross the border. Promise yourself to relax and soak in it: it's a glorious
mud puddle. Be militantly positive.

With so much history and art in Venice, Florence, and
Rome, you'll need to do some reading ahead here to maximize your experience. There are two Italys: the north is
relatively industrial, aggressive, and "time-is-money" in
its outlook. The Po River basin and the area between
Milan, Genoa, and Torino have the richest farmland and
comprise the industrial heartland. The south is more
crowded, poor, relaxed, farm oriented, and traditional.
Families here are very strong and usually live in the same
house for many generations. Loyalties are to the family,
city, region, soccer team, then country—in that order.
The Appenine mountains give Italy a rugged north-south
spine.

Economically, Italy has its problems, but things some-how work out. Statistically, it looks terrible (high infla-tion, low average income), but things work slick under the table. Italy is a leading wine producer and is sixth in the world in cheese and wool output. Tourism (your dol-lars) is big business in Italy. Cronyism, which complicates my work, is an integral part of the economy.

Italy, home of the Vatican, is Catholic, but the domi-nant religion is life—motor scooters, football, fashion, girl-watching, boy-watching, good coffee, good wine, and *la dolce far niente* (the sweetness of doing nothing).

The language is fun. Be melodramatic and move your hand with your tongue. Hear the melody, get into the flow. Fake it, let the farce be with you. Italians are outgo-ing characters; they want to communicate and try harder than any other Europeans. Play with them.

Italy, a land of extremes, is also the most thief-ridden country you'll visit. Tourists suffer virtually no violent crime—but plenty of petty purse-snatchings, pickpock-etings, and short-changings. Only the sloppy will be stung. Wear your money belt! Unfortunately, you'll need to assume any Gypsy woman or child on the street is after your wallet or purse.

Traditionally, Italy uses the siesta plan: people work from 8:00 or 9:00 to 13:00 and from 15:30 to 19.00, six days a week. Many businesses have adopted the govern-ment's new recommended 8:00 to 14:00 workday. In tourist areas, shops are open longer.

Sightseeing hours are always changing in Italy, and many of the hours given in this book will be wrong by the time you travel. Use the local tourist offices to double check your sightseeing plans. For extra sightseeing infor-mation, take advantage of the cheap, colorful, dry but informative city guidebooks sold on the streets all over. Also, use the information telephones you'll find in most historic buildings. Just set the dial on English, pop in your coins, and listen. The narration is often accompa-nied by a mini-slide show. Many dark interiors can be brilliantly lit for a coin. Whenever possible, let there be light.

Some important Italian churches require modest dress—no shorts or bare shoulders on men or women. With a little imagination (except at the Vatican), those caught by surprise can improvise something—a table-cloth for your knees and maps for your shoulders. I wear a super lightweight pair of long pants for my hot and muggy big city Italian sightseeing.

The Italian autostrada is lined with some of Europe's best rest stops, with gas, coffee bars, W.C.'s, long-distance telephones, grocery stores, restaurants, and often change facilities and tourist information. Italian trains are nor-mally on time when you aren't. Take advantage of the new computer grid train schedule planners in most Ital-ian stations.

While no longer a cheap country, Italy is still a hit with shoppers. Glassware (Venice), gold, silver, leather, and prints (Florence), and high fashion (Rome) are good souvenirs.

Many tourists are mind-boggled by the huge prices: 16,000 lire for dinner! 42,000 for the room! 126,000 for the taxi ride! That's still real money—it's just spoken of in much smaller units than a dollar. Since there are roughly 1,300 L in a dollar (at this writing), figure Italian prices by covering the last three zeros with your finger and taking about 75 percent of the remaining figure. That 16,000 L dinner costs $12 in U.S. money; the 42,000 L room, $30; and the taxi ride. . . oh-oh!

Beware of the "slow count." After you buy something, you may get your change back very slowly, one bill at a time. The salesperson (or bank teller) hopes you are con-fused by all the zeros and will gather up your money and say *"Grazie"* before he or she finishes the count. Always do your own rough figuring beforehand and understand the transaction. Only the sloppy are ripped off.

Italians eat a skimpy breakfast, a huge lunch between 12:30 and 15:30, and a light dinner around 20:00. Food in Italy is given great importance and should be thought of as sightseeing for your tongue. Focus on regional special-ties, wines, and pastas. In restaurants, you'll be billed a small cover charge (*coperto*) and a 10 to 15 percent service charge. A salad and minestrone or pasta, while not a proper meal, is cheap and filling. *Gelato* (ice cream) and coffee are art forms in Italy.

Bar procedure can be frustrating. Decide what you want, check the price list on the wall, pay the cashier, give the receipt to the bartender (whose clean fingers handle no dirty lire), and tell him what you want. *Panini* is sandwich. *Da portare via* is "for the road."

La dolce far niente is a big part of Italy. Zero in on the fine points. Don't dwell on the problems; accept Italy as Italy. Savor your cappuccino, dangle your feet over a canal (if it smells, breathe with your mouth), and imagine what it was like centuries ago. Ramble through the rubble of Rome and mentally resurrect those ancient stones. Look into the famous sculpted eyes of Michelangelo's David, and understand Renaissance man's assertion of himself. Sit silently on a hilltop rooftop. Get chummy with the winds of the past. Write a poem over a glass of local wine in a sun-splashed, wave-dashed Riviera village. If you fall off your moral horse, call it a cultural experience. Italy is for romantics.

Venice
See tomorrow.

VENICE

Soak—all day—in this puddle of elegant decay. Venice is
Europe's best-preserved big city, a car-free urban wonderland of 100 islands, laced together by 400 bridges and
2,000 alleys. Born in a lagoon 1,500 years ago as a refuge
from barbarians, Venice is overloaded with tourists and
slowly sinking (two unrelated facts). In the Middle Ages,
after the Venetians created a great trading empire, they
smuggled in the bones of St. Mark (San Marco), and
Venice gained religious importance as well.

Venice is home to about 75,000 people in its old city,
down from a peak population of around 200,000. While
there are about 500,000 in greater Venice counting the
mainland, not counting tourists, the old town has a small-
town feel. Try to see small-town Venice through the
touristic flack. Venice is worth at least a day on even the
speediest tour. This itinerary gives it two nights and a day.

Suggested Schedule	
8:00	Breakfast, banking.
9:00	Basilica dei Frari and/or Scuola di San Rocco—for art lovers—or free to browse and shop.
11:00	Visit Accademia Gallery.
12:30	Lunch. How about a picnic in the breeze while you circle the city on Vaporetto 5?
14:00	St. Mark's area—tour the Doge's Palace and the Basilica, ride to the top of the Campanile, glassblowing demonstration.
17:30	Siesta in your hotel.
19:30	Dinner, or commence pub crawl.

Orientation and Arrival

The island city of Venice is shaped like a fish. Its major
thoroughfares are canals. The Grand Canal snakes
through the middle of the fish, starting at the mouth
where all the people and food enter, passing under the

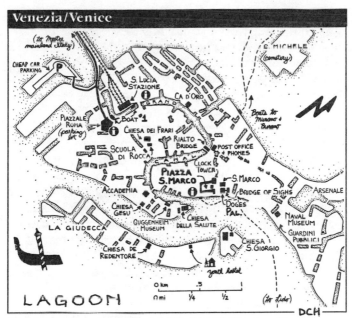

Rialto Bridge, and ending at St. Mark's Square (San Marco). Leave your car and twentieth-century perspective at the mouth and let Venice swallow you whole.

The city has no real streets, and addresses are hopelessly confusing. There are six districts, each with about 6,000 address numbers. Navigate by landmarks, not streets. Luckily, it's fairly easy to find your way, since nearly every street corner has a sign pointing you to the nearest major landmark (San Marco, Rialto, etc.), and most hotels and restaurants have neighborhood maps on their cards. (If you get lost, they love to hand them out to prospective customers.)

The 1:7000 scale, cheap, yellow Venice map is a good investment. Also consider the little sold-with-the-postcards guidebook with a city map and explanations of the major sights. Most people who have anything to sell to tourists (beds, meals, souvenirs) speak some English. Bank rates vary tremendously.

Only three bridges cross the Grand Canal, but several *traghetti* (little ferry gondolas) shuttle locals and smart tourists across the canal, where necessary.

The public transit system is a fleet of bus-boats called vaporetti. They work like city buses except that they never get a flat, the stops are docks, and if you get off between stops you may drown. Tickets are bought at the dock before you board and vary with the speed of the boat. Look into the cheap 24-hour and 3-day passes. Any city map shows the boat stops and routes. The TI or the boat information office at Piazzale Roma can give you the free ACTV Venice public transportation map.

Boat #1 is the slow boat down the Grand Canal (boats every ten minutes, making every stop from Piazzale Roma to San Marco in about 45 minutes). Number 34 is the best sightseeing boat, doing the entire Canale Grand, like #1 but with fewer stops (Piazzale Roma and the train station to San Marco in 20 minutes). Boat #2 is the fast Piazzale Roma-train station-Rialto-San Marco boat. Boat #5 gives you an interesting circular tour of this island city (ride clockwise from San Marco, and get off at Fondamenta Nuove to avoid the long lagoon trip).

If you've never been there, Venice is confusing. It's a carless kaleidoscope of people, bridges, and odorless canals. It's unique.

The best tourist information office is on St. Mark's Square (tel. 041/522 6356, hours variable, about 8:30 to 18:00 daily). Confirm your sightseeing plans and get a map and the latest museum hours. Anyone under 30 with a photo can get a free Carta Giovani (youth pass) giving you discounts all over town (about 30% off at museums, 10% off at Locanda Sturion, 15% off at Hotel San Gallo). Hotels publish and distribute a free periodical entertainment guide, *Un Ospite de Venezia*.

Accept the fact that Venice was a tourist town 400 years ago. It was, is, and always will be crowded. The crowds and tacky souvenir stalls vanish when you hit the back streets. Telephone code: 041.

Sightseeing Highlights—Venice

▲▲▲**Piazza San Marco**—Surrounded by splashy and historic buildings and filled with music, lovers, pigeons, and tourists from around the world by day and your private rendezvous with the Middle Ages late at night, Europe's greatest dance floor is the romantic place to be. This is the first place to flood, and it has the best tourist information office in town (in the rear corner), fine public rest rooms (behind the TI, see "Helpful Hints" below), and elegant cafés (7,000 L beer plus 3500 L for the music, but great people watching and live music; explore their fine interiors, mooch a W.C.).

▲▲**Doge's Palace (Palazzo Ducale)**—The former ruling palace has the second largest wooden room in Europe, virtually wallpapered by Tintoretto, Veronese, and other great painters. The attached Bridge of Sighs leads to the prison. Wave to the tourists gawking at you from the bridge (open 8:30-19:00, 5,000 L). No tours: buy a guidebook on the street, or use *Mona Winks*.

▲▲**St. Mark's Basilica**—For a thousand years, it has housed the saint's bones. Study the ceiling mosaics, the floor, and treasures. It's worth 2,000 L to go upstairs to see the newly restored bronze horses and enjoy the views of the square from the balcony. (Modest dress, no shorts or bare shoulders admitted, open 9:00-17:00, Sunday 14:00-17:00, free, tel. 041/522 2505, free English guided tours of the church Wednesday and Friday at 11:00, beautifully lit at the 18:45 mass on Saturday and 14:00-17:00 Sunday.)

▲**Campanile di San Marco**—Ride the elevator up 300 feet to the top of the bell tower for the best possible view of Venice. Notice the photos on the wall inside showing how this bell tower crumbled into a pile of individual bricks in 1902, one thousand years after it was built. For an ear-shattering experience, be on top when the bells ring. (Open 10:00-18:00, maybe later, 3,000 L.)

Clock Tower—See the bronze men (Moors) swing their huge clappers at the top of each hour. Closed for restoration. Notice the world's first "digital" clock on the tower facing St. Mark's Square.

▲▲**Ride the Vaporetti**—Venice's floating city buses take you anywhere in town for one ticket. Boats #34 and

Venice "Downtown"

#1 do the entire Grand Canal. There are plenty of boats
leaving from San Marco for the beach (Lido), as well as
speedboat tours of Burano (a quiet, picturesque fishing
and lace town), Murano (the glassblowing island), and
Torcello (has the oldest churches and mosaics but is an
otherwise dull and desolate island).

▲▲ **Grand Canal Tour**—Grab a front seat on boat #34
(fast, 20 minutes) or #1 (slow, 45 minutes) to cruise the
entire Canale Grande from the car park or train station to
San Marco. While Venice is a barrage on the senses that
hardly needs a narration, these notes will give the cruise a
little meaning and help orient you to this great city. The
small 2,500 L city map (on sale at most postcard racks)
has a handy Grand Canal map on its back side.

Venice is built in a lagoon, sitting on pilings—pine
trees driven 15 feet into the mud. Over 100 canals, about
25 miles in length, drain the city. If they are streams, the
Grand Canal is the river.

Venice is a city of palaces, and the most impressive were built fronting this canal. This ride is the only way to really appreciate this unique and historic chorus line of rich homes from the days when Venice was the world's richest city. Strict laws prohibit any changes in these buildings, so while landowners gnash their teeth, we can enjoy Europe's best-preserved medieval city. Many of the grand buildings are now vacant.

You'll start at Piazzale Roma (the bus and car park) or the train station. Each night the steps of the station are lined with backpackers in sleeping bags boycotting the city's expensive rooms. The gray building on the corner just before the station is the Mensa DLF, the public transportation workers cafeteria, very cheap and open to you.

The first bridge is at the station, one of only three that cross the Canale Grande.

Vaporetto stop #4 (San Marcuola-Ghetto) is near the old Jewish quarter. This district is the world's original ghetto.

As you cruise, notice the traffic signs. This is the main thoroughfare of the city, and it's busy with traffic. You'll see all kinds of boats: taxis, police boats, garbage, even brown-and-white UPS boats.

Venice has about 500 sleek, black, and graceful gondolas. They are a symbol of the city, cost about $35,000, and are built with a slight curve so they can be propelled by one oar in a straight line.

At the Ca d'Oro stop, notice the palace of the same name. For years it's been under a wooden case of scaffolding for reconstruction. Named the "House of Gold," it's considered the most elegant Venetian Gothic palace on the canal.

Just before the Rialto Bridge you'll see the outdoor produce market. It bustles with people in the morning but is quiet and sleepy with only a few grazing pigeons the rest of the day. The huge post office, usually with a postal boat moored at its blue posts, is on the left.

A symbol of Venice, the Rialto Bridge is lined with shops and tourists. Built in 1592, with a span of 42 meters, it was an impressive engineering feat in its day. Locals call the summit of this bridge the "ice box of Venice" for its cool breeze.

The Rialto was a separate town in the early days of Venice. It has always been the commercial district, while San Marco was the religious and governmental center. Today a street called the Merceria connects the two, providing travelers with a gauntlet of shopping temptations.

Take a deep whiff of Venice. What's all this nonsense about stinky canals? By the way, how's your captain? Smooth landings?

Notice how the rich marble facades are just a veneer covering no-nonsense brick buildings. Notice also the characteristic chimneys.

After passing the British consulate, you'll see the old wooden Accademia Bridge, leading to the Accademia Gallery, which is filled with the best Venetian paintings.

Cruising under the bridge you'll get a classic view of the Salute Church. They claim to have used over a million trees for the foundation alone. Much of the surrounding countryside was deforested by Venice. Trees were needed both to fuel the furnaces of its booming glass industry and to prop up this city in the mud.

The low white building on the right is the Peggy Guggenheim Gallery. She willed the city a fine collection of modern art.

As you prepare to de-boat at stop #15—San Marco— look from left to right out over the lagoon. The green area in the distance is the public gardens, the only sizable park in town. Farther out is the Lido, with its beaches, casinos, and cars. The dreamy church that seems to float is the architect Palladio's San Giorgio. And farther to the right is an island called the Guidecca.

▲▲ **Galleria dell' Accademia**—Venice's top art museum is packed with the painted highlights of the Venetian Renaissance (Bellini, Giorgione, Veronese, Tiepolo, and Canaletto). Just over the wooden Accademia Bridge (open

9:00-14:00, Sunday 9:00-13:00, expect delays as they allow in only 180 at a time, 8,000 L, tel. 041/522 2247).

▲**Museo Civico Correr**—The interesting city history museum offers fine views of Piazza San Marco. Entry is on the square opposite the church (9:00-19:00 daily, 5,000 L).

▲**Chiesa dei Frari**—A great church houses Donatello's wood carving of St. John the Baptist, a Bellini, Titian's *Assumption*, and more. Open 9:00-11:45, 15:00-17:30.

▲**Scuola di San Rocco**—Next to the Frari church, another lavish building bursts with art, including some fifty Tintorettos. View the splendid ceiling paintings with the mirrors available at the entrance. (9:00-13:00, 15:30-18:30, last entrance a half hour before closing, 6,000 L.)

▲**Peggy Guggenheim Collection**—A popular collection of far-out art that so many try so hard to understand, including works by Picasso, Chagall, and Dali. (11:00-18:00, closed Tuesdays, 5,000 L; Saturday 18:00-21:00, free.)

Also, for modern art fans: on even-numbered years, Venice hosts a "World's Fair" of art, the Biennale, at the fairgrounds on Venice's "tail" (vaporetto: Biennale).

▲**Gondola Rides**—This tradition is a must for many but a rip-off for most. Gondoliers charge about 70,000 L for a 50-minute ride. You can divide the cost—and the romance—by up to six people (some take seven if you beg and they're hungry). For cheap gondola thrills, stick to the 400 L one-minute ferry ride on the Grand Canal traghetti, or hang out on a bridge along the Gondola route and wave at the romantics.

▲**Glassblowing**—It's unnecessary to go all the way to Murano Island to see glassblowing demonstrations. Wait in the alley just 20 yards north of St. Mark's Square and follow any tour group into the glass factory outlets for a fun and free ten-minute show.

▲▲**Evening: The Stand-up Progressive Venetian Pub Crawl Dinner**—Venice's residential back streets hide plenty of characteristic bars with countless trays of interesting toothpick munchie food (*cicheti*). This is a great way to mingle and have fun with the Venetians. Real cicheti pubs are getting rare in these fast-food days, but locals can point you in the right direction, or you can follow the plan below.

Italian cicheti (hors d'oeuvres) wait under glass in bars; try fried mozzarella cheese, blue cheese, calamari, artichoke hearts, and anything ugly on a toothpick. Drink the house wines. A small beer (*birrino*) or house wine costs less than 1,000 L, meat and fish munchies are expensive, veggies are around 4,000 L for a meal-sized plate. When you're good and ready, ask for a glass of grappa. A good precaution might be to give each place 20,000 L (or whatever) for your group and explain you want to eat and drink until it's kaput. Bars don't stay open very late, so start your evening by 19:00. Ask your hotel manager for advice—or to join you.

First course: Find Campo Santa Maria di Formosa. Split a pizza with wine on the square (Bar all' Orologio, opposite the canal, has the worst pizza with the best setting. Pizzeria da Egidio and Cip Ciap cook their own delicious pizzas). When in doubt, I order the *capricioso*, the house specialty.

Second course: Fresh fruit and vegetables. After 50 years, Giuseppe's still actually enjoys selling fresh fruit and vegetables on the square next to the water fountain (open until about 20:30).

Third course: Cicheti and wine. From Bar Orologio, head down the street to Osteria Mascaron (Gigi's bar, closes at 21:30 and on Sunday).

Fourth course: More cicheti and wine. Go down the alley across from Gigi's bar (Calle Trevisana o Cicogua), over the great gondola voyeurism bridge, down Calle Brasano to Campo S. Giovanni e Paolo. Pass the church-looking hospital (notice the illusions on its facade, maybe with a drink under the statue at the Caffe Bar Cavallo). Go over the bridge to the left of the hospital to Calle Larga Gallina, and take the first right to Antiche Cantine Ardenghi de Luigi (another Gigi) Ardenghi at #6369 under the red telephone (no sign for tax reasons, tel. 041/523 7691).

This is a *cicheteria* (munchie bar supreme), and this Gigi is a great character. Open nightly, except Sunday, until 23:00.

Sixth course: gelati. The unfriendly but delicious gelateria on Campo di Formosa closes at about 20:00 and on Thursdays. Those on San Marco stay open very late.

You're not a tourist, you're a living part of a soft Venetian night. Street lamp halos, live music, floodlit history, and a ceiling of stars make St. Mark's magic at midnight. Shine with the old lanterns on the gondola piers where the sloppy Grand Canal splashes at the Doge's Palace. Comfort the four frightened tetrarchs (ancient Byzantine emperors) under the moon near the Doge's Palace entrance. Cuddle history.

Side Trips from Venice
Several interesting places hide out in the Venice Lagoon. Burano, famous for its lace making, is a sleepy island with a sleepy community, giving you a look at village Venice without the glitz. Torcello is another lagoon island. This one's dead except for its church, which claims to be the oldest in Venice. It's impressive for its mosaics but not

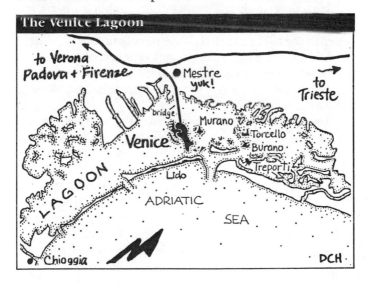

The Venice Lagoon

worth a look on a short visit. The Lido, a quick boat ride from San Marco, is the Venice beach strip with fancy hotels, casinos, nightlife, a fun, if congested, beach scene. . . and cars.

Farther away, interesting, but forgotten in the shadow of Venice, are Chioggia (Italy's top fishing port, a Venice with cars), Grado (a resort calling itself the "Mother of Venice," with lots of history and the fine Roman ruins of Aquileia), and Palmanova (a Renaissance planned town, the 1593 town of the future, with a unique snowflake street plan within a ten-sided wall).

Helpful Hints

Venetian churches and museums keep erratic hours. Double-check hours with the TI's help. Venice is the ideal town to explore on foot. Walk and walk to the far reaches of the town. Don't worry about getting lost. Get as lost as possible. Keep reminding yourself, "I'm on an island and I can't get off." When it comes time to find your way, just follow the directional arrows on building corners, or simply ask a local, "*Dov'è* (DOH-vay) *San Marco*?" (Where is St. Mark's?)

Try a siesta in the Giardini Publici (public gardens, in the tail area), on the Isle of Burano, or in your hotel. The area in the tail of the fish is completely untouristy, just canals, laundry, sleepy dogs, and Venetians.

Venetians pride themselves in having pure, safe, and tasty tap water, which is piped in from the foothills of the Alps.

The best shopping area is around the Rialto Bridge and along the Merceria, the road connecting St. Mark's and the Rialto. Things are cheaper on the non-San Marco side of the Rialto Bridge.

Laundry time? There's a handy family-run *lavanderia* (laundromat) near St. Mark's and most of my hotel listings. The full-service Laundry "Gabriella" (open Monday-Friday 8:00-19:00, Rio Terra Colonne, one bridge off the Merceria near San Zulian church, tel.

5221758) does 9 pounds of laundry, wash and dry, for 15,000 L. Drop it by in the morning, pick it up that afternoon.

Need cash after hours? There's a cash machine near the Rialto vaporetto stop that exchanges U.S. dollars, German marks, and Austrian schillings into lire at a good exchange rate.

If bombed by a pigeon, resist the initial response to wipe it off immediately—it'll just smear into your hair. Wait until it dries and flake it off cleanly.

Sleeping in Venice (about 1,300 L = U.S.$1)

Finding a room in Venice is actually easy if you go with one of my recommendations, call a few days in advance, reconfirm the morning of the day you plan to arrive, and arrive no later than midafternoon. From Germany, dial 0039/41/Venice number; from Austria, dial 04/041/Venice number (note in this unusual case the first zero in the area code is dialed even from out of the country). While many choose to stay in a nearby less crowded place and side-trip to Venice (Padua, just 30 minutes away by train works well), I can't imagine not sleeping with this beautiful city. If you come in on the overnight train, chances are your room won't be ready, but any hotel will happily store your bag and move it in when the room is vacant and ready while you enjoy the town.

There are clear hotel rules. The maximum price is posted in the lobby, including all extras; breakfast price is uncontrolled and, technically, must be optional. For any complaints, call 041/520 0911. Unless otherwise stated, all of the prices listed here include breakfast.

You can't find a sleepable double for much under 60,000 L in Venice. I've let location and character be my priorities. It's worth budgeting the money to stay in the old center and not in a dorm. The first listing overlooks the Rialto Bridge on the Grand Canal, the next seven are generally between the Rialto and San Marco, within 3 or 4 minutes walk of San Marco, and the last three are far from the action in quieter quarters of the island city.

Locanda Sturion (75,000-110,000 L doubles, S. Polo,
Rialto, Calle Sturion 679, 30125 Venezia, tel. 041/523
6243, fax 522 5702) is my home in Venice and the only
budget place on the Grand Canal. Sergio and Sandro
speak English and will hold a room until 16:00 with no
deposit. Their 700-year-old hotel is located 100 yards
and as many stairs from the Rialto Bridge (it's opposite the
vaporetto dock, go over the bridge, left along the canal
past four lamp posts, and you'll see the simple sign down
an alley). The Rialto/canal view from the breakfast room
makes the climb more bearable. Two 5-bed family rooms
also have canal views. You'll see this hotel's sign of the
sturgeon (*sturion*) in a 400-year-old painting in the
Accademia (or on their colorful business card). Read the
history on the breakfast wall.

Alloggi Gino (60,000 L with or without shower, Calle
Del Rimedio 4412, Castello, Venezia, tel. 041/5206232)
crouches almost namelessly down a narrow alley. A visual
Doppler effect almost takes your breath away as you step
through the door into a 600-year-old dark, fragile, chandeliered place. Half the rooms are plain and decent; the
others are richly attired with museum-piece furniture
(request one of the special rooms). The place is perfect
for aristocrats who like to camp. The young proprietor,
Renato, appreciates respect for this smoky-mirrored relic.
He'll hold a room with a phone call if you promise to
reconfirm a day or two before you arrive. It's four bridges
down from the Bridge of Sighs. Go over Ponte Remedio,
down Calle del Remedio past Hotel Atlantico, and take
the first right down the dark lane.

Hotel Rive (two 62,000 L shower-across-the-hall doubles on the fourth floor—campanile view but no elevator, 92,000 L doubles with very modern showers, Ponte
dell'Angelo, 5310, Venezia, tel. 041/522 7034) is entirely
redone, with gleaming marble hallways and bright modern rooms, and romantically situated on a canal along the
gondola serenade route. You could actually dunk your
breakfast rolls in the canal (but don't). Sandro will hold a
corner (*angolo*) room if you ask. If you looked down the

Rio di Palazzo from the Bridge of Sighs, Hotel Rive is at the end of the canal, halfway between San Marco and Campo Santa Maria Formosa.

Hotel San Gallo (85,000-120,000 L doubles, San Marco 1093/A, 30124 Venice, tel. 041/522 7311 or 528 9877, fax 522 5702) is your best splurge. It's about 50 yards off Piazza San Marco (kitty-corner from the bell tower) on a very quiet little square, clean, and serves breakfast on the chirpy breezy roof garden. English is spoken. Hotel San Gallo is run by the helpful managers, Luca and Sandro, the same people who bring you Locanda Sturion.

Albergo Doni (twelve 65,000 L doubles, showers down the hall cost extra, Riva Schiavoni, San Zaccaria N. 4656—Calle del Vin, tel. 041/5224267) is a dark, woody, clean, quiet little place run by a likable smart-aleck named Gina. One minute from San Marco, it's two bridges behind the church, or walk east along the San Marco waterfront (Riva Degli Schiavoni), over two bridges, take the first right, and follow the signs.

Locanda Casa Petrarca (60,000-80,000 L doubles without breakfast, Calle Schiavone 4386, near San Marco, two blocks south of Campo San Luco, just down Calle dei Fuseri, second turn on left, tel. 520 0430), wicker-cozy, and my closest listing to a private home, hangs like an ivy-framed painting over a dead-end alley. Nelli, a friend as well as a host, speaks English. With only six rooms and listed in seven guidebooks, she doesn't need to serve breakfast and holds rooms only until 13:00 with a phone call.

Alloggi Ai Do Mori (55,000 L doubles without breakfast, or 23,000 L in shared four-bed rooms, Calle Larga San Marco, 658 San Marco, tel. 041/520 4817) is incredibly central, one block off St. Mark's and the bell tower with the two Moors, which it's named after (next to Wendy's). The place has lots of long, narrow stairways and peeling green wallpaper and the finishing touches are pretty flimsy, but the rooms and facilities are clean and functional, the management is friendly, and it's much handier than the hostel.

Hotel Canada (115,000 L doubles, Castello San Lio 5659, 30122 Venezia, tel. 041/522 9912, fax 523 5852) has 25 rooms, all with private showers, W.C., phones, and air-conditioning. In a "typical noble Venetian home," it's ideally located on a quiet square, just behind Campo San Bartolomeo between the Rialto and San Marco.

Albergo alla Salute 'Da Cici (70,000-100,000 L, 222 Salute, behind the Salute church, one vaporetto ride from San Marco, tel. 041/523 5404) is a close, but off-the-beaten-path, alternative, with a peaceful garden and far fewer tourists littering your doorway.

Locanda Sant' Anna (70,000-80,000 L, Castello 269, tel. 041/528 6466) is a garden of peace tucked away from all the hustle and bustle of Venice out in the "tail of the fish." Go to the far end of Venice, walk down Via Garibaldi almost to Isolo di San Piero, turn left over a bridge onto Sant' Anna street. Son, Walter, speaks English.

The **Venice youth hostel** (18,000 L per person with sheets and breakfast in 4- to 6-bed rooms, on Giudecca Island, tel. 041/523 8211, "Zittele" stop on Boat #5) is crowded, clean, cheap, efficient, and newly remodeled. The reception accepts no telephone reservations but can tell you what's available (desk open 7:30-9:00, 18:00-21:00, lock-up at 23:00). Their budget cafeteria welcomes non-hostelers.

Each summer, the city uses a few elementary schools to house budget travelers with sleeping bags. The tourist office has a list of these options, but they're not much cheaper than simple pensions.

Eating in Venice, near Campo San Bartolomeo

These places are just off the very central Campo San Bartolomeo (a block toward San Marco from the Rialto Bridge). Directions are based on the statue in this square's center.

The very local, hustling **Rosticceria San Bartolomeo/ Gislon** (Calle della Bissa 5424, 40 yards to the statue's left, tel. 041/522 3569, open 10:00-14:30, 17:00-21:00, closed Monday) is a cheap and confusing self-service restaurant on the ground floor (5,000 L pasta, prices listed at door, stools along the window) with good but pricier meals in its full-service restaurant upstairs.

If the statue on the square were to jump off his pedestal, walk ahead 50 yards, and look down a narrow alley to the left, he'd see a fat hula girl. That's **Bora Bora**, a new pizzeria with a fun menu and good prices (less a 10% discount if you show them this book). Across the alley from Bora Bora is the **Devil's Forest Pub**, English decor and self-service Italian food (5,000 L pasta, no cover, open late, closed Monday).

If the statue stepped back a few feet, turned left, went over one bridge, to Campo San Leo, took a left past Hotel Canada and over another bridge, he'd hit **Alberto's Osteria**, called simply "Osteria" on Calle Malvasia (fine local-style bar snacks and cicheti, very cheap, self-service from bar, then sit or stand for same price, open until 20:30, closed Sunday, tel. 041/522 9038).

Ristorante Pizzeria da Nane Mora (behind the statue, past PTT, over the bridge, and right at the red Santuario Madonna della Grazie church, on a tiny triangular square) has good pizza and indoor/outdoor seating.

For low-stress budget meals, you'll find plenty of self-service restaurants (*Self-service* in Italian). One is right at the Rialto Bridge. Pizzerias are cheap and easy. The **Wendy's** just off San Marco on Calle Larga San Marco serves a 7,000 L all-you-can-eat salad bar. Another budget-saver is bar snacks. You'll find plenty of stand-up mini-meals in out-of-the-way bars. Order by pointing. (See today's pub crawl.)

For a splurge, try **Trattoria de Remigio** (Castello 3416, 8 minutes toward the tail from St Mark's, tel. 041/523 0089, reservations necessary). This popular place is wonderfully "local" and near the Arsenale, a great neighborhood for after-meal wandering.

FROM VENICE TO FLORENCE

Leave the splash and flash of Venice for Europe's noble art capital, Florence. While Florence can't be seen in 24 hours, if you're well organized, you can enjoy its highlights. After the three-hour trip south, get set up, take a siesta, and you'll be ready for a look at the greatest collection anywhere of Italian Renaissance paintings and a thrilling walk through the historic center of the birthplace of the Renaissance.

Suggested Schedule	
8:00	Leave Venice.
12:00	Arrive in Florence, set up, siesta.
15:00	Tour Uffizi Gallery for a look at Italy's best paintings.
17:00	Walk through the Renaissance core of downtown Firenze.

Transportation: Venice to Florence (150 miles)
By car, traveling from Venezia (Venice) to Firenze (Florence) is easy. It's autostrada (with reasonable tolls) all the way. From Venice, follow the signs to Bologna, and then head for Firenze. Take the Firenze Nord-Al Mare exit. (The modern church at this exit, dedicated to the workers who lost their lives building this autostrada, is worth a look.) Follow signs to Centro and Fortezza di Basso. After driving and trying to park in Florence, you'll understand why Leonardo never invented the car. Cars flatten the charm of Florence. Get near the *centro* and park where you can.

By train, things are much easier. The Venice-Florence (and Florence-Rome) trains are fast (four hours) and frequent, zipping you into the centrally located station (five-minute walk from the Duomo). Use train time to eat, study, and plan.

Orientation

Florence is a treasure chest of artistic and cultural wonders from the birthplace of our modern world. Since our time here is limited, we'll wait to get intimate with Italy later in the hill towns of Umbria and the salty ports of the Riviera. For us, Florence is a "supermarket sweep," and the groceries are the best art in Europe.

The Florence we're interested in lies mostly on the north bank of the Arno River. Everything is within a 20-minute walk from the train station, cathedral, or Ponte Vecchio (Old Bridge). Some of the best hotels and restaurants are on the more colorful, less awesome Oltrarno (south bank). Orient yourself by the red-tiled dome of the cathedral (the Duomo) and its tall bell tower (Giotto's Tower). This is the center of historic Florence.

Arrival: The train station is very central, with a tourist information center and plenty of reasonable but full-by-early-afternoon hotels nearby. Those arriving by car with a hotel reservation can make life a little easier by driving as close to the center as possible and hiring a taxi to lead them to their hotel.

Parking (and driving) is a problem in Florence. Garages are expensive (around 25,000 L a day; the cheapest and biggest garage is at Borgo Ognissanti 96 near the Amerigo Vespucci bridge). You can try Piazza del Carmine for a free spot if you're staying across the river. White lines are free, blue are not. I got towed once in the town of Michelangelo—an expensive lesson.

Tourist Offices: Normally overcrowded, under-informed, and understaffed. If the line's not too long, pick up a map, a current list of museum hours, and ideas for entertainment. You may find small temporary information booths around the town supplementing the main Informazione Turistica at the train station (open daily in summer 8:30-21:00, tel. 055/28 28 93). There's often a small information booth across from the Baptistry. While the tourist information people dawdle, Florence has particularly hardworking Gypsy thief gangs.

Firenze/Florence

Florence requires organization, especially for a blitz tour. There's so much to see. Local guidebooks are cheap and give you a decent commentary on the sights and a map. Remember, many museums call it a day at 14:00 and stop selling tickets 30 minutes before that. Most are closed Monday and at 13:00 on Sunday. Churches usually close from 12:30 to 15:00 or 16:00. Hours can change radically. No one knows exactly what's going on tomorrow. Street addresses throw visitors a curve by listing businesses in red and residences in black or blue. *Pensioni* are usually black but can be either. Taxis are expensive. Buses are cheap. An 800 L ticket lets you ride anywhere for 70 minutes.

If you arrive early enough, see everyone's essential sight, David, right off. In Italy, a masterpiece seen and enjoyed is worth two tomorrow; you never know when a place will unexpectedly close for a holiday, strike, or restoration. Late afternoon is the best time to enjoy the popular Uffizi Gallery without its crowds. Telephone code: 055.

Sightseeing Highlights—Florence

▲▲▲A Florentine Renaissance Walk—For a walk through the core of Renaissance Florence, start at the Accademia (home of Michelangelo's David) and cut through the heart of the city to the Ponte Vecchio on the Arno River. (A 10-page, self-guided tour of this walk is outlined in *Mona Winks*.) From the Accademia, walk to the Cathedral (Duomo). Check out the famous doors and the interior of the Baptistry. Consider climbing Giotto's Tower. Continue toward the river on Florence's great pedestrian mall, Via de' Calzaioli, which was part of the original grid plan given the city by the ancient Romans. Down a few blocks, notice the statues on the exterior of the Orsanmichele Church. Via de' Calzaioli connects the cathedral with the central square (Piazza della Signoria), the city palace (Palazzo Vecchio), and the great Uffizi Gallery.

After you walk past the statues of the great men of the Renaissance in the Uffizi courtyard, you'll get to the Arno River and the Ponte Vecchio. Your introductory walk will be over, and you'll know what sights to concentrate on tomorrow. You still have half a day to see a lifetime of art and history—or just to shop, people watch, and enjoy Europe's greatest ice cream.

▲▲▲The Accademia (Galleria dell' Accademia)—This museum houses Michelangelo's *David* and his powerful (unfinished) *Prisoners*. Eavesdrop as tour guides explain these masterpieces. More than any other work of art, when you look into the eyes of David, you're looking into the eyes of Renaissance man. This was a radical break with the past. Man is now a confident individual, no longer a plaything of the supernatural. And life is now more than just a preparation for what happens after you die. The Renaissance was the merging of art and science. In a humanist vein, David is looking at the crude giant of medieval darkness and thinking, "I can take this guy." Back on a religious track (and, speaking of veins), notice how big and overdeveloped David's right hand is. This is symbolic of the hand of God that powered David to slay the giant. . .and, of course, Florence to rise above its crude neighboring city-states.

There's also a lovely Botticelli painting. The newly opened second floor is worth a quick look for its beautiful pre-Renaissance paintings. (Via Ricasoli 60, open 9:00-14:00, Sunday 9:00-13:00, closed Monday, 10,000 L.)

There's a good book and poster shop across the street. Walk around behind the Accademia to the Piazza Santissima Annunziata, with its lovely Renaissance harmony, and the Hospital of the Innocents (Spedale degli Innocenti, not worth going inside) by Brunelleschi with terracotta medallions by della Robbia. Built in the 1420s, it is considered the first Renaissance building.

▲▲ **Museum of San Marco**—One block north of the Accademia on Piazza San Marco, this museum houses the greatest collection anywhere of dreamy medieval frescoes and paintings by the early Renaissance master, Fra Angelico. You'll see why he thought of painting as a form of prayer and couldn't paint a crucifix without shedding tears. Each of the monks' cells has a Fra Angelico fresco. Don't miss the cell of Savonarola, the charismatic monk who threw out the Medici, turned Florence into a theocracy, sponsored "bonfires of the vanities" (burning books, paintings, etc.), and was finally burned when Florence decided to change channels. (Open 9:00-14:00, Sunday 9:00-13:00, closed Monday, 6,000 L.)

▲▲ **The Duomo**—Florence's mediocre Gothic cathedral has the third longest nave in Christendom (open 10:00-12:30, 15:00-18:00, sometimes with no lunch break, daily, free). The church's neo-Gothic facade, from the 1870s, is covered with pink, green, and white Tuscan marble. Since all of its great art is stored in the Museo del

Duomo, behind the church, the best thing about the inside is the shade. But it's capped by Brunelleschi's magnificent dome—the first Renaissance dome and the model for domes to follow. When planning St. Peter's in Rome, Michelangelo said, "I can build a dome bigger but not more beautiful than the dome of Florence." You can climb to the top, but climbing Giotto's Tower (Campanile, open 9:00-17:30, sometimes until 19:30, 4,000 L) next to it is 50 less steps, faster, not so crowded, and offers a better view (including the dome).

▲▲**Museo dell' Opera del Duomo**—The underrated cathedral museum, just behind the church at #9, has masterpieces by Donatello (a gruesome wood carving of Mary Magdalene clothed in her matted hair and the *cantoria*, the delightful choir loft bursting with happy children), Luca della Robbia (another choir loft, lined with the dreamy faces of musicians praising the Lord), a late Michelangelo Pietà (Nicodemus, on top, is a self-portrait), Brunelleschi's models for his dome, and the original restored panels of Ghiberti's doors to the Baptistry. Great if you like sculpture. To get the most out of your sightseeing hours, remember that this is one of the few museums in Florence that stays open late. (Open in summer, 9:00-18:00, often until 19:30, closed Sunday, 4,000 L.)

▲**The Baptistry**—Michelangelo said its bronze doors were fit to be the gates of paradise. Check out the gleaming copies of Ghiberti's bronze doors facing the Duomo and the famous competition doors around to the right. Making a breakthrough in perspective, Ghiberti used mathematical laws to create the illusion of 3-D on a 2-D surface. Go inside Florence's oldest building, and sit and savor the medieval mosaic ceiling. Compare that to the "new, improved" art of the Renaissance. (Open 13:00-18:00, Sunday 9:00-13:00, free. Bronze doors always "open"; original panels are in the cathedral museum.)

▲**Orsanmichele**—Mirroring Florentine values, this was a combination church-grainery. The best 200 L deal in Florence is the light machine, for its glorious tabernacle. Notice the spouts for grain to pour through the pillars

inside. You can go upstairs through the building behind it
and over a sky bridge for the temporary exhibit and a fine
city view (free). Also study the sculpture on its outside
walls. You can see man literally stepping out in the great
Renaissance sculptor Donatello's *St. George*. (On via Calzaioli, 8:00-12:00, 15:00-18:00, free.) The original Orsanmichele statues will soon be stationed upstairs. When this
happens, it will be one of the great sights of Florence.

▲**Palazzo Vecchio**—The interior of the fortified palace,
which was once the home of the Medici family, is worthwhile only if you're a real Florentine art and history fan.
(Open 9:00-19:00, Sunday 8:00-13:00, closed Saturday.)
Until 1873, Michelangelo's *David* stood at the entrance,
where the copy is today. The huge statues in the square
are only important as the whipping boys of art critics and
as pigeon roosts. The important art is in the nearby Log-
gia dei Lanzi. Notice the bronze statue of Perseus (with
the head of Medusa) by Cellini. The plaque on the pave-
ment in front of the palace marks the spot where Savonarola was burnt.

▲▲▲**Uffizi Gallery**—The greatest collection of Italian
painting anywhere is a must, with plenty of works by
Giotto, Leonardo, Raphael, Caravaggio, Rubens, Titian,
Michelangelo, and a roomful of Botticellis, including his
Birth of Venus. There are no tours, so buy a book on the
street before entering (or follow *Mona Winks*). The
museum is nowhere near as big as it is great: few tourists
spend more than two hours inside. The paintings are displayed (behind obnoxious reflective glass) on one comfortable floor in chronological order from the thirteenth
through the seventeenth century.

Essential stops are the Gothic altarpieces by Giotto and
Cimabue (narrative, pre-realism, no real concern with
believable depth); Uccello's *Battle of San Romano*, an
early study in perspective; Fra Lippi's cuddly Madonnas;
the Botticelli room filled with masterpieces including the
small *La Calumnia* showing the *glasnost* of Renaissance
free thinking being clubbed back into the darker age of
Savonarola; two minor works by Leonardo; the octagonal

classical sculpture room with Praxiteles' *Venus de Medici*, considered the epitome of beauty in Elizabethan Europe; view of the Arno through two dirty panes of glass; Michelangelo's only easel painting, the round Holy Family; Raphael's *Madonna of the Goldfinch*; Titian's *Venus of Urbino*; and an interesting view of the palace and cathedral from the terrace at the end. (Open 9:00-19:00, Sunday 9:00-13:00, closed Monday, last ticket sold 45 minutes before closing, 10,000 L. Go very late to avoid the crowds and heat.)

Enjoy the Uffizi square, full of artists and souvenir stalls. The surrounding statues of the earthshaking Florentines of 500 years ago remind us that the Florentine Renaissance was much more than just the visual arts.

▲▲▲ **Bargello (Museo Nazionale)**—The city's underrated and greatest sculpture museum is behind the Palazzo Vecchio (a four-minute walk from the Uffizi) in a former prison that looks like a mini-Palazzo Vecchio. It has Donatello's *David*, the very influential, first male nude to be sculpted in a thousand years, works by Michelangelo, and much more. (At Via del Proconsolo 4; open 9:00-14:00, Sunday 9:00-13:00, closed Monday, 6,000 L.) Dante's house, just around the corner, is interesting only to his Italian-speaking fans.

Medici Chapel (Cappelle dei Medici)—This chapel is drenched in incredibly lavish High Renaissance architecture and sculpture by Michelangelo. (Open 9:00-14:00, Sunday 9:00-13:00, closed Monday.) It's surrounded by a lively market scene that, for some reason, I find more interesting.

Museo di Storia della Scienza (Science Museum)—This is a fascinating collection of Renaissance and later clocks, telescopes, maps, and ingenious gadgets. A highlight for many is Galileo's finger in a little shrinelike bottle. English guidebooklets are available. It's friendly, comfortably cool, never crowded, and just upstream from the Uffizi. (At Piazza dei Giudici 1; open Monday, Wednesday and Friday 9:30-13:00, Wednesday and Friday 14:00-17:00, 6,000 L.)

Michelangelo's Home, Casa Buonarroti—Fans will
enjoy Michelangelo's house at Via Ghibellina 70 (open
9:30-12:30, closed Tuesday, 5,000 L).

The Pitti Palace—Across the river, it has the giant
Galleria Palatina collection with works of the masters
(especially Raphael), plus the enjoyable Galleria d'Arte
Moderna (upstairs) and the huge landscaped Boboli
Gardens—a cool refuge from the city heat. (Five
museums; open 9:00-14:00, Sunday 9:00-13:00, closed
Monday.)

▲**Piazzale Michelangelo**—Across the river overlooking the city (look for the huge statue of David), this
square is worth the half-hour hike or the drive for the
view. After dark it's packed with local school kids sharing
slices of watermelon with their dates. Just beyond it is the
strikingly beautiful, crowd-free, romanesque San Miniato
church. (Bus 13 from the station.)

▲▲**Gelato**—Gelato is a great Florentine edible art form.
Italy's best ice cream is in Florence. Every year I repeat
my taste test. And every year Vivoli's (on Via Stinche, see
map) wins. Festival del Gelato and Perche Non! just off
the pedestrian street running from the Duomo to the
Uffizi are almost as good. That's one souvenir that can't
break and won't clutter your luggage. Sample Vivoli's
zabaglione (eggnog), then the *riso* (rice). To me, rice is
the best.

Shopping
Florence is a great shopping town. Busy street scenes and
markets abound, especially near San Lorenzo, on the
Ponte Vecchio, and near Santa Croce. Leather, gold, silver,
art prints, and tacky plaster "mini-Davids" are most
popular. Check out the leather school in the Santa Croce
church, to the right of the altar (10:00-18:00).

Sleeping in Florence (about 1,300 L = US$1)
Even in crowded and overpriced Florence, with a little
information and a phone call ahead, you can find a simple, cheery, and comfortable double for around 50,000

to 65,000 L. For 90,000 L, you'll get roof garden elegance. If you're staying for three or more nights, ask for a discount. The technically optional and definitely overpriced breakfast can be used as a bargaining chip. Prices I've listed include 10,000 L for each breakfast. In practice, most places require it, but if it's not too busy, it doesn't hurt to ask. While the hottest months, July and August, are less crowded, and prices don't seem very firm, most hotels claim they are full every day from mid-March to mid October. Call ahead. I repeat, call ahead. Places will happily hold a room until early afternoon. If they say they're full, mention you're using this book. Use the crowded station room-finding service only if you lose this book.

Near the Station: While there are scads of inexpensive (one star) *pensioni* near the station (Via Fiume and Via Faenza), I'd choose something on or near Piazza Santa Maria Novella (behind the church, which is directly in front of the station) or on neighboring Via della Scala.

Casa Rabatti (46,000 L doubles or 20,000 L per bed in shared quad or quint for travelers with this book, no breakfast, Via San Zanobi 48, 50129 Florence, tel. 055/21 23 93, no English spoken) is the ultimate if you always wanted to be a part of a Florentine family. Simple, clean, very friendly, four blocks northeast of the station, this is my best rock-bottom listing.

Hotel Enza (55,000 L to 65,000 L doubles, no breakfast, Via San Zanobi 45, 50129 Florence, tel. 055/49 09 90) is clean, cheery, halfway between the station and *David*, and run by English-speaking Eugenia.

Let's Go and Arthur Frommer (the basic English-language guides to Florence) each rave about the same places two blocks from the station on Via Faenza. The street is filled with English-speaking tourists and good 50,000 L to 60,000 L doubles. No. 56 is a slumber mill, filled with these heavily recommended English-speaking places: **Albergo Azzi** (48,000 L doubles, 22,000 L per bed in shared quads and quints, no breakfast, Via Faenza 56, tel. 055/21 38 06), very accommodating, with a small terrace, is better than a hostel and will hold a room until 16:00. Not quite as good are **Merlini** (tel. 055/21 28 48), **Paola** (tel. 055/21 36 82), **Armonia** (tel. 055/21 11 46), and **Anna** (tel. 055/29 83 22).

Hotel Pensione Elite (70,000 L doubles, with modern showers but no breakfast, Via della Scala 12, second floor, a block off Piazza S. Maria Novella, and just two blocks from the station) has none of the backpacking flavor of Via Faenze and is a good basic value; run warmly by Maurizio.

Casa Cristina (65,000-70,000 L doubles, with this book, Via Bonifacio Lupi 14, just off the ring road near Piazza della Liberta, right side of courtyard, second floor, tel. 055/49 67 30) is farther away, a brisk ten-minute walk from the station and center. It's elegant and spotless and offers free, easy parking on its quiet street. Richly and traditionally decorated and run by Mr. Holtz, this place is a rare value in Florence.

Pensione Sole (50,000-60,000 L, no breakfast, Via del Sole 8, 3rd floor, no lift, tel. 055/239 6094) is a clean, cozy, family-run place with kids, caged birds, and a few bright rooms. Well located halfway between the station and the Ponte Vecchio, but there are lots of stairs.

Hotel Loggiato dei Serviti (160,000 L with everything, Piazza SS. Annunziata 3, Firenze, tel. 055/28 95 92, fax 055/28 95 95, guarantee reservations with AmExCo cards), which has about the most prestigious address in Florence, right on the most Renaissance square in town, has done a fine job of giving you Renaissance romance with a place to plug in your hair dryer. Stone stairways lead you under open beam ceilings through this sixteenth-century monastery's elegantly appointed public rooms. (It also has an Otis elevator.) The cells, with air-conditioning, TVs, mini-bars, and telephones, wouldn't be recognized by their original inhabitants. Stepping out onto the square into a traffic-free Brunelleschi world is a splurge-worthy treat.

On the River Arno: Pensione Bretagna (85,000-100,000 L doubles, west of the Ponte Vecchio, just past

Ponte San Trinita, at Lungarno Corsini 6, 50123 Firenze, tel. 055/28 96 18, English spoken) is a classy, Old World, elegant place for similar tourists. Imagine breakfast under a painted, chandeliered ceiling with an Arno view. To reserve, call first and follow up with a bank draft in lire for the first night. Or call in the morning, and they'll hold a room until noon.

Hotel Rigatti (95,000-110,000 L doubles, just east of the Ponte Vecchio at Lungarno Diaz 2, 50122 Firenze, tel. 055/21 30 22) is another well-run, peaceful splurge.

Soggiorno Cestelli (70,000-75,000, Borgo SS. Apostoli 25, 50123 Florence, tel. 21 42 13), in the old center, one block off the river, is the closest thing to living in a Botticelli painting a budget traveler will find in Florence. Luciano and his aunt rent 4 doubles and 3 singles and serve breakfast in the room. They like, but don't allow, children in their pint-sized palace. The rooms are huge, many with grand matrimonial beds, tassles on the hutches, candelabra, and hard wood floors framing rich old carpets. Their room #2 is the best deal in Florence.

Rooms in Oltrarno, Over the River: Across the river in the Oltrarno area, between the Pitti Palace and the Ponte Vecchio, you'll still find small traditional crafts shops, neighborly piazzas hiding a few offbeat art treasures, family eateries, two distinctive, clean, friendly, moderately priced hotels and three decent hostels. Each of these places is only a few minutes walk from the Ponte Vecchio.

Pensione Sorelle Bandini (80,000-90,000 L doubles with breakfast, Piazza Santo Spirito 9, 50125 Firenze, tel. 055/21 53 08), a ramshackle 500-year-old palace on a perfectly Florentine square, is two blocks from the Pitti Palace with cavernous rooms, museum warehouse interiors, a musty youthfulness, a balcony lounge-loggia with a view and an ambience that is, for me, a highlight of Florence. Mimmo, Monica, or Sr. Romeo will hold a room until 16:00 with a phone call.

Hotel La Scaletta (82,000-102,000 L doubles, Via Guicciardini, 13 black, 50125 Firenze, straight up the

street from the Ponte Vecchio, next to the AmExCo, tel.
055/28 30 28, fax 055/28 95 62) is more elegant, friendly,
clean, with a dark, cool, labyrinthian floor plan and lots
of Old World lounges. Owner Barbara and her children,
Manfredo and Diana, speak English and elevate this well-
worn place with brute charm. Your journal becomes
poetry when written on the highest terrace of La
Scaletta's panoramic roof garden.

Also in Oltrarno are some of the best rock-bottom
budget deals in town: **Institute Gould** (50,000 doubles,
with or without private shower, 20,000 L beds in shared
2- to 4-bed rooms, 49 Via dei Serragli, tel. 055/21 25 76,
office open Monday-Friday 9:00-13:00, 15:00-19:00,
Saturday 9:00-12:00, closed Sunday) is a Protestant
church-run place with 72 beds in 24 rooms. The facilities, whether in the room or down the hall, are modern
and clean. They'll hold a room until noon with a phone
call. Since you must arrive during their office hours,
there's no way to check in on Sundays.

Pensionato Pio X-Artigianelli (15,000 L beds in 2-
to 10-bed rooms, 3,000 L extra if you want a single or a
private shower, Via dei Serragli 106, tel. 055/22 50 44) is
Catholic-run and a little more free-wheeling and ramshackle, with 35 beds in 15 rooms, cheap meals served,
and a midnight curfew.

Ostello Santa Monaca (15,000 L beds, 2,500 for
sheets, without breakfast, 6 Via Santa Monaca, a few
blocks past Ponte Alla Carraia, tel. 055/26 83 38 or 055/
239 6704), with over 100 beds in 8- to 20-bed dorms,
takes no reservations. Sign up for available beds from
9:30-13:00 or when it reopens after 16:00. You can leave
bags (without valuables) there until it opens after siesta.
This and the classy **IYHF hostel** (tel. 055/601 4151) on
the outskirts of Florence should be last alternatives.

Eating in Florence
There are several good and colorful restaurants in
Oltrarno near Piazza Santo Spirito. **Trattoria Casalinga**
(9 Via dei Michelozzi) is an inexpensive and popular

standby, famous for its home cooking. Good values but more expensive are **Trattoria Sabitino** at Borgo S. Frediano and **Osteria del Cinghiale Bianco** at Borgo S. Jacopo 43 (closed Tuesday and Wednesday). **Trattoria Oreste** (right on Piazza S. Spirito at 16), with a renowned new cook and on-the-piazza ambience, may have the best 30,000 L dinner in the area. The **Ricchi** bar on the same square has some of the best homemade gelati in Firenze and a particularly pleasant interior. The best places change, and I'd just wander in a colorful neighborhood and eat where you see locals eating.

Trattoria il Contadino (55 via Palazzuolo, a few blocks south of the train station) offers an inexpensive but hearty fixed-price menu with a bustling working-class, family-style atmosphere.

I keep lunch in Florence fast and simple, eating in one of countless self-service places or Pizza Rusticas (holes in the wall that sell cheap delicious pizza by weight) or just picnicking (juice, yogurt, cheese, roll: 8,000 L). Try the local Chianti Classico.

Many locals enjoy catching the bus to the breezy hill town of Fiesole for dinner, a sprawling Florence view, and a break from the city heat. **Ristorante La Romagnola** (Via A. Gramsci 43, tel. 055/59258, closed Monday) serves fine meals and inexpensive pizza.

FROM FLORENCE TO ITALIAN HILL TOWNS

Today, see more of Florence, then trade big-city bustle for hill town snooziness. The hill towns of Tuscany and Umbria are a welcome breather from the frantic Venice-Florence-Rome scramble that spells "Italy" in most itineraries. By early evening, you'll be in Italy's ultimate hill town, Città di Bagnoregio, stranded alone on a pinnacle in a vast canyon.

Suggested Schedule

8:00	Half a day free in Florence. See David and the Bargello sculpture museum, shop, eat more gelati.
13:00	Picnic and drive south.
16:00	Set up at Angelino's.
17:00	Evening walk through Città.
20:00	Dinner in town or at Angelino's.

Transportation: Florence to Città di Bagnoregio (120 miles)

Leaving Florence, cross the St. Nicolo Bridge and follow the green autostrada signs south toward Roma. Drive two hours south to Orvieto, then leave the freeway, pass under hill-capping Orvieto (on your right, signs to Lago di Bolsena, on Viale I Maggio), take the first left, winding up past great Orvieto views, the Orvieto Classico vineyard, through Canale, and through fields of giant shredded wheat and farms to Bagnoregio, where the locals (or rusty old signs) will direct you to Angelino Catarcia's Al Boschetto, just outside town. Just before Bagnoregio, follow the signs left to Lubriano and pull into the first little square by the church on your right for a breathtaking view of Città.

By train, touring the hill towns is more difficult. Italy's small-town public transportation is slow. You can take the

Hills Towns of Central Italy

GENOA
LA SPEZIA
BOLOGNA ↑   VENICE ↑   RAVENNA
CARRARA   RIMINI
FIESOLE
CINQUE TERRE   LUCCA   FLORENCE   SAN MARINO
PISA   ARNO   POPPI   URBINO
SAN GIMIGNANO   AREZZO   ANCONA
VOLTERRA   SIENA   GUBBIO
CORTONA   PERUGIA
TUSCANY   ASSISI
UMBRIA   TREVI
ELBA   SORANO   SPOLETO
PITIGLIANO   TODI
ORVIETO   ←TIBER R.
CIVITA   BOMARZO   PESCARA
DI BAGNOREGIO
TARQUINIA   LAZIO   BRINDISI ↘ & GREECE
CERVETERI   TIVOLI
ROMA
OSTIA
ITALY'S REGIONS   ↓ NAPLES   —DCH—

0 KM 50 100
0 MI 50

MARCHES

very cheap one-hour bus trip from Orvieto (the nearest train station) to Bagnoregio (departures from Orvieto's Piazza Cahen and then its train station daily except Sunday, buy tickets on the bus) at 6:25, 7:50, 9:10, 12:40, 13:55, 14:30, 15:45, and 18:35, with a quick look at the great Civitá view from Lubriano, or hitchhike. From Bagnoregio, walk out of town past the gate, turn left at the pyramid monument, and right at the first fork to get to Angelino's hotel.

Sightseeing Highlights

▲▲▲**Civitá di Bagnoregio**— Yellow signs direct you through Bagnoregio to its older neighbor, Civitá (a pleasant 45-minute walk from Angelino's). You can drive through Bagnoregio and park at the base of the steep donkey path up to the traffic-free, 2,500-year-old, canyon-swamped pinnacle town of Civitá di Bagnoregio.

Civitá is terminally ill. Only 20 residents remain, as bit by bit it is being purchased by rich big-city Italians who will escape to their villas here.

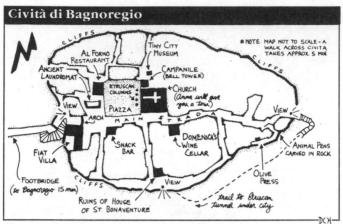

Civita di Bagnoregio

NOTE: MAP NOT TO SCALE - A WALK ACROSS CIVITA TAKES APPROX. 5 MIN

CLIFFS

AL FORNO RESTAURANT

TINY CITY MUSEUM

ANCIENT LAUNDROMAT

CAMPANILE (BELL TOWER)

ETRUSCAN COLUMNS

+CHURCH (Anna will give you a tour.)

VIEW

ARCH

PIAZZA

MAIN STRADA

VIEW

FIAT VILLA

SNACK BAR

DOMENICA'S WINE CELLAR

ANIMAL PENS CARVED IN ROCK

FOOTBRIDGE (to Bagnoregio 15 min)

CLIFFS

VIEW

OLIVE PRESS

RUINS OF HOUSE OF ST. BONAVENTURE

trail to Etruscan tunnel under city

—DCH—

Apart from its permanent (and aging) residents and those who have weekend villas here, there is a group of Americans, mostly Seattle-ites, introduced to the town through the small University of Washington architecture program, who have bought into the rare magic of Civita. When in session, fifteen students live with residents and study Italian culture and architecture.

Al Forno (green door on main square) is the only restaurant in town. Ask for Anna: she'll give a tour of the little church (tip her and buy your postcards from her). Maria runs a cute little *museo* (ask for "moo-ZAY-oh,") around the corner, to the left of the church. Around the other corner, on the main street, is a cool and friendly wine cellar, where Domenica serves local wine on a dirt floor with stump chairs—1,000 L a glass and worth it only for the atmosphere. (Civita's white wine tastes like dirty socks. The red tastes better, like clean socks.) Down the street is a garden with a huge old olive press and an even bigger view. Victoria (knock on the door across the lane) is willing, if not eager, to show you around . . . for a tip. Civita offers lots more; it's an Easter egg hunt, and you're the kid. The Ferrari family owns the house at the town gate—complete with Civita's only hot tub, for now.

Evenings on the town square are a bite of Italy. The same people sit on the same church steps under the same moon night after night, year after year. I love my cool late evenings in Civita. Listen to the midnight sounds of the

valley from the donkey path. If you know how to turn the
volume up on the crickets, do so.

▲ **Bagnoregio**—While lacking the pinnacle-town
romance of Città, Bagnoregio rings true as a pure bit of
small-town Italy. It's actually a healthy vibrant community (unlike the suburb it calls "the dead city"). Enjoy the
view from the park at the Città end. Get a haircut, sip a
coffee on the square, walk down to the old laundry (ask
"*Dov'è la lavandaria vecchia?*").

▲ **Etruscan Tomb**—Driving from Bagnoregio toward
Orvieto, stop just past Purano to tour an Etruscan tomb.
Follow the yellow road signs, reading Tomba Etrusca, to
Giovanni's farm (a sight in itself). If the farmer's home
(which is iffy), he'll take you out back and down into the
lantern-lit, 2,500-year-old tomb discovered 100 years ago
by his grandfather. His Italian explanation is fun. Tip him
4,000 to 5,000 L. (He's often in the town. Ask for Sr. Giovanni at Purano's Castello Robelli.) New excavations on
the site may turn it into the usual turnstile-type visit.

Orvieto

Umbria's grand hill town is no secret but still worthwhile.
Just off the freeway with three popular gimmicks (its ceramics, cathedral, and "Classico" wine), it's loaded with
tourists. Still, Orvieto is fun for a quick look.

From the train station (check your bag and your connection) ride the newly restored funicular (every 15
minutes, 1,000 L with the connecting mini-bus transfer
from the top, Piazza Cahen, to the cathedral square, or
Piazza Duomo, where you'll find the TI, and everything
that matters). The Tourist Information (tel. 0763/43884,
daily 10:00-19:00 with a lunch break, shorter hours on
Sunday) has a good free map.

The Orvieto cathedral has Italy's most striking facade.
It's a fascinating mass of mosaics and sculpture that
deserves some study. The rest of the church seems to be
there only to keep it from falling down, but in a chapel
next to the altar you'll find some great Signorelli frescoes
(7:00-13:00, 15:00 to 20:00, earlier in off-season).

Surrounding the striped cathedral are a fine Etruscan
museum (free, 9:00-13:30, 15:00-19:00), a great gelati

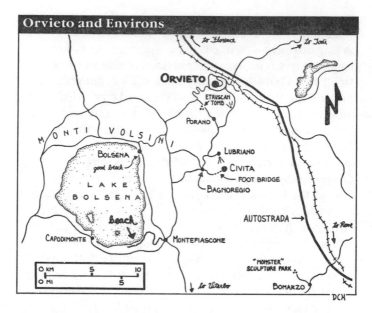

Orvieto and Environs

shop, and unusually clean public toilets. A shot of wine in a ceramic cup while gazing up at the cathedral lets you experience all of Orvieto's claims to fame at once.

Take a quick medieval wander into its back streets. The town sits majestically on a tufa rock, and its buildings are made of the dark volcanic stuff, so many streets seem like they're still in the dark ages. Piazza Cahen is only a transportation hub at the entry to the hilltop town. It has a ruined fortress with a garden, a commanding view, and a popular well that is an impressive hole but not worth the steep entry fee.

Sleeping in Orvieto

While you should do what you can to enjoy a true back door experience sleeping in Bagnoregio, many will end up spending the night in Orvieto. While it's touristy, it's far more relaxed and affordable than Florence or Rome. I found two fine cheap hotels.

Albergo Posta (36,000-56,000 L doubles, no breakfast, Via Luca Signorelli 18, Orvieto, tel. 0763/41909) is in the center of the hill town, two minutes' walk from the cathedral. It's a big, old, formerly elegant, but well-cared-for-in-its-decline building with a breezy garden, a grand old lobby, and spacious, clean, plain rooms.

Albergo Picchio (35,000-55,000 L doubles, breakfast 3,000 L in its classy little bar, Via G. Salvatori 17, 05019 Orvieto Scalo, tel. 0763/90246) is a shiny, modern, concrete-and-marble place, more comfortable and family run but with less character. It's in the lower, ugly part of town, 300 yards from the train station.

How about a swim? For a fun and refreshing side trip, take a dip in Lake Bolsena, which is nestled within an extinct volcano, 30 minutes by car from Bagnoregio. Ristorante Il Faro, directly below the town of Montefiascone, offers good meals on a leafy terrace overlooking the lake. Good swimming! Nearby in Bomarzo is the gimmicky monster park (Parco di Mostri), filled with stone giants and dragons. Built about two centuries ago, it proves that Italy has a long and distinguished tradition of tacky.

Tour a Winery? Orvieto Classico wine is justly famous. For a great look at a local winery, visit Tanuta Le Velette where Julia Bottai and her English-speaking son, Corrado, welcome those who'd like a look at their winery and a taste of the final product (tel. 0763/29090 or 29144, daily 8:00-12:00 and 14:00-17:00, closed Sunday). You'll see their sign five minutes past Orvieto at the top of the switchbacks on the Bagnoregio road.

Tuscany—The province just to the north also has some exciting hill towns, many of which are served by trains and more frequent buses. Whatever you do, rip yourself out of the Venice-Florence-Rome syndrome. There's so much more to Italy! Experience the slumber of Umbria, the texture of Tuscany, and the lazy towns of Lazio. Seek out and savor uncharted hill towns. For starters, the accompanying map lists a few of my favorites.

Food and Lodging near Città (about 1,300 L = U.S.$1)

When you leave the tourist crush, life as a traveler in Italy becomes very easy and prices tumble. You should have no trouble finding rooms in the small towns of Italy.

Just outside Bagnoregio, you'll find Angelino's **Al Boschetto**. Angelino speaks no English; he doesn't need to. Have an English-speaking Italian call him for you from Venice or Florence (about 45,000 L doubles, Strada Monterado, Bagnoregio [Viterbo], Italy, tel. 0761/79 23 69). Most rooms have private showers (no curtains; slippery floors, be careful not to flood the place; as you sing, find its great resonant frequency).

Angelino's family (wife Perina, sons Gianfranco and Dominico, and their wives, Giuseppina and Rosella, and the grandchildren) is wonderful and, if you so desire, he'll get the boys together and take you deep into the gooey, fragrant bowels of the *cantina*. Music and *vino* kill the language barrier in Angelino's wine cellar. Angelino will teach you his theme song, "Trinka, Trinka, Trinka." The lyrics are easy (see the previous sentence). Warning: Angelino is Bacchus squared, and his boys have learned well. Descend at your own risk. There are no rules unless the female participants set them. If you are lucky enough to eat dinner at Angelino's (20,000 L, "bunny" is the house specialty), ask to try the *dolce* (sweet) dessert wine. Everything at Angelino's is deliciously homegrown—figs, fruit, wine, rabbit, pasta. This is traditional rural Italian cuisine at its best.

Hotel Fidanza (50,000 L doubles with shower and breakfast, Via Fidanza 25, Bagnoregio [Viterbo], tel. 0761/ 79 34 44 or 79 34 45) is new, comfortable, normal, and right in town. (Rooms 206 and 207 have views of Cività.)

(A general midtrip note: By now, you've probably discovered your own traveling pace. I hope I haven't lost the readers who refuse to accept blitz travel as a realistic option for the overworked American who can get only three weeks off and who desperately wants to see the all-stars of European culture. So we'll unashamedly accept our time limitations and do our darnedest—resting when we get home. Now, on to Rome!)

ROME

Rome is magnificent. Your ears will ring, your nose will
turn your hankie black, you'll be run down or pickpock-
eted if you're careless enough, and you'll be frustrated by
chaos that only an Italian can understand. But you must
see Rome. If your hotel provides a comfy refuge; if you
pace yourself, accept, and even partake of, the siesta plan;
if you're well organized for sightseeing; and if you protect
yourself and your valuables with extra caution and dis-
cretion, you'll do fine. You'll see the sights and leave satisfied. You may even fall in love with the Eternal City.

Suggested Schedule

Day 12

8:00	Tour Orvieto or Città, or relax at Angelino's.
11:00	Drive into Rome.
14:00	Get set up in your hotel, siesta.
16:00	Walk through ancient Rome: Colosseum, Forum, Capitoline Hill.
20:00	Dinner in Campo dei Fiori.

Day 13

9:00	Pantheon.
10:00	Curious sights near Pantheon.
12:00	Self-service or picnic lunch.
14:00	Siesta, free afternoon. Options: Ostia, EUR, Villa Borghese, shopping.
18:00	Taxi to Trastevere for dinner. Walk through Rome at night: Campo dei Fiori, Piazza Navona, Trevi Fountain, Spanish Steps, subway home (last ride, 23:30).

Day 14

9:00	Vatican Museum and Sistine Chapel, postal chores.
12:00	Picnic in Via Andrea Doria Market. Catch the Vatican bus to St. Peter's.
14:00	St. Peter's Basilica. Church, crypt, hike to top of dome (allow one hour), treasury, square.
18:00	The "Dolce Vita stroll" down the Via del Corso. Nocturnal museums on Capitoline Hill?

Transportation: Bagnoregio-Orvieto-Rome (90 miles)

After an easy morning in hill town Italy, wind back to Orvieto for the quick, one-hour autostrada drive to Rome. At the edge-of-Rome rest stop, there's a freeway room-finding service. If it's open, buy the cheap Rome book, and pick up a city map.

Greater Rome is circled by the Grande Raccordo Anulare. This ring road has spokes that lead you into the center. Entering from the north, take the Via Salaria and work your way doggedly into the Roman thick-of-things. (You may want to follow a taxi to your hotel.) Avoid driving in Rome during rush hour. Drive defensively: Roman cars stay in their lanes like rocks in an avalanche. Parking in Rome is dangerous: choose a well-lit busy street or a safe neighborhood. Get advice at your hotel. My favorite hotel is next to the Italian "Pentagon"—guarded by machine gunners. You'll pay about 20,000 L a day in a garage. In many cases, it's well worth it.

Or consider this. Your car is a worthless headache in Rome. Avoid a pile of stress by parking it at the huge, new, free, easy, and relatively safe lot behind the Orvieto station (drive around about a half mile south), and catch the train to Rome.

By train, things are much easier. The Orvieto-Rome trains (70-minute ride, only a couple of departures a day, 18,000 L round-trip) zip you straight into the centrally located Roma-Termini station. Use train time to eat, study, and plan.

Orientation—Rome

Rome at its peak meant civilization itself. Everything was either civilized (part of the Roman Empire, Latin- or Greek-speaking) or barbarian. Today, Rome is Italy's leading city, the capital of Catholicism, and a splendid . . . "junkpile" is not quite the right word . . .of Western Civilization. As you wander, you'll find its buildings, people, cats, laundry, and traffic endlessly entertaining. And then, of course, there are its magnificent sights.

The ancient city is easy, if hot, on foot. The best of the classical sights stand in a line from the Colosseum to the Pantheon. The medieval city lies between the Pantheon and the river. The nightlife and ritzy shopping twinkle on or near the Via del Corso, Rome's main drag. Vatican City is a compact world of its own, as is the seedy/colorful wrong-side-of-the-river Trastevere neighborhood— village Rome at its best. The modern sprawl of Rome is of no interest to us. Our Rome is the old core—basically within the triangle formed by the train station, Colosseum, and Vatican.

Tourist Information: The Ente Provinciale Per il Turismo (EPT) has three offices (open 8:15-19:00, except Sunday): at the airport, in the train station (very crowded, only one open Sunday, tel. 06/487 1270), and the central office (5 Via Parigi, just a five-minute walk from the station, off Piazza della Republica, less crowded and more helpful, air-conditioned with comfortable sofas and a desk to plan on, tel. 06/488 3748 or 488 1851). Get the free EPT city map with bus lines and the monthly *Carnet di Roma* periodical guide (recommended hotels Nardizzi and Alimandi carry this map, hopefully saving you a stop here). Rome's attractions have a mysterious system of rotating opening hours. Confirm sightseeing plans on arrival.

The Termini station has many services: a late-hours bank, a day hotel, luggage lockers, the bus station, 24-hour thievery, and a subway stop. Handy multilingual charts make locations very clear. Telephone code: 06.

Transportation in Rome

Never drive in Rome if you can avoid it. This plan groups most of your sightseeing into neighborhoods, so you'll be on foot a lot. Still, use public transportation whenever you can. It's logical, inexpensive, and part of your Roman fertility rite. Bus routes are charted on the EPT map and

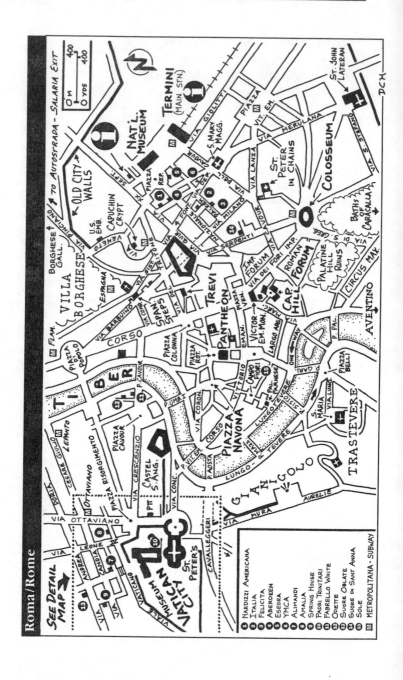

are clearly listed at the stops. Bus 64 is particularly useful, connecting the station, the Victor Emmanuel monument (near the Forum), and the Vatican. Ride it for a city overview. Buy tickets at *tabac* shops or at major bus stops but not on board (800 L, punch them yourself on board). Learn why the system is named ATAC. There are very cheap half-day and full-day tickets. Learn which buses serve your neighborhood. Buses, especially the touristic #64, are havens for thieves. Assume any commotion is a thief-created distraction.

The Roman subway system (Metropolitan) is just two simple, clean, cheap, and fast lines. While much of Rome is not served by its skimpy subway, these stops may be helpful to you: Termini (central train station, tourist office, National Museum), Barberini (Hotel Nardizzi, Cappuccin Crypt, Trevi Fountain), Spagna (Spanish Steps, Villa Borghese, classiest shopping area), Flamino (Piazza del Popolo, start of the Via del Corso Dolce Vita stroll), Ottaviano (the Vatican, several recommended hotels), Colosseo (the Colosseum, Roman Forum), and E.U.R. (Mussolini's futuristic suburb). Buy your 800 L subway tickets at tabacs or from machines in some stations (they take coins while neighboring machines change 1,000 L bills).

Metered taxis have a big drop charge (7,000 L), but it covers you for 3 kilometers. From the station to the Vatican costs about 10,000 L. Three or four traveling together with more money than time should taxi almost everywhere. Rather than wave and wave, ask in local shops for the nearest taxi stand. As long as they use the meter, they're fair.

Save time and legwork whenever possible by telephoning. When the feet are about to give out, sing determinedly, "Roman, Roman, Roman, keep those doggies movin'. . ."

Sightseeing Highlights—Rome
▲▲▲**Colosseum**—This is the great example of Roman engineering, 2,000 years old. Putting two theaters together, the Romans created an amphitheater capable of

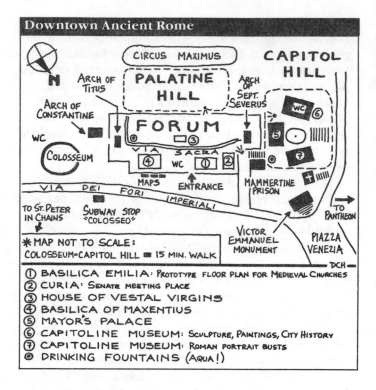

Downtown Ancient Rome

① BASILICA EMILIA: Prototype floor plan for Medieval Churches
② CURIA: Senate meeting place
③ HOUSE OF VESTAL VIRGINS
④ BASILICA OF MAXENTIUS
⑤ MAYOR'S PALACE
⑥ CAPITOLINE MUSEUM: Sculpture, Paintings, City History
⑦ CAPITOLINE MUSEUM: Roman portrait busts
◎ DRINKING FOUNTAINS (Aqua!)

seating 50,000 people. Read up on it. Climb to the top.
Watch out for Gypsy thief gangs—children or mothers
with babies. (Open daily 9:00-19:00 or an hour before
sunset, Sunday and Wednesday 9:00-13:00, free, 3,000 L
to go upstairs.)

▲▲▲ **Roman Forum (Foro Romano)**—Ancient Rome's
birthplace and civic center, the Forum was the common
ground of Rome's famous seven hills. To help resurrect
this confusing pile of rubble, study the before-and-after
pictures in the cheap city guidebooks sold on the streets.
(Check out the small red books with plastic overleafs to
un-ruin the ruins. They're priced at 25,000 L—pay no
more than 15,000 L.) Start at the Basilica Aemilia, on your
right as you walk down the entry ramp. The floor plan of
this ancient palace shows how medieval churches
adopted this basilica design. Then walk the Via Sacra, the

main street of ancient Rome running from the Arch of
Septimus Severus on the right, past Basilica Aemilia, up to
the Arch of Titus and the Colosseum on the left. Only the
giant barrel vault remains of the huge Basilica Maxentius
looming crumbly and weed-eaten to the left of Via Sacra
as you walk to the Arch of Titus. At the Arch of Titus,
walk to the right up the Palatine Hill to the remains of the
Imperial palaces, a pleasant garden with a good Forum
view, and, on the far side, a view of the dusty old Circus
Maximus. (Open 9:00-18:00 or an hour before sunset,
Sunday and Thursday 9:00-13:00, 9:00-15:00 in off-
season, 10,000 L.) Just past the entry there's a W.C. and a
handy headless statue for you to pose behind.

▲**Gypsy Thief Gangs**—If you know what to look out
for, the omnipresent groups of children picking the
pockets and handbags of naive tourists are not a threat
but an interesting, albeit sad, spectacle. Gangs of children, too young to really prosecute but old enough to be
very effective at ripping you off, troll through the tourist
crowds around the Forum and Colosseum. Watch them
target tourists distracted with their video camera or overloaded with bags. They look like beggars, hold newspa-
pers or cardboard signs to distract, and wear colorful
Gypsy-type clothing. Every year they get bolder, but
they'll still scram like stray cats if you're on to them. A
fast-fingered mother with a baby is often nearby. With
every visit to Rome, I meet tourists who've been ripped
off. Be on guard.

**St. Peter-in-Chains Church (San Pietro in Vin-
coli)**—On exhibit are the original chains and Michelangelo's *Moses* in an otherwise unexceptional church.
Just a short walk from the Colosseum. (Open 6:30-12:30,
15:00-19:00.)

▲**Mammertine Prison**—The 2,500-year-old converted
cistern that once imprisoned Saints Peter and Paul is
worth a look. On the walls are lists of prisoners (Christian
and non-Christian) and how they were executed (Stran-
golati, Decapitato, Morto di Fame). At the top of the stairs
leading to the Campidoglio you'll find a refreshing water

fountain. Block the spout with your fingers; it spurts up for drinking. Prison open 9:00-12:30, 14:30-18:00.

▲▲**Capitoline Hill (Campidoglio)**—This hill was the religious and political center of ancient Rome and has been the home of the civic government for 800 years. Michelangelo's lovely Renaissance square is bounded by two fine museums and the mayoral palace.

The Capitoline Museum in the Palazzo Nuovo (the building closest to the river) is the world's oldest museum (500 years old) and more important than its sister (opposite). Outside the entrance, notice the marriage announcements. You may see a few blissfully attired newlyweds as well. Inside the courtyard, have some photo fun with chunks of a giant statue of Emperor Constantine. (A rare public toilet hides near the museum ticket taker.) The museum is worthwhile, with lavish rooms housing several great statues including the original (500 B.C.) Etruscan Capitoline wolf and the enchanting Commodus as Hercules. Across the square is a museum full of ancient statues—great if you like portrait busts of forgotten emperors. (Both open Tuesday to Saturday 9:00-13:30, Tuesday 17:00-20:00, Saturday 20:00-23:00, Sunday 9:00-13:00, closed Monday, 5,000 L.)

Don't miss the great view of the Forum from the terrace just past the mayor's palace on the right. Walk halfway down the grand stairway toward Piazza Venezia. From here, walk back up to approach the great square the way Michelangelo wanted you to. At the bottom of the stairs, look up the long stairway to your right for a good example of the earliest style of Christian church. (If you climb up, let me know what you think of the church.)

Way down the street on your left you'll see a modern building built around surviving ancient pillars and arches. Farther on, look into the ditch (on the right) and see how everywhere modern Rome is built on the countless bricks and forgotten mosaics of ancient Rome.

Piazza Venezia—This square is the focal point of modern Rome. The Via del Corso, starting here, is the city's axis, surrounded by the classiest shopping district. From the Palazzo di Venezia's balcony above the square, Mussolini whipped up the nationalistic fervor of Italy. (Fifteen years later, they hung him from a meat hook in Milan.) **Victor Emmanuel Monument**—Loved only by the ignorant and his relatives, most Romans call this over sized memorial to the Italian king "the wedding cake," "the typewriter," or "the dentures." It wouldn't be so bad if it weren't sitting on a priceless acre of Ancient Rome. The soldiers there guard Italy's Tomb of the Unknown Soldier.

▲▲▲ **Pantheon**—For the greatest look at the splendor of Rome, this best-preserved interior of antiquity is a must (open 9:00-14:00, but often later, Sunday 9:00-13:00, tel. 369831, free). Walk past its one-piece granite columns and through the original bronze door. Sit inside under the glorious skylight and study it. The dome, 140 feet high and wide, was Europe's tallest until Brunelleschi's dome was built in Florence 1,200 years later. You'll understand why this wonderfully harmonious architecture was so inspirational to the artists of the Renaissance, particularly Raphael who, along with Italy's first two kings, chose to be buried here. As you leave, notice the "rise of Rome"—about 15 feet since the Pantheon was built. This is the only continuously used building of ancient Rome.

▲ **Curiosities near the Pantheon**—In a little square behind the Pantheon to the left, past the Bernini elephant and the Egyptian obelisk statue, is Santa Maria sopra Minerva, Rome's only Gothic church (built *sopra*, or over, a pre-Christian Temple of Minerva) with a little-known Michelangelo statue, *Christ Bearing the Cross*, and Fra Angelico's grave inside. Nearby (head out the church's rear door behind the Michelangelo statue and turn left) you'll find the church, Chiesa di Ignazio, with a fake (and flat) cupola. Stand on the round spot halfway down the nave for the right perspective. (Both of these churches are open until 19:00, with a siesta.)

Just past the busy street a few blocks south is the very rich and baroque Gesu Church, headquarters of the Jesuits.

There are also three dramatic Caravaggio paintings (each showing a scene from the life of St. Matthew, in the fifth chapel on the left) in the nearby church of San Luigi dei Francesi (open 7:30-12:30, 15:30-19:00, closed Thursday afternoon).

▲**Piazza Navona**—Rome's most interesting night scene features street music, artists, fire eaters, local Casanovas, ice cream, outdoor cafés (splurge-worthy if you've got time to sit and enjoy the human river of Italy), hippies, and three fountains by Bernini, the father of baroque art. This oblong square is molded around the long-gone stadium of Domitian, an ancient chariot racetrack. (There's a fine view from the Museum of Rome's top-floor windows.)

Piazza Navona is famous for its chocolate ice cream specialty, Tartufo. Two places on the square offer homemade Tartufo for about the same steep price. Tre Scalini is most famous ("to go" is much less expensive) and Ai Tre Tartufi, next door, makes its special softer variation with less chocolate and more sugar and cream. Factory-made tartufos are cheaper 20 yards away, just down the lane from the square.

The nearby Campo dei Fiori (Field of Flowers) offers a good look at village Rome, colorful produce and flower market by day and a romantic outdoor dining room after dark (several decent restaurants).

▲▲**The Dolce Vita Stroll down Via del Corso**—The city's chic and hip "cruise" here from the Piazza del Popolo down a wonderfully traffic-free section of the Via del Corso and up Via Condotti to the Spanish Steps each evening around 18:00. Shoppers, take a left on Via Condotti for the Spanish Steps and Gucci (shops open after siesta from 16:30 to 19:30). Historians, continue down the Via del Corso to the Victor Emmanuel Monument, climb Michelangelo's stairway to his glorious Campidoglio Square, and visit Rome's Capitoline Museum, open Tuesday and Saturday evenings. Catch the lovely view of the Forum (from past the mayor's palace on the right) as the horizon reddens and cats prowl the unclaimed rubble of ancient Rome.

▲**Villa Borghese**—Rome's "Central Park" is great for
people watching (plenty of modern-day Romeos and
Juliets). Take a row on the lake, or visit its fine museums.
The Borghese Gallery has some world-class baroque art,
including the exciting Bernini statue of Apollo chasing
Daphne and paintings by Caravaggio and Rubens (free,
9:00-19:00, Sunday 9:00-13:00, closed Monday, often
closed for restoration, call 06/854 8577 before going
out). The nearby Museo di Villa Giulia is a fine Etruscan
museum (same hours, also often closed, 8,000 L, call
06/320 1951).

▲**National Museum of Rome (Museo Nazionale
Romano delle Terme)**—Directly in front of the station,
it houses much of the greatest ancient Roman sculpture.
(Open 9:00-14:00, Sunday until 13:00, closed Monday,
4,000 L.)

▲**Trastevere**—The best look at medieval village Rome
is across the Tiber River. Witness colorful street scenes:
pasta rollers, streetwise cats, and crinkly old political
posters caked like graffiti-laden baklava on the walls.
There are motionless men in sleeveless T-shirts framed
by open windows, cobbles with centuries of life ground
into their cleavages, kids kicking soccer balls into the cars
that litter their alley-fields. The action all marches to the
chime of the church bells. Go there and wander. Wonder.
Be a poet. This is Rome's Left Bank.

Santa Maria in Trastevere, from the third century (open
8:00-12:00 and 16:00-19:00), is one of Rome's oldest
churches. Notice the ancient basilica floor plan and early
Christian symbols in the walls near the entry.

▲▲**Ostia Antica**—Rome's ancient seaport (80,000 people in the time of Christ, later a ghost town, now exca-
vated) is the next best thing to Pompeii and, I think,
Italy's most underrated sight. Start at the 2,000-year-old
theater, buy a map, and explore the town, finishing with
its fine little museum. Get there by taking the subway's B
Line to the Magliana stop and catching the Lido train to
Ostia Antica (twice an hour). Walk over the overpass and
go straight to the end of that road and follow the signs to
Ostia Antica. Open daily except Monday from 9:00 to

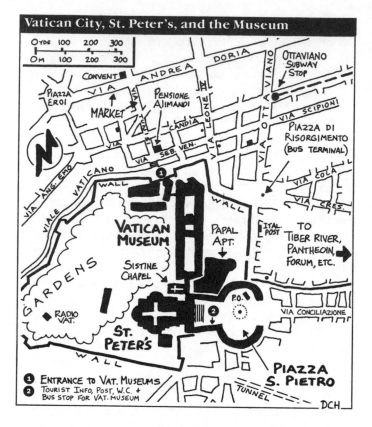

Vatican City, St. Peter's, and the Museum

❶ Entrance to Vat. Museums
❷ Tourist Info, Post, W.C. + Bus stop for Vat. Museum

one hour before sunset. The entry fee includes the museum (which closes at 14:00). Just beyond is the filthy beach (Lido), an interesting anthill of Roman sun worshipers.

▲▲ **The Vatican City**—This tiny independent country of just over 100 acres is contained entirely within Rome. Politically powerful, the Vatican is the religious capital of 800 million Roman Catholics. If you're not Catholic, becoming one for your visit makes it a much better experience. Start your visit by dropping by the helpful tourist office just to the left of St. Peter's Basilica. (Open Monday-Saturday, 8:30-19:00, tel. 06/698 4466; 2,000 L map of the country and church). Telephone them if you're interested in the Pope's schedule, or their sporadic but very good tours of the Vatican grounds, or the church interior. Very handy buses shuttle visitors between the church and the museum twice an hour from 8:45 to 13:45 for 2,000 L. This is far better than the exhaust-filled walk around the Vatican wall, and it gives you a pleasant peek at the garden-filled Vatican grounds.

▲▲▲**St. Peter's Basilica**—There is no doubt: this is the biggest, richest, and most impressive church on earth. To call it vast is like calling God smart. Marks on the floor show where the next largest churches would fit if they were put inside; the ornamental cherubs would dwarf a large man. Birds roost inside, and thousands of people wander about, heads craned heavenward, hardly noticing each other. Don't miss Michelangelo's *Pietà* (behind bulletproof glass) to the right of the entrance. Bernini's altar work and huge bronze canopy (the *baldacchino*) are brilliant. The treasury and the crypt are also important.

The dome, Michelangelo's last work, is (of course) the biggest anywhere. Taller than a football field is long, it's well worth the sweaty climb (330 steps after the elevator, allow an hour to go up and down) for a great view of Rome, the Vatican grounds, and the inside of the Basilica. (Last entry is about an hour before closing. Catch the elevator just outside around to the right.) The church strictly enforces its dress code. Dress modestly—a dress or long pants, shoulders covered. St. Peter's is open daily from 8:00 to 19:00; crypt, treasury, and dome close an hour

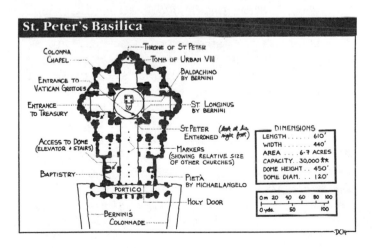

St. Peter's Basilica

THRONE OF ST. PETER
COLONNA CHAPEL
TOMB OF URBAN VIII
BALDACHINO BY BERNINI
ENTRANCE TO VATICAN GROTTOES
ENTRANCE TO TREASURY
ST. LONGINUS BY BERNINI
ST. PETER (look at his right foot) ENTHRONED
ACCESS TO DOME (ELEVATOR + STAIRS)
MARKERS (SHOWING RELATIVE SIZE OF OTHER CHURCHES)
BAPTISTRY
PIETÀ BY MICHAELANGELO
PORTICO
HOLY DOOR
BERNINI'S COLONNADE

DIMENSIONS
LENGTH . . . . . 610'
WIDTH . . . . . 440'
AREA . . . . 6-7 ACRES
CAPACITY . 30,000 ft
DOME HEIGHT . . 450'
DOME DIAM. . . 120'

0 m 20 40 60 80 100
0 yds. 50 100

-DCH

early. All are welcome to join in the mass (daily at 17:00). Volunteers who want you to understand and appreciate St. Peter's give free 90-minute "Pilgrim Service" tours in English most days at 10:15 and 15:00. Check at the desk just after the dress code check as you're entering for today's schedule. Seeing the *Pietà* is neat, understanding it is divine.

▲▲▲ **The Vatican Museum**—Too often, the immense Vatican Museum is treated as an obstacle course, with 4 miles of displays separating the tourist from the Sistine Chapel. Even without the Sistine, this is one of Europe's top three or four houses of art. It can be exhausting, so plan your visit carefully, focusing on a few themes, and allow several hours. Required minimum stops, in this order: Etruscan Gallery, Egyptian mummies and statues; *Apollo Belvedere* and *Laocoön* in Octagonal Courtyard, *Belvedere Torso* (all three very influential to Renaissance artists); School of Athens and neighboring Raphael rooms; modern Catholic art; Sistine Chapel; and the Pinacoteca painting collection with Raphael's *Transfiguration* and Caravaggio's *Deposition*. The museum clearly marks out four color-coded visits of different lengths. Rentable headphones (6,000 L) give a recorded tour of the Raphael rooms and Michelangelo's Sistine masterpiece. These rooms are the pictorial culmination of the Renaissance. (Easter, July, August, September hours: 8:45-17:00, Saturday 8:45-14:00, closed Sunday, except last Sunday of month when museum is free; off-season: 8:45-14:00. Last entry an hour before closing. Many minor rooms close from 13:45 to 14:45 or from 13:30 on. The Sistine Chapel is closed 30 minutes before the rest of the museum. It takes 8 minutes to slalom through the tourists from the Sistine to the entry/exit, 10,000 L.)

The museum's excellent book and card shop offers a priceless (9,000 L) black-and-white photo book of the *Pietà*—great for gifts. The Vatican post has an office in the museum and one on the Piazza San Pietro (comfortable writing rooms, open Monday-Friday 8:30-19:00, Saturday 8:30-18:00); the Vatican post is the most reliable mail service in Italy, and the stamps are a collectible bonus. (Vatican stamps are good throughout Rome; Italian stamps are not good at the Vatican.)

▲**Cappuccin Crypt**—If you want bones, this is it: below Santa Maria della Concezione on Via Veneto, just off Piazza Barberini, are thousands of skeletons, all artistically arranged for the delight—or disgust—of the always wide-eyed visitor. Read the monastic message on the wall near the entry so you'll understand this as more than just a macabre exercise. Pick up a few of Rome's most interesting postcards. (Open 9:00-12:00, 15:00-18:30.) A bank with long hours and good exchange rates is next door and the American Embassy is just up the street.

▲**E.U.R.**—Mussolini's planned suburb of the future (60 years ago) is a ten-minute subway ride from the Colosseum to Magliana. From the subway stop, walk through the park up to the Palace of the Civilization of Labor (Pal. di Civilta di Concordia), the essence of Fascist architecture with its giant, no-questions-asked, patriotic statues and its this-is-the-truth simplicity. (Remember this when similar art decorates your favorite mall, it's too late.) On the far side is the Museo della Civilta Romana (history museum, Piazza G. Agnelli, metro: EUR Fermi, 9:00-13:30, Tuesday and Thurday 15:00-18:00, closed Monday, 5,000 L), including a large-scale model of ancient Rome.

Historical and Religious Walks and Talks—The Ladies of Bethany offer free walking tours and slide show lectures on various Roman sites of religious and historical interest and help set visitors up with papal audiences. Since the future of this service is uncertain, call for an update. (Foyer Unitas Ecumenical Centre, Via S. Maria dell'Anima 30, just off Piazza Navona, tel. 06/686 5951 only Monday-Friday from 9:00-12:00 and 16:30-18:30.)

Overrated Sights—The Spanish Steps (with Italy's first, and one of the world's largest, McDonald's—McGrandeur at its greatest—just down the street) and Trevi Fountain (but very central, free and easy to see, best at night) are famous only because they are famous. The commercialized Catacombs, which contain no bones, are way out of the city and not worth the time or trouble.

Entertainment

Nighttime fun in Rome is found in the piazzas, along the river, and at its outdoor concerts and street fairs. Pick up the local periodical entertainment guide, the English-language monthly *Carnet di Roma* for a rundown on special events.

A highlight for many is a grand and lavish opera performance on the world's biggest opera stage, the ruins of the ancient Baths of Caracalla (Terme di Caracalla). (Shows start at 21:00 and finish after midnight several nights a week throughout July and August; tickets 25,000-50,000 L; English scripts available; tel. 06/488 1755.) This spectacle is taking its toll on the ruins of the baths and will be stopped soon. "Soon" in Rome is kind of like the Second Coming.

The social whirlpools make the famous floodlit night spots (Piazza Navona, Trevi Fountain, Spanish Steps, Via del Corso) endlessly stimulating. Sit in a café and watch the world stay young. La dolce vitamin! The places to meet a rich, sexy, and single Italian (or 2 or 3 out of the 4) are the streetside cafés of Via Veneto, near America's fortress-embassy.

Helpful Hints—Rome

The are no absolutes in Italy, and the hours I've listed will invariably vary. Museums are generally open 9:00 to 14:00. Most museums close on Mondays (except the Vatican) and at 13:00 on Sundays. Outdoor sights like the Colosseum, Forum, and Ostia Antica are open 9:00 to 19:00 (or one hour before sunset), often closed one day a week. The Capitoline Hill museums are Rome's only nocturnal museums, open Tuesdays 17:00 to 20:00 and Saturdays 20:00 to 23:00. By the way, in museums, "A.C." (*Avanti Cristo*, or Before Christ) after a year means the same as our B.C. "D.C." (*Dopo Cristo*) is what we call A.D.

Churches open very early, close for lunch, and reopen for a few hours around 16:00. Dress modestly—no bare shoulders or shorts. Kamikaze tourists maximize their sightseeing hours by visiting churches very early, seeing the major sights that don't close for siesta (St. Peter's and the Forum) when all good Romans are taking it cool and easy, and doing the nocturnal museums after dark.

Shops and offices are usually open 9:00 to 13:00 and 16:00 to 20:00. In the holiday month of August, many shops and restaurants close up—*Chiuso per feria* signs decorate locked doors all over town. Closed for Restoration is another sign you'll see all too often, especially in the winter.

One final theft alert: With seemingly likable, sweet-talking con artists, thieves on buses and at the station, and Gypsy gangs at the ancient sights, Rome is a mine field of rip-offs. But, unless you are really looking for trouble, no one is going to mug you. If you keep on guard (remember that thieves strike when you're distracted), don't trust kind strangers, and keep nothing important in your pockets, you have nothing to fear in Rome.

The siesta is a key to survival in summertime Rome. Lie down and contemplate the extraordinary power of gravity in the Eternal City.

Sleeping in Rome (about 1,300 L = U.S.$1)

The absolute cheapest doubles in Rome are 40,000 L, without shower or breakfast. A nicer hotel, providing an oasis/refuge, makes it easier to enjoy this intense and grinding city. If you're going door to door, prices are soft—bargain. Easter, September, and October are the crowded times. July and August are too hot for crowds. I've focused on three areas. Most of the places are small with huge, murky entrances that make you feel like a Q-tip. Except for the convents, most of them speak a little English and will hold a room with a phone call.

Near the Station: The cheapest hotels in town are on either side of the station (lining Via Palestro and Via Principe Amedeo). But, while you could probably manage without a problem, the area just doesn't feel safe. I'd spend as little time in the Termini Station area as possible These recommendations are about a ten-minute walk toward the old town and river.

Hotel Nardizzi Americana (85,000-107,000 L doubles, less 10% for 22 Days readers, Via Firenze 38, 00184

Roma, classic elevator to the fifth floor, tel. 06/488 0368,
or 474 5090) is my longtime favorite. Most of the beds are
springy cots, and the traffic noise in the front rooms
reminds you you're in a city of 4 million, but it's a tran-
quil haven, safe, handy, and central, a short walk from the
central station and Piazza Barberini, on the corner of Via
Firenze and Via XX Septembre. Sr. Nardizzi and his wife
speak English, stock the TI's free Rome maps, and provide a homey-and-you-belong atmosphere. Parking is
actually workable here. Double park below the hotel
until a space becomes available and grab it. The defense
ministry is across the street, and you've got heavily
armed guards all night. The nearby **Residence Adler**
(90,000-120,000 L doubles, Via Modena 5, 00184 Roma,
tel. 06/488 0940) is also good, but not as good.

   Hotel Pensione Italia (120,000 L doubles with
shower, promises a 20,000 L discount for 22 Days
readers, Via Venezia 18, just off Via Nazionale, tel. 06/482
8355, fax 06/474 5550) is in a busy, interesting, handy
locale, placed safely next to the Ministry of the Interior.
It's pleasant, clean, and friendly, and English is spoken.

   Hotel Felicita (100,000 L doubles, all with showers,
price guaranteed for my readers through 1992, Via
Palermo 73, 00184 Roma, tel. 06/48 59 15 and 474 7363)
is a friendly and happy place with quiet rooms.

   Hotel Aberdeen (150,000 L doubles, Via Firenze 48,
00184 Roma, tel. 06/481 9340) with mini-bars, phones,
TVs, and showers in its modern rooms and a first class
breakfast buffet, is my classiest hotel listing and a good
value for Rome.

   Hotel Pensione Esedra (60,000 L doubles without
shower, 47 Piazza della Repubblica, third floor, tel.
06/488 3912), on a formerly elegant piazza, a cigarette
butt's toss from the station, is the best cheap deal close to
the station I found. The place is spacious enough to make
its dumpiness acceptable.

   The **YWCA Casa Per Studentesse** (24,000 L per person in 3- and 4-bed rooms, 30,000 L per person in spacious doubles, with breakfast and showers down the hall,
locked up from midnight to 7:00, Via C. Balbo 4, 00184

Roma, 5 blocks toward the Forum from the station, tel.
06/488 0460 or 488 3917) accepts women, couples, and
couples with children. It's a gray and institutional place,
filled with maids in white and 75 single beds, with a
raggedy fruit market out the front door; a great value for
central Rome.

Near the Vatican: These hotels, except for the last listing, are handy to the Ottaviano metro stop near the Vatican museum entry, surrounded by good places to eat and
a shopping district favored by locals.

Pension Alimandi (65,000 to 95,000 L doubles,
optional 10,000 L breakfast, great roof garden; one block
in front of the Vatican Museum, Via Tunisi 8, 00192 Roma,
tel. 06/38 45 48, fax 06/31 44 57, credit card accepted to
secure telephone reservation) is a great value, run by
friendly and hardworking Paolo and Enrico and perfectly
located. They stock the free TI map.

Pensione Amalia (66,000 doubles, 8% discount to
my readers who stay at least two nights, showers all down
the hall, 12,000 L breakfast optional, Via Germanico 66,
00192 Roma, tel. 06/31 45 19 or 06/372 1968, accepts
Visa cards), run by friendly, English-speaking Amalia, is
another rare value.

Hotel Spring House (120,000 L doubles, Via
Mocenigo 7, one block from Alimandi, tel. 06/302 0948)
offers clean, quiet rooms with balconies, TVs, and
refrigerators, and a fine sixth-floor breakfast terrace but
no personality. If you need a normal hotel, this is a good
value.

Padri Trinitari (70,000 L doubles, all with private
showers and breakfasts, Piazza Santa Maria alle Fornaci 31,
00165 Roma, tel. 06/637 0736) is attached to the church
but run like a large, impersonal hotel. Its 42 rooms are
spacious, simple, clean, and popular with German
groups. This place is on a pleasant square three blocks
south of St. Peter's Square (far from my other listings), a
godsend to the budget traveler.

Near Ponte Cavour (on the Vatican side): This is a
normal, untouristy, livable neighborhood far from the
station and the Forum but just ten minutes from the Vati-

can, Via del Corso, the Pantheon, and the old medieval quarter, just over the Cavour Bridge.

Hotel Pensione Fabrello White (100,000 L doubles with shower and breakfast in your room, Via Vittoria Colonna 11, tel. 06/320 4446 or 320 4447, fax 06/562 1667) is comfortable, clean, peaceful, with high ceilings, Old World elegance, and New World bathrooms. It's a rare case where the entry is classier than the interior.

Pensione Residence Odette (45,000 L doubles, extra for shower and breakfast, Via Marianna Dionigi 17, 4th floor, with elevator, tel. 06/320 4507, some English spoken) is funky/ramshackle but friendly, clean, and safe, and the best doubles I found in this price range. The **Pensione Anita** (45,000 doubles, no breakfasts, showers extra, Via Marianna Dionigi 17, fifth floor with elevator, tel. 06/320 4677) is as cheap with rooms big enough to dance in. Even with dirty walls and bare bulbs it beats the Rome youth hostel.

Get Thee to a Nunnery: The convents of the city are your most interesting budget bet. The Protezione delle Giovane (in the train station near the day hotel, erratic hours, tel. 06/482 7594) is a helpful—to pilgrim-looking women—convent and budget room-finding service. Convents operate tax-free and are therefore cheaper; these are peaceful, safe, and clean, but sometimes stern, and they rarely speak English.

Suore Oblate dell Assunzione convent (25,000 L per bed, no meals, Via Andrea Doria 42, three blocks in front of the Vatican Museum entrance, buzz at the big gray gate, tel. 06/372 9540, French and Italian spoken). Just across the street from the Vatican Museum is a **convent** (20,000 L per person, in 1- to 4-bed rooms, Viale Vaticano 92, tel. 06/372 0209). They take men and women but no reservations and are normally full. It's worth a try if you have a good prayer life or know the people at Pension Alimandi, around the corner.

Near the Forum, the **Suore di Sant Anna** (25,000 L per bed in singles and doubles, including breakfast, lunch, or dinner—a great 15,000 L value—at Piazza Madonna dei Monti 3, 00184 Roma, tel. 06/48 57 78, three blocks from the Forum at Via Serpentine and Via Baccina) was built for Ukrainian pilgrims, so it's rarely full (groups in June, July, and September; empty in August). The sisters who speak Italian, Portuguese, Ukrainian, and a little English are sweet. The male staff doesn't seem to want your business. If you land a spot, your blessings will include great atmosphere, heavenly meals, unbeatable location—and a rock bottom price.

Similar places near the Vatican are: **Casa Valdese** (Via Alessandro Farnese, 18, tel. 06/321 1843), **Emaus** (Via di S. Maria alle Fornace 23, tel. 06/638 0370), and **Franciscan Sisters of the Atonement** (Via Monte del Gallo 105, tel. 06/63 07 82). Near Via Veneto is the convent **Nôtre Dame de Lourdes** (Via Sistina 113, tel. 06/474 5324.)

A few scattered recommendations in Rome: Albergo del Sole (65,000-90,000 L doubles, no breakfast, Via del Biscione 76, 00186 Roma, tel. 06/654 0873 or 06/687 9446) is just off the colorful Campo dei Fiori, right in the seedy Roman thick of things. It's clean and very well run with 65 rooms, a roof garden, and lots of Germans.

The Aventino hill is a high-class and peaceful residential neighborhood just beyond the Circus Maximus (bus 94 to center or metro: Circus Maximus). If you want to leave the big city but stay close, these two listings are a good bet. **Hotel Aventino** (121,000 doubles, Via San Domenico 10, tel. 06/574 5174, fax 06/578 3604) is run by security camera from a classier hotel next door. It's a sweet place with a garden, pastel-and-baroque frills, and modern showers in every room. **Souvenir Hotel** (125,000 L doubles, a few small 100,000 L doubles, 10% discount to travelers with this book, all with shower, breakfast in a small garden) is closer to the noise and bus and not as elegant.

Eating in Rome

The cheapest meals in town are **picnics** (from *alimentari* shops or open-air markets), self-serve **rôtisseries**, and stand-up or takeout meals from a **Pizza Rustica** (pizza slices sold by the weight). Most alimentari will slice and stuff your sandwich (*panini*) for you if you buy the stuff there. Hotels can recommend the best nearby cafeteria or restaurant. My best dinner tip is to go for Rome's Vespa street ambience and find your own place in Trastevere or on Campo di Fiori.

Near the Pantheon: Il Delfino is a handy self-service cafeteria on the Largo Argentina square (7:00-21:00, closed Monday, not cheap but fast). Classier (two blocks in front of the Pantheon, down Via Maddalena, left on Via della Coppelle) is **Hostaria La Nuova Capannina** (Piazza della Coppelle 8, tel. 06/654 3921, open for diner at 19:00, closed Monday), with good, moderately priced, sit-down, indoor or outdoor meals. The alimentari on the Pantheon square will make you a sandwich for a temple porch picnic.

Near the Station, Nardizzi's, and Piazza Barberini: Italy Italy on Piazza Barberini is a good value for Italian fast food. The nearby **Trattoria Il Giardino** (25,000 L for dinner, Via Zucchelli 29, one block down Via del Tritone then right, tel. 4885202, open at 19:00, closed Monday) is a good Roman splurge.

Near the Vatican Museum and Pension Alimandi: Ristorante dei Musei (15,000 L menu, indoor/outdoor, corner of Via Sebastiano Veneiro and Via Santamaura, closes at 17:00), or one of several good places along Via Sebastiano Veniero, such as **La Rustichella da Carlo** (more expensive but fine food, especially fish) at Via Angelo Emo 1 and the **Cipriani Self-Service Rosticceria** at the corner of Via Vespasiano and Viale Giulio Cesare (cheap, easy, with pleasant outdoor seating). Don't miss the wonderful Via Andrea Doria marketplace in front of the Vatican Museum two blocks between Via Tunisi and Via Andrea Doria (closed by 13:00). If your convent serves food, sup thee there.

NORTH TO PISA AND THE ITALIAN RIVIERA

Speed north from Rome, with a stop in Pisa for lunch and a look at that leaning tower. Then it's on to the sunny and remote chunk of the Italian Riviera called the Cinque Terre where you'll set up for two nights. This is a much-needed break after the intensity of Venice, Florence, and Rome. You couldn't see a museum here if you wanted to—just sun, sea, sand, wine, and pure unadulterated Italy.

Suggested Schedule	
8:00	Drive north to Pisa (or maximize beach time and skip Pisa).
13:00	Picnic lunch, climb the tower, sightsee in Pisa.
15:00	Drive to La Spezia.
16:30	Train to Cinque Terre.
Evening	Free time in Vernazza.

Transportation: Rome to Cinque Terre (250 miles)
With breakfast and plenty of cappuccino under your belt, hit the autostrada and drive north for about five hours, turning left at Florence, stopping at Pisa for lunch. You might consider beating the traffic by leaving before breakfast. The quickest way out of Rome, regardless of which way you're heading, is the shortest way to the ring road (Raccordo). Ask your hotel for advice. From the Vatican area, go west on Via Candia and follow the green autostrada signs. Exit the Raccordo toward Firenze. At Florence, you'll exit "al Mare." Pisa, a 30-minute drive out of the way, can be seen in an hour or two. Since you can no longer climb the tower, and traffic around Pisa can be a problem, seriously consider streamlining your day and going straight to the Cinque Terre.

One hour north is the port of La Spezia, where you'll park your car. You can leave your car near the station in

any spot with white lines and no sign. The far side of the
station lot has open parking spots, as do the nearby
streets. Confirm that it's okay and leave nothing to steal
inside. Catch the 1,200 L half-hour train ride into the Cinque Terre, Italy's Riviera wonderland. The villages of the
Cinque Terre are now accessible by car, but don't try it in
August or any summer weekend. Parking is strung out
forever leading into each town. Vernazza does have a few
parking lots a ten-minute hike out of town, which works
fine off-season, if you survive the scenic but treacherous
little road.

Pisa

Pisa was a regional superpower in her medieval heyday
(eleventh, twelfth, and thirteenth centuries), rivaling
Florence and Genoa. But its fleet was beat and its port
silted up, leaving it high and dry with only its Piazza of
Miracles keeping it on the map.

Pisa's three important sights float regally on a lush
lawn—the best grass in Italy, ideal for a picnic. The Piazza
del Duomo (also called Campo dei Miracoli, "Field of
Miracles") is the home of the famous Leaning Tower and
the textbook example of the town's unique Pisan Romanesque architecture. The 294 tilted steps to the top are
now closed. The tower was leaning even before its com-
pletion. Notice how the architect, for lack of a better
solution, kinked up the top section. The huge cathedral
with its richly carved pulpit by Pisano (open 7:45-12:45,
15:00-18:45) is actually more important artistically than
its more famous tipsy bell tower. Finally, the Baptistry
with more Pisano work (same hours as the church) is
interesting for its great acoustics; if you ask nicely and
leave a tip, the doorman uses its echo power to sing
haunting harmonies with himself. (Worth waiting until
15:00 if you're into acoustics.)

There's a large parking lot right at the sights, just outside the wall on the north end of town, so those coming
in by freeway don't actually have to drive into Pisa.

Train travelers will find the major Rome and Florence
trains stop in Pisa, and many will have to change there

whether they plan to see the tower or not. Getting from the station to the tower is very easy: bus #1 leaves from the bus circle to the right of the station every ten minutes. Buy your ticket from the magazine kiosk in the station's main hall or, more rewarding, from the yellow machine just outside to the left (push *corsa semplice*) outside the Tourist Information door (9:30-13:00, 15:00-19:00 daily, tel. 050/56 04 64).

Cinque Terre Train Schedule
Trains leaving La Spezia for the Cinque Terre villages: 1:40, 4:31, 5:29, 6:38, 7:24, 7:45, 9:03, 10:37, 11:20, 12:22, 13:03, 13:33, 14:17, 15:00, 15:34, 17:05, 17:35, 18:12, 18:53, 19:10, 19:50, 21:18, 22:35, 23:10
Trains leaving Vernazza for La Spezia: 1:13, 4:59, 5:18, 6:04, 6:44, 7:13, 8:33, 8:58, 9:56, 10:44, 11:37, 12:11, 13:01, 13:52, 14:23, 15:43, 17:10, 18:12, 19:06, 19:33, 19:43, 20:42, 21:36, 22:23, 22:52.

The trains listed above stop at all Cinque Terre towns, which are just a few minutes apart. They are in the *locale* class (Italian for "milk run") and often run late. The schedule is as stable as a mink in heat. Any station can give you an up-to-date schedule.

Cinque Terre Sightseeing Highlights
Riomaggiore—town #1: The most substantial non-resort town of the group, Riomaggiore is a disappointment from the station. But walk through the tunnel (or take the high road, straight up and to the right), and you land in a fascinating tangle of pastel homes leaning on each other as if someone stole their crutches. There is homemade gelati at the Bar Central. Its beach is just a few black pebbles, but that's enough to give the gang at Mama Rosa's a place for a midnight dip.

From the Riomaggiore station, the Via del' Amore affords a film-gobbling fifteen-minute promenade (wide enough for baby strollers) around the coast to Manarola. While there's no beach here, a stairway leads the way for sunbathing on the rocks.

Manarola—town #2: Like town #1, #2 is attached to its station by a 200-yard-long tunnel. Manarola is tiny and rugged, a tumble of buildings bunny-hopping down its ravine to the tiny harbor that somebody, sometime, must have called the "Devil's Caldron." An uppity crowd seems to hang out on the congested waterfront of Manarola. This is a good place to buy your picnic before walking to the beaches of town #3, Corniglia. As you leave, the low trail is a scenic dead end. Take the high one from the harborfront. This is a more rugged walk that any fit person could enjoy.

Cinque Terre—The Italian Riviera

This chart shows hiking time between the five villages of the Cinque Terre, as numbered on the map above. (Thinking of towns as numbers simplifies your beach life.)

Corniglia—town #3: A zigzag series of stairs that looks worse than it is leads up to the only town of the five not on the water. For that reason, Corniglia is the most remote and is rarely visited. It has a windy belvedere, a few restaurants, and a handful of often empty private rooms for rent.

The Corniglia beach below the station is where I do my 5-Terre swimming. It's rocky and narrow with a couple of buoys to swim to, relatively clean, and less crowded than town #5. The beach bar has showers, drinks, and snacks. Between the station and the beach you'll pass a bungalow village filled with Italians doing the Cinque Terre in 14 days.

Vernazza—town #4: With the closest thing to a natural harbor, overseen by a ruined castle and an old church, and only the occasional noisy slurping up of the train by the mountain to remind you these are the 1990s, Vernazza is my 5-Terre home base.

The action is at the harbor, where you'll find a kids' beach with showers, plenty of sunning rocks, outdoor restaurants, a bar hanging on the edge of the castle (great for evening drinks), the tiny town soccer field, and the busiest foosball game in Italy.

The hike from #3 to #4 is the wildest of the coast. The trail from Vernazza to #5 is a scenic, up-and-down-a-lot hour. The hourly boat service connects #4 and #5 (4,000 L, 6,000 L round-trip). A five-minute hike in either direction from Vernazza gives you a classic village photo stop.

In the evening, wander down the main (and only) street to the harbor to join the visiting Italians in a sing-along. Have a gelato, a cappuccino, or a glass of the local Cinque Terre wine at a waterfront café or on the bar's patio that overlooks the breakwater (follow the rope railing above the tiny soccer field, notice the photo of rough seas just above the door inside). Stay up as late as you like because tomorrow you're actually on holiday—nothing scheduled!

The expensive Castello (Castle) restaurant serves good food just under the castle with Vernazza twinkling below you. The town's only gelati shop is good, and most harborside bars will let you take your glass on a breakwater stroll. The pizza bar on the main street serves a great blend of crust, sauce, cheese, and spice—by the 2,500 L slice.

Monterosso al Mare—town #5: This is a resort with cars, hotels, rentable beach umbrellas, and crowds. Still, if you walk east of the station to the section through the tunnel, it has its charm. If you want a sandy beach, this is the only place you'll find it. Adventurers may want to rent a rowboat or paddleboat and find their own private cove. There are several between #4 and #5. One has its own little waterfall. (Tourist office, 10:00-12:00, 17:00-19:00, closed Sunday afternoon, tel. 0187/81 75 06.)

Sleeping in the Cinque Terre (about 1,300 L = U.S.$1)
While the Cinque Terre is unknown to the international mobs that ravage the Spanish and French coasts, plenty of Italians come here, so room-finding can be tricky. August and summer weekends are tight. August weekends are miserable. But the area is worth planning ahead for. If you arrive without a room and the hotels are full, ask anyone on the street or in the local bars for *affitta camere* (rooms in private homes). If you go direct, it's usually

easy to talk the price down. The hotels, enjoying more demand than they can handle, are high-priced and don't try very hard. With some luck, you can get a more comfortable room with a magnificent view for half the price in a private home. Off-season, you can just drop in and ask around. In summer, I'd always call long in advance and reconfirm a day before my arrival.

Sleeping in Vernazza: Vernazza is the essence of the Cinque Terre, my favorite town. There is just one real pension, but three restaurants have about a dozen simple rooms each. There must be 40 private homes that rent rooms, mostly through the local restaurants and pensions. If you arrange a private room directly, you'll save about 10,000 lire.

I stay at **Pension Sorriso** (50,000 L per person including a fine dinner and breakfast, last night's bread and a cappuccino, 19018 Vernazza, Cinque Terre, La Spezia, just up the street from the train station, tel. 0187/81 22 24, English spoken, train noise is a problem for some in the front rooms). It's the only real pension in town, and Sr. Sorriso knows it. He's a bit jaded but having a tough time retiring. Don't expect an exuberant welcome. Sr. Sorriso and his nephew, Giovanni, will hold a room for you without a deposit, if you give him a call and reconfirm a few days before your arrival with another call. If he's full or too expensive, Sr. Sorriso will help you find a private room (25,000 L per person). You can ask around yourself at the local bars and save a little money. If you like sweet wine, you'll love his *Sciachetre* (shock-ee-tra).

Trattoria Gianni Franzi (60,000-75,000 doubles, no breakfast, good modern showers, Piazza Marconi, 5, 19018 Vernazza, tel. 0187/81 22 28) has 14 simple, comfortable doubles up lots of stairs near the castle, where it's very quiet and the views are Mediterranean blue. The restaurant/reception is right on the harbor square. Their pension business is kept very simple.

Locanda Barbara is run by Giacomo at the Taverna del Apitano (45,000 doubles, no breakfast, Piazza Marconi 5, tel. 0187/81 22 01), which is also on the harbor square. His 9 quiet, basic doubles are on the top floor of what seems like a vacant city hall, with lots of stairs, low sloping ceilings, and small windows with wide harbor views.

Trattoria da Sandro (45,000 doubles, no breakfast, Via Roma 62, tel. 0187/81 22 23) has a line on 10 rooms scattered in the back alleys of Vernazza close to the train station. These are off the water a few hundred yards but more *tipico*.

Sleeping in Riomaggiore: Riomaggiore is a bit more substantial than Vernazza, with almost all of the same magic. Unfortunately, the accommodations are in the less colorful concrete part of town near the station. A short walk through the tunnel puts you in the heart of town.

Youth Hostel Mama Rosa (15,000 L beds, Plaza Unita 2, across from the station on the right, tel. 0187/92 00 50) is a splash of Mother Theresa and a dash of John Belushi, offering you the only cheap dorm on the Cinque Terre. Run by Rosa Ricci, an effervescent and friendly character who welcomes backpackers at the train station (whether they know they're staying with her or not), her husband, Carmine, and English-speaking son, Silvio. The 5 coed rooms with 8 to 10 beds are plain and basic, but a family atmosphere rages with a self-serve kitchen, laundry facilities, plenty of showers, free "beauty soap," and Silvio's 20 unnamed cats (available as bed partners upon request). Rosa also runs **Pensione Alloggiate** (40,000 L doubles, no breakfast, Via Signorini 41, tel. 0187/92 00 50), 4 very simple, quiet, and clean rooms with a kitchenette in her apartment, a steep three-minute hike away from the train tracks, up the hill in view country.

Affitta Camere "da Mario" (50,000 L doubles, 45,000 L for two nights, no breakfast, just to the left of the Riomaggiore station, tel. 0187/92 06 92, call in a reservation) is the best place for anyone needing privacy and quiet. Federica and Angela have 5 very comfortable rooms. (Don't let Mama Rosa lasso you if you're heading their way.)

For a stay in the characteristic center of Riomaggiore, ask at the Central Bar.

Sleeping in Manarola: Marina Piccola has fine rooms right on the water (tel. 0187/92 01 03, 75,000 L doubles, no breakfast) but lacks a personal touch.

The new **Albergo ca' d'Andrean** (75,000 L doubles with showers, breakfast extra, Via A. Discovolo 25, tel. 0187/92 10 40) is quiet, almost sterile, businesslike, comfortable, modern, with a cool garden, in the village center.

Casa Capellini (45,000 L doubles, 40,000 L for two nights, no breakfast, Via Antonio Discovolo 6, tel. 0187/92 08 23) farther up the street, just off the church square, is the best private home I found. Run by a bouncy elderly woman, with a prize-winning village-Mediterranean-vineyards-church bell tower view from its terrace, a self-service kitchenette, and modern facilities down the hall, this place is worth the language hassles.

Sleeping elsewhere in or near the Cinque Terre: Some enjoy staying in Monterosso al Mare, the most beach-resorty and least friendly of the five Cinque Terre towns. There are plenty of hotels. This is the forbidden city, and if you want to sleep here (**Pensione al Carugio**, tel. 0187/81 74 53, and **Albergo Punta Mesco**, Via Molinelli 35, tel. 0187/81 74 95 are decent), may you meet in hell all the hitchhikers you never picked up.

Nearby Lerici is a pleasant town with several reasonable harborside hotels and a daily boat connection to Vernazza. Boat in, train and bus home. The youth hostel in Finale Ligure, down the coast, is a friendly, deluxe castle.

When all else fails, you can stay in a noisy bigger town like La Spezia. **Hotel Terminus** (36,000-45,000 L doubles, no breakfast, Via Paleocapa 21, next to the station, tel. 0187/37204) has an elegant, arcaded, old lobby used by old locals to watch soccer, worn-out carpets, yellow walls, old plumbing, and basic rooms; **Albergo Parma** (40,000-50,000 L doubles, without breakfast, Via Fiume 143, 19100 La Spezia, tel. 0187/74 30 10), brighter but lacking the character, is located 200 yards from the station, down the stairs.

THE ITALIAN RIVIERA—BEACH DAY

Take a free day to enjoy the villages, swimming, hiking, sunshine, wine, and evening romance of one of God's great gifts to tourism, the Cinque Terre. Pay attention to the schedules, and take advantage of the trains.

Helpful Hints
Pack your beach and swim gear, wear your walking shoes, and catch the train to Riomaggiore (town #1). Walk the cliff-hanging Via dell' Amore to Manarola (#2) and buy food for a picnic, then hike to Corniglia (#3) for a rocky but pleasant beach. The swimming is great, and there's a train to zip you home to Vernazza later on. Or train all the way to Monterosso (#5) and hike or catch the boat back.

If you're into *la dolce far niente* and don't want to hike, you could enjoy the blast of cool train tunnel air that announces the arrival of every Cinque Terre train and go directly to Corniglia to maximize beach time.

If you're a hiker, hike from Riomaggiore all the way to Monterosso al Mare (the forbidden town #5), where a sandy "front door"-style beach awaits. Each beach has showers that probably work better than your hotel's. (Bring soap and shampoo.) Wash clothes today (in Switzerland, your laundry won't dry as fast).

It's your last night in Italy. Sit on the Vernazza breakwater, wine or whatever in hand, and get mushy. Do the church lights look like three ladies on a beach and a very interested man? Can a mountain slurp spaghetti trains? Do we have to go to Switzerland tomorrow?

Optional Itinerary
Hurried train travelers can take the overnight train from Rome to La Spezia (midnight to 5:30), check their bags at any Cinque Terre station for 1,500 L, and have 14 hours of fun in the Cinque Terre sun. (Hike from Riomaggiore to Monterosso in the cool morning hours, midday on the

beaches of towns #5 and #3, dinner on Vernazza water-front or up in the castle.) Then travel overnight again up to Switzerland (Genova-Luzern 23:25-4:48, scenic Luzern-Interlaken 6:05-8:19).

By car, you can enjoy the day and drive north after din-ner to Tortona, a nothing town just off the freeway half-way to Switzerland which (trust me) always has rooms available for late-night drop-ins.

From the Cinque Terre, you could trade Switzerland for France and spend a day in Nice, Cannes, and Monte Carlo. Take the night train from Nice to Chamonix via Aix-les-Bains (20:22-10:00) for the best of the French Alps (Mont-Blanc) and take the night train (20:58-6:42) directly into Paris from there. This plan is much better by train than by car.

FROM THE ITALIAN RIVIERA TO THE ALPS

Today's long drive takes you from palm trees to snow-balls. It's scenic along the Mediterranean coast, boring during the stretch from Genova to Milan, and thrilling through the Alps. By sunset you'll be nestled down in the very heart of the Swiss Alps—a cathedral even more glorious than St. Peter's.

Suggested Schedule	
7:00	Catch the train back to your car.
8:00	Drive the freeway north to Switzerland.
12:30	Lunch in Bellinzona area.
13:30	Drive to Interlaken with a snowball-and-hot-chocolate break at Sustenpass.
16:00	Stop in Interlaken for two hours of banking, tourist information, and shopping (or tour the Ballenberg Folk Museum).
18:10	Leave Interlaken for Stechelberg.
18:55	Catch the gondola to Gimmelwald.
19:00	Learn why they say, "If heaven isn't what it's cracked up to be, send me back to Gimmelwald."
19:30	Dinner at Walter's.

Transportation: Cinque Terre to Gimmelwald in the Alps (250 miles)

Catch the early train. (Skip Sorriso's breakfast; you'll hurt no one's feelings. There's coffee and a roll at the La Spezia station bar.) If your car's where you left it, drive by autostrada along the stunning Riviera (expensive tolls because of the many bridges and tunnels; the route via Parma is a bit cheaper and faster but less interesting). Skirt Christopher Columbus's hometown of Genova, noticing the crowded high-rise living conditions of the Italy that most tourists choose to avoid. Turn north through Italy's industrial heartland, past Milano's hazy black halo, and on into Switzerland. This is Amaretto country: it's very cheap at any truck stop. Just over the border is the Italian speaking "Swiss Riviera," with famous resorts like Lugano and Locarno. At the border, you'll be sold the 30 SF (Swiss franc) annual Swiss autobahn use permit. (Worthwhile, and required if you'll be using the Swiss freeways. Those caught on Swiss freeways without the decal on their window are ticketed.)

Bellinzona is a good town for a lunch break (great picnic rest stop a few miles south of Bellinzona, turn right off the freeway) before climbing to the Alps. After driving through the Italian-speaking Swiss *canton* (state) of Ticino—famous for its ability to build just about anything out of stone—you'll take the ten-mile-long St. Gotthard Pass Tunnel under Europe's Continental Divide. It's so boring it's exciting. It hypnotizes most passengers into an open-jawed slumber until they pop out into the bright and slaphappy, green, and rugged German-speaking Alpine world. Say *"ciao"* to Italian and *"guten Tag"* to German.

At Wassen (a good place to change money and famous among railroad buffs as the best place in Europe for train-watching), turn onto the Sustenpass road (closed in winter). Higher and higher you'll wind until you're at the snowbound summit—a good place for a coffee or hot chocolate stop. Give your intended hotel a call, toss a few snowballs, pop in your "Sound of Music" cassette, and roll on to Brienz.

When Sustenpass is closed, follow the autobahn around the mountain and along the scenic lake toward Lucerne (Luzern). Be careful to exit at the Stans-Nord exit (follow the signs to Interlaken) along the Alpnachersee south toward Sarnen, continue past Sarnensee to Brienzwiller before Brienz. A sign at Brienzwiller directs you to the Ballenberg Frei Luft (Swiss Open-Air) Museum (described below).

From Brienzwiller, drive along the congested but scenic north side of Lake Brienz (or save 20 minutes by taking the new autobahn to Interlaken on the south side). From the north shore road, follow the blue, not green, exit sign into Interlaken. Turn right after the bridge, and cruise through the old resort town down its main street, past the cow field with a great Eiger-Jungfrau view on your left and grand old hotels, the TI, post office, and banks on your right. At the end of town you'll hit the West Bahnhof. Park there.

To get to Gimmelwald (from downtown Interlaken or from the autobahn), follow signs south to Lauterbrunnen, pass through Lauterbrunnen town, noticing the train station on your left and the funicular across the street on your right, and drive to the head of the valley, a glacier-cut cradle of Swiss-ness, where you'll see the base of the Schilthornbahn (a big, gray gondola station). This parking lot is safe and free. Allow 30 minutes to drive from Interlaken to the Stechelberg gondola parking lot. Ride the 18:55 lift (five minutes, 6.20 SF, two trips an hour) to Gimmelwald. A steep 200-yard climb brings you to the chalet marked simply "Hotel." This is Walter Mittler's Hotel Mittaghorn. You have arrived.

Eurailers should go to La Spezia to catch a fast train to Milan (4 hours with a change in Genova) where there are regular 4-hour rides to Spiez and easy hourly 20-minute rides to Interlaken Ost (east). This is a messy trip. There is a Genova-Luzern night train with a two-hour connecting trip to Interlaken. Let an Italian train information person recommend the best route.

While most major trains leave from the Interlaken-West station, private trains (not covered by Eurailpass) go from the Interlaken-East station into the Jungfrau region. Ask at the station about discount passes and special fares. Spend some time in Interlaken before buying your ticket to Lauterbrunnen. It's a pleasant walk between the East and West stations.

Take the train to Lauterbrunnen and cross the street to catch the funicular to Mürren. You'll ride up to Grütschalp where a special scenic train (*panorama fahrt* in German) rolls you along the cliff into Mürren. From there, walk an easy, paved 45 minutes downhill or walk 10 minutes across town to catch the gondola (7 SF and a five-minute, steep, uphill backtrack) to Hotel Mittaghorn

If you walk, there's just one road leading out of Mürren (well marked for Gimmelwald), and your hotel greets you at the edge of Gimmelwald. A good bad-weather option is to ride the post bus from Lauterbrunnen to the base of the Stechelberg-Schilthorn gondola and ride up to Gimmelwald from there. The hike from Stechelberg to Gimmelwald is well marked and as enjoyable as a steep two-hour hike can be. (Note that for a week or so from late April to early May and from late November to early December the Schilthornbahn is closed for servicing. During this time, Gimmelwald is a serious headache to get to, and Hotel Mittaghorn is closed. Schilthornbahn tel. 036/23 14 44.)

SWITZERLAND (Schweiz, Suisse, Svizzera)
• 16,000 square miles (half the size of Ireland, or 13 Rhode Islands).
• About 6 million people (400 people per square mile, declining slightly).
• One Swiss Franc = about U.S.$.70, 1.5 SF = about U.S.$1.
Switzerland, Europe's richest, best-organized, and most mountainous country, is an easy oasis and a breath of fresh Alpine air, particularly refreshing after intense Italy. Like Boy Scouts, the Swiss count cleanliness, neatness, punctuality, tolerance, independence, thrift, and hard work as virtues and love pocket knives. They appreciate the awesome nature that surrounds them and are proud of their little country's many achievements.

The average Swiss income (among the highest in the world), a great social security system, and their super-strong currency, not to mention the Alps, give them plenty to be thankful for.

Switzerland, 40 percent of which is uninhabitable rocks, lakes, and rugged Alps, has distinct cultural regions and customs. Two-thirds of the people speak German, 20 percent French, 10 percent Italian, and a small group of people in the southeast speak Romansch, a direct descendant of ancient Latin. Within these four language groups, there are many dialects. The singsongy Swiss German,

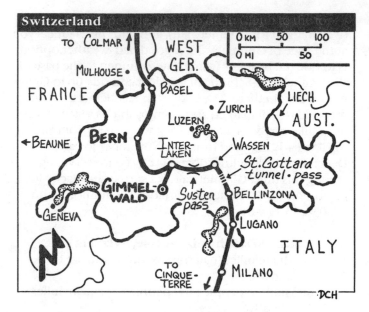

the spoken dialect, is quite a bit different from High German, which is Switzerland's written German. An interest in these regional distinctions will win the hearts of locals you meet. As you travel from one valley to the next, notice changes in architecture and customs.

Historically, Switzerland is one of the oldest democracies. Born when 3 states, or cantons, united in 1291, the Confederation Helvetica as it was called in Roman times (the "CH" decal on cars doesn't stand for chocolate) grew to the 23 of today. The government is decentralized, and cantonal loyalty is very strong.

Switzerland loves its neutrality and stayed out of both world wars, but it is far from lax defensively. Every fit man serves in the army and stays in the reserve. Each house has a gun and a bomb shelter. There are 600,000 rifles in homes and 12,000 heavy guns in place. Swiss vacuum-packed emergency army bread, which lasts two years, is said to also function as a weapon. Airstrips hide inside mountains behind Batmobile doors. With the push of a button, all road, rail, and bridge entries to the country can be destroyed, changing Switzerland into a formidable mountain fortress. Notice the explosive patches checkerboarding the roads at key points like mountain summits (and hope no one invades until you get past). Sentiments are changing, and in 1989, Switzerland came close to voting away its entire military. August 1 is the very festive Swiss national holiday.

Switzerland has a low inflation rate and a strong franc. Gas is less than $3 a gallon, cheap for Europe. Dormitory accommodations are plentiful and cheap, groceries are reasonable, and hiking is free, but Alpine lifts and souvenirs are expensive. Shops throughout the land thrill tourists with carved, woven, and clanging mountain knickknacks, clocks, watches, and Swiss army knives (Victorinox is the best brand).

The Swiss eat when we do and enjoy a straightforward, no-nonsense cuisine. Specialties include delicious fondue, rich chocolates, a melted cheese dish called *raclette*, fresh dairy products (try müesli yogurt), 100 varieties of cheese, and Fendant, a good crisp local white wine, too expensive to sell well abroad but worth a taste here. The Co-op and Migros grocery stores are the hungry hiker's best budget bet.

You can get anywhere quickly on Switzerland's fine road system (the world's most expensive to build per mile) or on its scenic and efficient trains. Families should take advantage of the supersaver Family Pass, available free at Swiss stations for train and Alpine lift discounts.

Tourist information offices abound. While Switzerland's booming big cities are cosmopolitan, the traditional culture lives on in the Alpine villages. Spend most of your time getting high in the Alps. On Sundays, you're most likely to enjoy traditional sports, music, clothing, and culture.

Sightseeing Highlights on the Road to Gimmelwald

▲▲▲ **Ballenberg**—The Swiss Open-Air Museum Ballenberg is a rich collection of traditional and historic farmhouses from every region of the country. Each house is carefully furnished, and many feature a traditional craftsperson at work. The sprawling 50-acre park, laid out roughly as a huge Swiss map, is a natural preserve providing a wonderful setting for this culture-on-a-lazy-Susan look at Switzerland.

The Thurgau house (#621) has an interesting wattle-and-daub (half-timbered construction) display and a fun bread museum upstairs. Use the 2 SF map/guide. The more expensive picture book is a better souvenir than guide. Open daily 10:00 to 17:00, mid-April through late October, 10 SF entry, two-hour private tours are 50 SF (by prior arrangement), tel. 036/51 11 23, reasonable outdoor cafeteria inside the west entrance, and fresh baked bread, sausage, and mountain cheese, or other cooked goodies available at several houses. Picnic tables and grills with free firewood are scattered throughout the park.

Before leaving, drive through the little wooden village of Brienzwiller (near the east entrance). It's a museum in itself with a lovely little church. (Trains go regularly from Interlaken to Brienz, where buses connect you with Ballenberg.)

▲**Interlaken**—When the nineteenth-century romantics redefined mountains as something more than cold and troublesome obstacles, Interlaken became the original Alpine resort. Ever since then, tourists have flocked to the Alps "because they're there." Interlaken's glory days are long gone, its elegant old hotels eclipsed by the new, more jet-setty Alpine resorts. Today, its shops are filled with chocolate bars, Swiss army knives, and sunburned backpackers.

But it's a good administrative center. You'll find a handy post office with boxes, a late hours (7:00-21:30 daily), long-distance phone booth (next to the post office, easy 1.5 SF/minute calls to the U.S., even cheaper on Saturday, Sunday, and after 21:00), plenty of banks (the West train station exchange desk has fair rates and is open daily until 18:00), and major trains to all corners of Europe.

Interlaken is a handy place to wash your filthy clothes. Helen Schmocker's Wascherei Laundry has a change

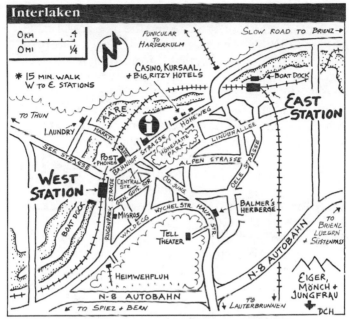

machine, soap, English instructions, and a pleasant riverside place to hang out (from the post office follow Markt-
gasse over two bridges to Beatenbergstrasse, open 7:00-
22:00 daily for self-service, 8 SF to wash and dry 10
pounds; Monday-Friday 8:00-12:00 and 13:30 to 18:00
for full service: drop off 10 pounds and 12 SF in the
morning and pick it up clean that afternoon; tel. 036/22
15 66).

Interlaken is your best Swiss shopping town. I'd take
care of business, give the town a quick look, and head for
the hills. The big Migros supermarket across from the
West station is handy. The tourist office (on the main
street, open 8:00-12:00, 14:00-19:00, Saturday 8:00-
12:00, 14:00-17:00, Sunday 17:00-19:00 from July
through mid-September; shorter hours and closed Saturday afternoon and Sunday in the off-season; tel. 036/22
21 21) has good information for the whole region and
advice on Alpine lift discounts. Pick up a Bern map, a
Jungfrau region map, and a Jungfrau region timetable. For
mountain train information, tel. 036/26 42 33

Luzern—Train travelers may pass through Luzern. Near
the station is the tourist office and the pleasant lakeside
old center with its charming covered bridges—worth a
walk. The sightseeing highlight, apart from ogling the
50,000 SF watches in the shop windows near the lake-
front (only the cheaper 10,000 SF ones are left out at
night), is Luzern's huge Museum of Transportation (Ver-
kehrshaus der Schweiz) outside town on the lake (boats
and cable cars go there from the center). Europe's best
transport museum, it's open daily from 9:00 to 18:00
(November-February, 10:00 to 16:00), 12 SF.

Sleeping and Eating in Gimmelwald (4,500 feet; 1 SF = about U.S.$.60)

To inhale the Alps and really hold it in, sleep high in
Gimmelwald. Poor, stuck happily in the past, avalanche-
zone Gimmelwald has a youth hostel, a pension, and a
hotel. The only bad news is that the lift costs about 7 SF
each way.

The **"Mountain Hostel"** (7 SF per bed in 2- to 15-bed
rooms, 2 SF for sheets, open all year, tel. 036/551704) is
simple, less than clean, rowdy, cheap, and very friendly.
Its 45 beds are often taken in July and August, so call
ahead to Lena, the elderly woman who runs the place.
The hostel has low ceilings, a self-serve kitchen, enough
hot water for ten (1 SF, five minutes) hot showers a day (or
you can drop by the Mürren Sports Center with a towel
and 2 SF), and coed washrooms. It's 50 yards from the lift
station.

This relaxed hostel is struggling to survive. Please read
the signs, respect its rules, leave it cleaner than you found
it, and treat it and Lena with loving care. Without Lena,
I'm afraid there's no hostel in Gimmelwald. The place,
because of the spirit of its rugged but sensitive visitors
and the help of Brian (a local Texan), almost runs itself.

The **Pension Gimmelwald** (with a cheap dorm on its
top floor and decent 70 SF doubles, two-night minimum,
tel. 036/55 17 30) next door serves meals.

Hotel Mittaghorn (59 SF doubles, with breakfast,

cheaper triples, quads, and quints, loft beds with breakfast are 20 SF, CH-3826 Gimmelwald (Bern), tel. 036/55 16 58, phone reservations are a good idea, call a few days ahead), the treasure of Gimmelwald, is run by Walter Mittler, a perfect Swiss gentleman (and former chef for Swiss Air).

It's a classic, creaky, Alpine-style place with memorable beds, ancient (short) down comforters, and a million-dollar view of the Jungfrau Alps. The hotel has one room with a shower (and it has two) and a single communal shower. Walter is careful not to get too hectic or big and enjoys sensitive, back door travelers. He runs the hotel with the help of Don von Gimmelwald (actually "von" Winnipeg) keeping it simple but with class. This is a good place to receive mail from home.

To some, Hotel Mittaghorn is a fire just waiting to happen, with a kitchen that would never pass code, terrible beds, nowhere near enough plumbing, run by an eccentric man. These people enjoy Interlaken, Wengen, or Mürren, and that's where they should sleep. Be warned, you'll meet maybe more of my readers than you hoped for, but it's a fun crowd, an extended family. (Walter closes his place for a week or so around May 1 and November 20, when the local lift is closed for servicing.)

Gimmelwald feeds its goats better than its people. The hostel has a decent members' kitchen but serves no food, and the village grocery is open only every other morning. The wise and frugal buy and pack in food from the Co-ops in Mürren or Lauterbrunnen. Walter, at Hotel Mittaghorn, is Gimmelwald's best cook (not saying much, but he is good). Dinners must be preordered and prepaid by 16:00. His salad is best eaten one leaf at a time with your fingers. There's no menu, and dinner's served at 19:30 sharp. When Walter's in the mood, his place is the best bar in town. Cheap and good beer, strong *kaffee fertigs* (coffee with schnapps). Otherwise, you can eat at the pension in the center of the village. For a rare bit of ruggedness and the best budget food in the center of Mürren, eat at the "Stägerstübli."

Sleeping in Mürren (5,500 feet)

Mürren is as pleasant as an Alpine resort can be. It's
traffic-free, filled with old-timers with walking sticks and
Japanese making movies of each other with a snowy
backdrop. Its chalets are prefab-rustic. It sits on a ledge
2,000 feet above the Lauterbrunnen valley and is surrounded by a brilliant chorus of mountains. It has all the
comforts of home and then some, with very high prices.

Mürren's best value is **Chalet Minerva** (75 SF doubles
with breakfast, view and kitchenette, tel. 036/55 29 84)
where owner, Denise, makes you feel right at home and
will, for a small price, do your laundry.

Hotel Alpina (110 SF doubles with shower, breakfast,
and the great view, baths more expensive, no view
cheaper, CH-3825 Mürren, tel. 036/55 13 61) is clean,
friendly, modern, like something you'd expect in Port-
land but hanging literally on the cliff. The big, basic
Pension Regina (100 SF doubles, tel. 036/55 14 21) is
located a block from the Schilthorn station.

Sleeping in Wengen (4,200 feet)

Wengen is just a "Mürren" on the other side of the valley.
Both are traffic-free and an easy lift ride above Lauter-
brunnen. Wengen is halfway up to Kleine-Scheidegg and
Männlichen. It has more tennis courts than budget beds.

Hotel Bernerhof (75 SF doubles with breakfast, tel.
036/55 27 21) has 16 SF dorm beds. The **Hotel Jung-
fraublick** has dorm beds for 30 SF with breakfast, tel.
036/55 27 55. The **Chalet Schweizerheim Garni** (100
SF doubles, tel. 036/55 15 81) is the cheapest hotel in
Wengen.

Sleeping below Gimmelwald near the Stechelberg Lift (2,800 feet)

Chalet Alpenglühn (50 SF per room for two or three,
kitchenette but no breakfast, 3824 Stechelberg across
from the Breithorn Campground, tel. 036/55 18 21), a
tiny drive before the Schilthornbahn, is on the valley
floor surrounded by the meadow, waterfalls, and birds
and features low ceilings and simple Alpine elegance.

This is the home of Theo Van Allmen, who makes art with leather and budget travelers happy.

The local **Naturfreundehaus Alpenhof** (cheap dorm, Stechelberg, tel. 551202) is a rugged Alpine lodge for local hikers at the far end of Lauterbrunnen Valley which I've never felt very welcome in.

Sleeping in Lauterbrunnen town (2,600 feet)

Masenlager Stocki (8 SF a night in an easygoing little coed dorm, with a kitchen, tel. 036/55 17 54) is a great value, across the river from the tourist office. **Gasthaus Bären** (60 SF doubles, tel. 036/55 17 23) is at the far end near the waterfall. Two campgrounds just south of town work very hard to provide 15 to 25 SF beds. They each have dorms, 2-, 4-, and 6-bed bungalows, no sheets, kitchen facilities, and big English-speaking tour groups. **Camping Jungfrau** (tel. 036/55 20 10) is romantically situated just beyond the stones hurled by Staubbach Falls, huge and well organized, with clocks showing the time in Sydney and Vancouver and even a "Heidi Shop." They also have fancier cabins and trailers for the classier camper. **Schützenbach Campground** (tel. 036/55 12 68), on the left just past Lauterbrunnen toward Stechelberg, is simpler.

Sleeping in Interlaken, Brienz, or Halfway to the Jungfrau

Balmer's Herberge, an Interlaken institution (16 SF dorm beds, 25 SF per person in simple doubles with breakfast, and even cheaper in overflow on-the-floor accommodations, Haupstrasse 23, in Matten, a 15-minute walk from either Interlaken station, tel. 036/22 19 61) is run by a creative tornado of entrepreneurial energy named Eric Balmer. With movies, Ping-Pong, laundromat, a secondhand English book-swapping library, rafting excursions, plenty of tips on budget eating and hiking, and a friendly, hardworking, mostly American staff, the place is home for those who miss their fraternity while making sure travelers of all ages feel welcome.

For 25 SF dorm beds with breakfast high in the mountains, you can sleep at Kleine Scheidegg (**Bahnhof Buffet**, tel. 036/55 11 51) or at Männlichen (**Berg Restaurant Männlichen**, dorm and double rooms, tel. 036/55 10 68).

If you get sidetracked in Brienz, its lakeside **hostel** (cheap, on Strandweg, tel. 036/51 11 52) is great. And for something really different—almost weird—drive or bus up the frighteningly narrow and winding Rosenlaui Valley road south from Meiringen (near Brienz) to the mountain climbers' Hilton. At 4,000 feet, in the middle of nowhere, is the Old World, tattered but elegant **Berg-Gasthaus Rosenlaui** (60 SF doubles, open June-early October, tel. 036/71 29 12). At the head of that valley, you can hike from there (or catch the mountain goat bus) over Grosse Scheidegg and down to Grindelwald.

FREE DAY IN THE ALPS—HIKE!

Today is your vacation from this go-go vacation. And a great place to recharge your touristic batteries is up here high in the Alps where distant avalanches, cowbells, the fluff of a down comforter, and the crunchy footsteps of happy hikers are the dominant sounds.

If the weather's good, ride the lift from Gimmelwald to a classy breakfast at Schilthorn's 10,000-foot revolving restaurant. Linger among Alpine whitecaps before riding or hiking down (5,000 feet) to Mürren and home to Gimmelwald.

Suggested Schedule	
8:00	Ride the Gimmelwald-Schilthorn lift.
8:30	Breakfast on the Schilthorn, ride or walk down to Mürren, browse, buy a picnic lunch. Hike to Gimmelwald via Gimmelen.

Sightseeing Highlights

▲▲▲ **Gimmelwald**—So undeveloped because of its "avalanche zone" classification, Gimmelwald is one of the poorest places in Switzerland. Its economy is stuck in the hay, and many of the farmers, unable to make it in their disadvantaged trade, are subsidized by the "kinder and gentler" Swiss government. There's little to see in the village. Be sure to take a walk, noticing the traditional log-cabin architecture. The numbers on the buildings are not addresses but fire insurance numbers. The cute little hut near the station is for storing and aging cheese, not youth hostelers (the stone plates under it work to keep bugs out). Be careful not to confuse obscure Gimmelwald with very touristy and commercialized Grindelwald just over the Kleine Scheidegg ridge.

Evening fun in Gimmelwald is found at the hostel (lots of young Alp-aholics and a good chance to share information on the surrounding mountains) and up at Walter's. Walter's bar is a local farmer's hangout. When they've

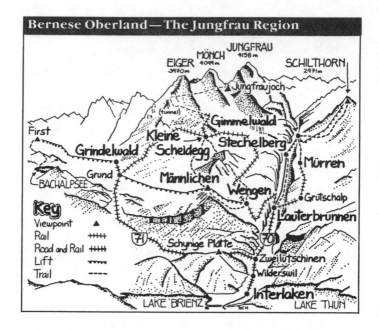

Bernese Oberland—The Jungfrau Region

made their hay, they come here to play. They look like what we'd call "hicks" (former city slicker Walter still isn't fully accepted by the gang), but they speak some English and can be fun to get to know. Walter knows how many beers they've had according to if they're talking, singing, fighting, or snoring. For less smoke and some powerful solitude, sit outside (benches just below the rails, 100 yards down the road from Walter's) and watch the sun tuck the mountaintops into bed as the moon rises over the Jungfrau.

▲ ▲ ▲ **Hike 1: The Schilthorn, Hikes, Lifts, and a 10,000-foot Breakfast**—Walter serves a great breakfast, but if the weather's good, skip his and eat atop the Schilthorn, in the slowly revolving, mountain-capping restaurant (of James Bond movie fame). The early-bird special gondola tickets (rides before 9:00) take you from Gimmelwald to the Schilthorn and back with a great continental breakfast on top for 50 SF. (Get discount tickets from Walter.) Bear with the slow service, and ask for more hot drinks if necessary. For a lighter meal, try the Birchermüesli-yogurt treat.

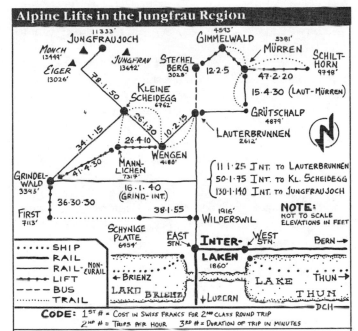

Alpine Lifts in the Jungfrau Region

JUNGFRAUJOCH 11333'
GIMMELWALD 4593'
MÜRREN 5381'
SCHILTHORN 9748'
MÖNCH 13449'
JUNGFRAU 13642'
EIGER 13026'
STECHEL BERG 3028'
KLEINE SCHEIDEGG 6762'
GRÜTSCHALP 4879'
LAUTERBRUNNEN 2612'
WENGEN 4180'
MANN-LICHEN 7317'
GRINDEL-WALD 3393'
FIRST 7113'
SCHYNIGE PLATTE 6454'

78·1·50
12·2·5
47·2·20
15·4·30 (LAUT-MÜRREN)
26·1·30
10·2·15
34·1·15
26·4·10
41·4·30
16·1·40 (GRIND-INT.)
36·30·30
38·1·55
1916' WILDERSWIL

11 1·25 Int. to Lauterbrunnen
50·1·75 Int. to Kl. Scheidegg
130·1·140 Int. to Jungfraujoch

NOTE: NOT TO SCALE ELEVATIONS IN FEET

EAST STN.
WEST STN.
INTER-LAKEN 1860'
BERN →

···· SHIP
─── RAIL
─── RAIL NON-EURAIL
•┼•┼ LIFT
─ ─ ─ BUS
···· TRAIL

← BRIENZ
LAKE BRIENZ
LAKE THUN
THUN →
↓ LUZERN
DCH →

CODE: 1ST # = COST IN SWISS FRANCS FOR 2ND CLASS ROUND TRIP
2ND # = TRIPS PER HOUR   3RD # = DURATION OF TRIP IN MINUTES

Round-trip price in Swiss francs—Departures per hour—Length of ride in minutes (e.g., 13-1-40 is 13 SF round-trip, 1 per hour, 40 minutes long).

Since round-trips are discounted only above towns (e.g., to Kl. Scheidegg & Schilthorn), buy one-way between towns for flexibility. Maps, schedules, and price lists are available at any station. Lifts run from about 7 a.m. to 8 p.m. Groups of five or more receive about a 20 percent discount. Early and late Jungfraujoch trains (leaving Kl. Scheidegg at 8:02, 15:02, and 15:56) are discounted 38 SF. Stechelberg to Gimmelwald lifts go at :25 and :55 past the hour, until 19:25, after that hourly in summer.

The Gimmelwald-Schilthorn hike is free, if you don't mind a 5,000-foot altitude gain. I ride up and hike down or, for a less scary hike, go halfway down by cable car and walk down from the Birg station. Lifts go twice an hour, and the ride takes 30 minutes. Watch the altitude meter in the gondola. (The round-trip excursion early-bird fare is cheaper than the Gimmelwald-Schilthorn-Birg ticket. If you buy that ticket, you can decide at Birg if you want to hike or ride down.)

Linger on top. There's a souvenir shop, the rocks of the region on the restaurant wall, a chart showing the engineering of this rugged mountain perch, the best toilet view in all of Europe, telescopes, and very thin air. Watch hang gliders set up, psych up, and take off, flying 30 minutes with the birds to distant Interlaken. Walk along the ridge out back to the No High Heels signpost. You can even convince yourself you climbed to that perch and feel pretty rugged (and take a picture to prove it). For another cheap thrill, ask the gondola attendant to crank down the window, stick your head out, and pretend you're hang gliding (ideally, over the bump going down from Gimmelwald).

Think twice before hiking down from the Schilthorn (weather can change, have good shoes). Most people have more fun hiking (steeply) down from Birg. Just below Birg is a mountain hut. Drop in for soup, cocoa, or a coffee schnapps. You can spend the night in the loft (40 mattresses, open July-September, tel. 036/55 26 40). Youth hostelers scream down the ice fields on plastic bag sleds from the Schilthorn. (English-speaking doctor in Mürren.)

The most interesting trail from Birg (or Mürren) to Gimmelwald is the high one via Suppenalp, Schiltalp, Gimmeln, and the Sprütz waterfall. Mürren has plenty of shops, bakeries, tourist information, banks, and a modern sports complex for rainy days. Ask at the Schilthorn station in Mürren for a souvenir pin or sticker.

▲▲▲ **Hike 2: The Männlichen-Kleine Scheidegg Hike**—This is my favorite easy Alpine hike, entertaining you all the way with glorious Eiger, Mönch, and Jungfrau views.

If the weather's good, descend from Gimmelwald bright and early. Drive (or catch the post bus) to the Lauterbrunnen train station, parking at the large multistoried pay lot behind the station. Buy a ticket to Männlichen and catch the train. Ride past great valley views to Wengen, where you'll walk across town (don't waste time here if it's sunny), buy a picnic if you like, and catch the Männlichen lift (departing every 15 minutes) to the top of the ridge high above you.

From the tip of the Männlichen lift, hike (10 minutes north) to the little peak for that king-of-the-mountain feeling. Then walk (very easy) about an hour around to Kleine Scheidegg for a picnic or restaurant lunch. If you've got an extra 78 SF and the weather's perfect, ride the train through the Eiger to the towering Jungfraujoch and back. Check for discount trips up to Jungfraujoch; three trips a day (one early, two late, telephone information 036/26 41 11, weather 036/55 10 22). Jungfraujoch crowds can be frightening. Until the new rolling stock is in place (late 1992), expect long waits and unruly mobs at the top on sunny days.

From Kleine Scheidegg, enjoy the ever-changing Alpine panorama of the North Face of the Eiger, Jungfrau, and Mönch, probably accompanied by the valley-filling mellow sound of alp horns and distant avalanches, as you ride the train or hike downhill (two hours) to the town of Wengen. If the weather turns bad, or you run out of steam, catch the train early at one of two little stations along the way. The trail is steep and, while not dangerous, requires a good set of knees. Wengen is a fine shopping town. The boring final descent is knee-killer steep, so catch the train from Wengen to Lauterbrunnen. Trails are often snowbound into early summer. Ask about conditions at lift stations. If the Männlichen lift is closed, take the train straight from Lauterbrunnen to Kleine Scheidegg.

▲▲▲ **Hike 3: Schynige Platte to First**—The best day I've had hiking in the Berner Oberland is the six-hour ridge walk high above Lake Brienz on one side and all that Jungfrau beauty on the other. Start at Wilderswil where you catch the little train up to Schynige Platte (2,000 meters). Walk through the Alpine flower display garden and into the wild Alpine yonder. The high point is Faulhorn (2,680 meters, with its famous mountaintop hotel). Your destination is a chair lift called First (2,168

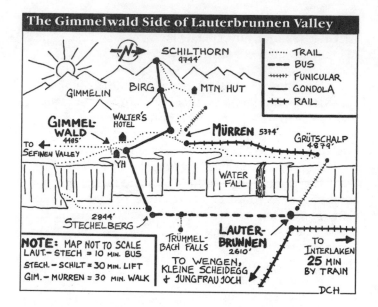

The Gimmelwald Side of Lauterbrunnen Valley

SCHILTHORN 9744'

BIRG   MTN. HUT

GIMMELIN

WALTER'S HOTEL

GIMMEL-WALD 4485'

MÜRREN 5374'   GRÜTSCHALP 4879'

TO SEFINEN VALLEY

YH

WATER FALL

2844' STECHELBERG

LAUTER-BRUNNEN 2610'

TO INTERLAKEN 25 MIN BY TRAIN

TRÜMMEL-BACH FALLS

TO WENGEN, KLEINE SCHEIDEGG & JUNGFRAU JOCH

······· TRAIL
BUS
++++ FUNICULAR
GONDOLA
++++ RAIL

NOTE: MAP NOT TO SCALE
LAUT- STECH = 10 MIN. BUS
STECH. - SCHILT = 30 MIN. LIFT
GIM. - MÜRREN = 30 MIN. WALK

DCH

meters), where you descend to Grindelwald and catch a
train back to your starting point, Wilderswil (or if you
have no car, a regional train pass, or endless money,
return to Lauterbrunnen from Grindelwald over Kleine
Scheidegg).

▲ **Other Hikes from Gimmelwald**—For a level
3-hour walk with great Jungfrau views and some mountain farm action, ride the funicular from Mürren to
Allmenhübel (1,934 meters), walk to Marchegg, Saustal,
and Grütschalp (1,500 meters), where you catch the
panorama train back to Mürren.

An easy, go-as-far-as-you-like trail from Gimmelwald is
up the Sefinen Valley. Or, you can wind from there down
to Stechelberg. Don von Gimmelwald is writing a small
Gimmelwald guidebook with more details and other
good hikes (available at Hotel Mittaghorn).

Rainy Day Options
If all the waterfalls have you intrigued, sneak a behind-
the-scenes look at the valley's most powerful one, Trüm-
melbach Falls (7 SF, on the Lauterbrunnen-Stechelberg

7:30 Bfast
8:30 Gondola
Drive to Lauderbrunen
Train to Wengen
Hike across Town
Gondola to Mannliche
1 hr. Hike to
  Kleine Schiedegg

Walk 2½hr. to Wengen

road, 9:00-18:00 daily, April-October). You'll ride an elevator up through the mountain and climb through several caves to see the melt of the Eiger, Mönch, and Jungfrau grinding like God's bandsaw through the mountain at the rate of up to 20,000 liters a second (that's faster than the beer is consumed at Oktoberfest)! The upper area, "shoots 6 to 10" are the best, so if your legs ache, you can skip the lower ones and ride the lift down.

Lauterbrunnen's Heimatmuseum (3 SF, 14:00-17:30, Tuesday, Thursday, Saturday, and Sunday, mid-June through September, just over the bridge) shows off the local folk culture.

Mürren's slick Sports Center (mid-June through mid-September) offers a world of indoor activities, for a price.

MORE ALPS, THEN ON TO FRANCE

This morning, get your last fill of the Alps. Take a quick look at the Swiss capital of Bern and head into France, to Alsace.

Suggested Schedule	
7:30	Breakfast.
8:00	Lift to car, drive to Lauterbrunnen. Lift to Männlichen (via Wengen), hike down to Wengen. (See Hike #2, Day 18.)
12:00	Lunch in Wengen, train to car.
13:00	Drive to Bern.
14:00	Explore downtown Bern.
16:00	Drive into France, set up in Colmar.

Transportation: Alps to Alsace (130 miles)
From Lauterbrunnen, drive north catching the autobahn (direction Spiez, Thun, Bern) just before entering Interlaken. After Spiez, the autobahn will take you right to Bern; there signs will direct you to Basel, where Switzerland, Germany, and France snuggle.

To go into Bern, circle the city on the autobahn, taking the (fourth) Bern exit, Neufeld Bern, into the center. Signs to Zentrum will take you to the station. Turn right just before the station into the Bahnhof Parkplatz (2-hour meter parking outside, all-day lot inside, 2 SF per hour). You're just an escalator ride from a great tourist information center and Switzerland's compact, user-friendly capital.

Before Basel (just after a long tunnel), you'll come to Restate Pratteln Nord, a strange orange structure that looks like a huge submarine laying eggs on the freeway. Park here for a look around one of Europe's great freeway stops: there's a bakery and grocery store for picnickers, a restaurant, and a change desk open daily until 21:00

(almost fair rates). Spend some time goofing around, then carry on (Interlaken to Colmar is a four-hour drive).

In Basel, follow signs to France. Over the border, head north to Colmar, where you'll follow *Centre Ville* signs to a huge square called Place Rapp. Park there and check into the nearby Hotel Le Rapp. Wander around the old town, then savor an Alsatian meal with the local wine.

By train, there are hourly Interlaken East or West to Bern trains (60 minutes); the same trains continue to Basel (90 minutes from Bern). The 60-minute ride from Basel to Colmar leaves nearly hourly. It's an hour from Bern to Lausanne, 2 hours from Lausanne to Dijon, and 30 minutes from there to Beaune.

Bern
The charming Swiss capital fills a peninsula bounded by the Aare River, giving you the most (maybe even only) enjoyable look at urban Switzerland. Just an hour from Interlaken, directly on your way to Murten, it's worth a stop, especially if disappointing weather cuts your mountain time short.

For a short, well-organized visit, park your car at the train station, visit the tourist office inside (open 8:00-20:30 daily, until 18:30 in winter, tel. 031/22 76 76), pick up maps for Bern and Murten, a list of city sights, information on the Parliament, the clock, or whatever you're interested in, and confirm your plans. Follow the walking tour explained in the handy city map while browsing your way downhill. Visit Einstein's house. Finish with a look at the bear pits (*Bärengraben*) and a city view from the Rose Garden across the river. Catch trolley #12 back up to the station (buy the cheapest, yellow-button ticket from the machine at the stop). Telephone code: 031.

Sightseeing Highlights—Bern
▲▲ **The Old Town**—Window shopping and people watching through the lovely arcaded streets and busy market squares is Bern's top attraction. This is my favorite shopping town: prices are so high there's no danger of buying. Great browsing. The clock tower (Zytglogge-

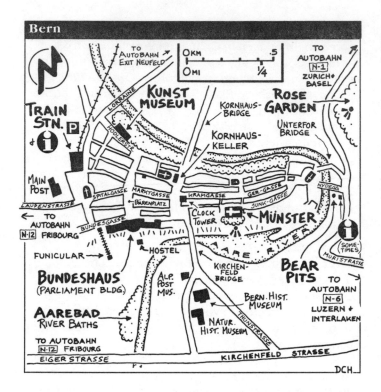

turm) performs at 4 minutes before each hour. Apparently this slowest moving 5-minute nonevent in Europe was considered entertaining in 1530. To pass the time during the performance, read the TI's brochure explaining what's so interesting about the fancy old clock. Enthusiasts can tour the medieval mechanics daily at 16:30 in the summer (tickets 4 SF at the TI or on the spot).

The 1421 Swiss late Gothic Münster, or cathedral, is worth a look (closed from 12:00-14:00). Climb the spiral staircase 100 yards above the town for a great view and good exercise and a chance to meet a live church watch-man. Peter Probst and his wife, Sigi, live way up there watching over the church, answering questions, and charging tourists for the view.

Nearby is the imposing Parliament building (Bundes-haus) of Switzerland (free 45-minute tours most days at 9:00, 10:00, 11:00, 14:00, 15:00, and 16:00, tel. 031/61 85

22 to confirm; closed about March, June, September, and December; five people minimum group size). Don't miss the view from the Bundeshaus terrace. You may see some national legislators, but you wouldn't know it—everything looks very casual for a national capital.

Einstein did much of his most important thinking while living in a house on the old town's main drag. It was just another house to me, but I guess everything's relative (Kramgasse 49, 10:00-17:00, Saturday until 16:00, closed Sunday, Monday, December, and January, free).

▲**Bear Pits and Rose Garden**—The symbol of Bern is the bear, and some lively ones frolic their days away (7:00-18.00) to the delight of locals and tourists alike in the big, barren, concrete pits, or *Graben*. Up the paved pathway is the Rosengarten. Worth the walk for the great city view. The Rosengarten restaurant (tel. 031/41 32 06) has a great view and serves a fine 15 SF lunch special.

▲▲▲**The Berner Swim**—For something to write home about, join the local merchants, legislators, publishers, students, and carp in a lunchtime float down the Aare River. The Bernese, proud of their very clean river and their basic ruddiness, have a tradition—sort of a wet, urban *paseo*—of hiking upstream 5 to 30 minutes and floating playfully or relaxed back down to the excellent (and free) riverside baths and pools (Aarebad) just below the Parliament building. If the river is a bit much, you're welcome to enjoy just the Aarebad. If the river is not enough, a popular day trip is to raft all the way from Thun to Bern.

▲▲**Museum of Fine Arts (Kunstmuseum)**—Located four blocks from the station, it features 1,000 years of local art and some impressionism, but the real hit is its fabulous collection of Paul Klee's playful and colorful paintings. If you don't know Klee, I'd love to introduce you. (Open 10:00-17:00, Tuesday until 21:00, closed Monday.)

Other Bern Museums—Across the bridge from the Parliament building on Helvetiaplatz are several museums (Alpine, Berner History, Postal) that sound more interesting than they are. Nearly all are closed on Monday.

Sleeping in Bern

Each of these places is in the old town within a fifteen-minute walk from the station. Except for the hostel, there are no alternatives to good, comfortable, clean, and expensive hotels in the entire city. The places listed are right in the old center. Since they are not modernized and are the only ones offering rooms with showers down the hall, they are far cheaper than other places. Get parking advice locally. Supposedly, non-Swiss cars aren't given parking tickets.

Hotel Hospiz sur Heimat (82 SF small doubles without showers, 106 SF big doubles with showers, Gerechtigkeitsgasse 50, on the main street near the bridge and bears, 15 minutes walk from the station or tram 12, tel. 031/22 04 36) is Bern's best budget hotel value. Its restaurant, next door, serves a good 11 SF lunch special (daily, except Sunday, 11:30-14:00).

Hotel Goldener Schlüssel (95 SF doubles, Rathausgasse 72, CH-3011 Bern, tel. 031/22 02 16, fax 031/22 56 88) and **Hotel Glocke** (94 SF doubles, Rathausgasse 75, 3011 Bern, tel. 031/22 37 71, Fax 031/22 10 08) are basic, crank-em-out, old hotels in the center.

Bern's big, newly renovated, sterile, well-run **IYHF hostel** (10 SF beds, nonmembers 18 SF, Weihergasse 4, 3005 Bern, tel. 031/22 63 16) has 8- to 26-bed rooms and is about a 10-minute walk from the station, down the stairs from the Parliament building, by the river. It provides an all-day lounge, laundry machines, and cheap meals (office open 7:00-9:30 and 17:00-23:00).

Itinerary Options

From Interlaken, train travelers can go directly to Paris on the overnight train.

Franco-phobes or those saving France for a later trip can mosey back to Amsterdam via more of Switzerland, the Bodensee, the Black Forest, Trier, Mosel Valley, Luxembourg, Brussels, and Bruges. This is mostly small-town and countryside travel, so it's best by car.

Or, you may decide to sell your plane ticket and perma-

nently join Heidi and the cows waiting for eternity in
Europe's greatest cathedral—the Swiss Alps.

FRANCE
- 210,000 square miles—as big as Texas.
- 58 million people (276 people per square mile, 78% urban).
- U.S.$1 = about 6 francs, 1 franc = about U.S.$.17.

You may have heard that the French are mean and cold.
Don't believe it. If anything, they're pouting because
they're no longer recognized as the world's premier culture. It's tough to be crushed by the Big American Mac
and keep on smiling. Be sensitive and understanding. The
French are cold only if you choose to perceive them that
way. Look for friendliness, give people the benefit of the
doubt, develop an appetite for French-ness, and you'll
remember France with a smile.

Learn some French—at least the polite words—and try
to sound like Maurice Chevalier or Inspector Clouseau.

The French don't speak much English, but they speak much more English than we speak French. Be patient about any communication problems. Start conversations with *"Bonjour Madame/Monsieur. Parlez-vous Anglais?"* The French are experts in the art of fine living. Their cuisine, their customs, even their vacationing habits, are highly developed. Since the vacation is such a big part of the French life-style (nearly every worker gets 5 weeks of vacation a year), you'll find no shortage of tourist information centers, hotels, transportation facilities, and fun ways to pass free days.

The French eat lunch from 12:00 to 14:00 and dinner from 19:00 to 22:00. And they eat well. A restaurant meal, never rushed, is the day's main event. Each region has its *haute cuisine* specialties, and even the "low cuisine" of a picnic can be elegant, with fresh bread and an endless variety of tasty French cheeses, meats, pâtés, freshly roasted chickens, store-bought quiches, salads, rich pastries, and, of course, wine. The best approach to French food is to eat where locals eat and be adventurous. Eat ugly things with relish!

French hotels are not as cheap or as carefully regulated as in the past. A few tips are helpful. Double beds are cheaper than twins; showers are cheaper than baths; breakfast in the dining room, while handy, is expensive, usually optional, and not included in the prices listed here. Each hotel is rated by stars on a plaque near its door. The star system (0-4; I stick to the 1- and 2-star places) tells general standards and price. Countryside prices are substantially less. If you're on a budget, insist on cheaper rooms, shower down the hall, and skip breakfast.

French Money: The French franc (FF or F) is divided into 100 centimes (c). A franc is worth about U.S.$.17. There are about 6 francs in a U.S. dollar. So, divide prices by about 6 to get dollars (e.g., 65F is about $11).

France's nearly extinct coin-op public telephones are being replaced by super efficient, vandal-resistant, card-operated models. Upon entry into France, buy a phone card (*telecarte*) from a post office or tabac shop, and take advantage of the phone. The smallest card is 40F. To use the phone booths (for hotel and restaurant reservations and confirmations, tourist and train information, museum hours, calling home, etc.), the little screen will instruct you to (1) pick up receiver, (2) "introduce" card, (3) "fermez le lid" over your card, (4) have "patientez." Then, (5) the amount of money you have will show on the little screen (e.g., credit: 4.80F), (6) dial your "numéro." After you hang up, "retirez" your card. You've got coin-free use of the French telephone system until your card expires.

In France's number system, calls within Paris and within the countryside need no prefix. From Paris to the countryside, dial 16 first; from the countryside into Paris, dial 16-1 and then the eight-digit number, which, in Paris, starts with 4. Any non-Paris to non-Paris area calls need no prefix.

Alsace

The French province of Alsace stands like a flower child referee between Germany and France. Bounded by the Rhine River on the east and the softly rolling Vosges Mountains on the west, this is a lush land of flowery villages, vineyards, ruined castles, and an almost naive cheeriness. Wine is the primary industry, topic of conversation, dominant mouthwash, perfect excuse for countless festivals, and a tradition that provides the foundation for the rest of the Alsatian culture.

Because of its location, natural wealth, naked vulnerability, and the fact that Germany thinks the mountains are the natural border and France thinks the Rhine River is, nearly every other Alsatian generation has weathered an invasion. A thousand years as a political pawn between Germany and France has given Alsace a hybrid culture. This Gallic-Teutonic mix is seen in many ways. Most locals who swear do so bilingually, and many of the towns have German names. Half-timbered restaurants serve sauerkraut with fine sauces.

Colmar

See tomorrow.

COLMAR AND THE ROUTE DU VIN

The morning is yours to explore Colmar's old center and impressive art. Shoppers love Colmar. Your afternoon will be filled with storks on rooftops and the cutest wine villages in Europe. Whatever you do, work up an appetite for a first-class Alsatian dinner.

Suggested Schedule	
8:30	Orientation walk ending at the tourist office.
9:00	Unterlinden Museum.
10:30	Free time to cruise Colmar, lunch.
13:30	Exploration of wine road and villages by car or bike.
19:30	Dine Alsatian-style back in Colmar.

Colmar

Colmar is a well-preserved old town of 70,000, offering heavyweight sights in a warm, small-town package. It's a perfect base for exploring the nearby villages, castles, and Route du Vin (Wine Road).

Historic beauty was usually a poor excuse to be spared the ravages of World War II, but it worked for Colmar. The American and British military were careful not to bomb the half-timbered old burghers' houses, characteristic red-and-green tiled roofs, and cobbled lanes of Alsace's most beautiful city.

Today, Colmar thrives, offering visitors historic buildings, impressive art treasures, and the popular Alsatian cuisine. And Colmar has that special French talent of being great but cozy at the same time. Schoolgirls park their rickety horse carriages in front of the city hall ready to give visitors a clip-clop tour of the old town. Antique shops welcome browsers, and hotel managers run down the sleepy streets to pick up fresh croissants in time for breakfast.

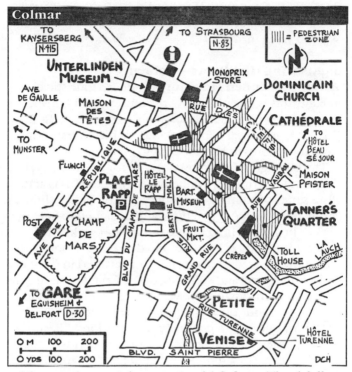

There isn't a straight street in old Colmar. Thankfully, it's a lovely town to be lost in. Navigate by the high church steeples. The TI, next to the Unterlinden Museum, has a board listing all the hotels, with *Complet* signs posted if they're full (not always accurate). They can get you a room in a hotel or in a private home (*chambre*) in Colmar or in a nearby village for 10F. Pick up their Route du Vin map, the free little Alsatian wines guide booklet, and, if you lack wheels, ask for *Colmar Actualités*, a booklet with bus schedules. Ask about organized wine road tours and Colmar's folklore Tuesdays (weekly in summer). Autumn is a festive time, with Colmar's Sauerkraut Days in late August/early September and local wine festivals throughout the countryside. (Open weekdays in July and August from 9:00-12:30 and 13:30-19:00, Saturday 9:00-12:00 and 14:00-17:00, and Sunday

9:00-12:30. Otherwise Monday-Friday 9:00-12:00 and
14:00-18:00, Saturday 9:00-12:00. Tel. 89 41 02 29. Public
W.C. 20 yards from TI.)

Sightseeing Highlights—Colmar

▲▲▲**Unterlinden Museum**—Colmar's touristic claim
to fame, this is one of my favorite museums in Europe. Its
extensive yet manageable collection ranges from Roman
Colmar to medieval wine-making exhibits to traditional
wedding dresses to babies' cribs to Picasso.

The highlight of the museum (and for me, the city) is
Grunewald's gripping Isenheim Altarpiece. This is actually a series of paintings on hinges that pivot like shutters
(study the little model on the wall). Designed to help people in a hospital—long before the age of painkillers—
suffer through their horrible skin diseases, it's one of the
most powerful paintings ever. Stand petrified in front of it
and let the agony and suffering of the Crucifixion drag its
gnarled fingers down your face. Just as you're about to
break down and sob with those in the painting, turn to
the happy ending—a psychedelic explosion of Resurrec-
tion happiness. It's like jumping from the dentist's chair
into a Jacuzzi. For a reminder that the Middle Ages didn't
have a monopoly on grief, stop at the museum's tapestry
copy of Picasso's famous *Guernica*. (Open 9:00-18:00
daily, fewer hours off-season, 25F.)

▲**Dominican Church**—Here you'll find another medieval mind-blower. Martin Schongauer's angelically beautiful *Virgin of the Roses* holds court on center stage, looking
like it was painted yesterday. (Open 10:00-18:00 daily, 8F.)

Tanners' Quarters—This refurbished chunk of the old
town is a delight, day or night. There is outdoor wine
tasting here on many summer evenings.

Bartholdi Museum—An interesting little museum
about the life and work of the local boy who gained fame
by sculpting our Statue of Liberty. You'll notice several of
his statues, usually with one arm raised high, gracing Colmar's squares. (Open April-October 10:00-12:00, 14:00-
18:00, off-season weekends only, 30 rue des Marchands.)

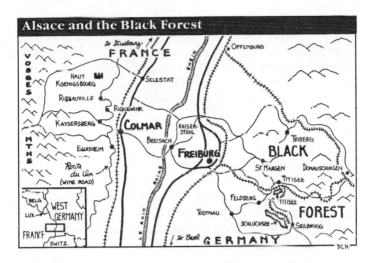

▲▲Route du Vin Side Trip—Alsace's wine road, the
Route du Vin, is an asphalt ribbon tying ninety miles of
vineyards, villages, and feudal fortresses into an under-
standably popular tourist package. The dry, sunny climate
makes for good wine and happy tourists. It's been a wine
center since Roman days. As you drive through 30,000
acres of vineyards blanketing the hills from Marleheim to
Thann, you'll see how vinocentric this area is. If you have
only one afternoon, limit yourself to Eguisheim and
Kaysersberg.

Throughout Alsace, you'll see *Dégustation* signs.
Dégustation means "come on in and taste," and *gratuit*
means "free"—otherwise, there's a very small charge.
Most towns have wineries that give tours, or at least tastings, and a friendly welcome. Eguisheim's and Riquewihr's are good. Bennwihr's modern cooperative, created
after the destruction of World War II, gives a fascinating
look at a more modern and efficient method of production. Your hotel receptionist or the people at the TI can
give you advice or even telephone a winery for you to
confirm tour times. You may have to wait for a group, and
tag along for a tour and free tasting. Be sure to try Cremant, the Alsatian "champagne."

The easiest approach to the Route du Vin is to leave

Colmar following signs to Strasbourg and Selestat (N-83).
Exit at signs to Kaysersberg, and you're in the heart of the
wine route. Michelin's regional map is very helpful. Public buses connect Colmar with most Route du Vin villages
(more detail below). The schedules are convenient, particularly to Kaysersberg and Riquewihr. Ask at the TI for
the *Actualités Colmar* to get schedules, and remember
that more than one company often provides service to
the same town, so check all the schedules.

You can rent a bike at the train station (tel. 89 23 17 17)
or at the Peugeot bike store next to the Unterlinden. Kaysersberg and Eguisheim, just three or four level miles
apart, are fine biking destinations.

▲**Eguisheim**—Just a few miles from Colmar, this scenic
little town is best explored by walking around its circular
road, then cutting through the middle. Visit the Eguisheim
Wine Cooperative. (Cave Vinicole d'Eguisheim, 6 Grand
Rue, tel. 89 22 20 20, folklore and tastings summer Wednesdays 17:00-19:00, open 10:00-11:00, 14:00-17:00). It's a
very easy bike ride from Colmar. Nearby, at Husseren
Château, you can climb the medieval towers for a great
view.

▲**Kaysersberg**—Albert Schweitzer's greatest act of self-
sacrifice was leaving his wonderful hometown. Climb the
castle, browse through the art galleries, enjoy the colorful
bundle of fifteenth-century houses near the fortified
town bridge, visit Dr. Schweitzer's house, check out the
church with its impressive 400-year-old altarpiece, taste
some wine, and wander along nearby vineyards. (TI tel.
89 78 22 78.)

▲**Riquewihr**—Very cute and very commercial, this little walled village is filled with shops, cafés, art galleries,
cobbles, and flowers. For tasting and a tour, visit the
Caves Dopff et Irion (Cour du Château, tel. 89 47 92 51).
TI tel. 89 47 80 80.

Helpful Hints
Colmar is a good place for mailing things if your parcel is
under about 10 pounds. (Posting in Paris can be a headache.) The post office near place Rapp is a good place to

lighten your load, with post boxes for sale and postal clerks as cheery, speedy, and multilingual as yours at home (open 8:00-19:00). Colmar is also a good place to do laundry (two self-serve laundromats: at 1 rue Ruest, just off the pedestrian street rue Vauban, and on rue Turenne, in Petite Venise, open daily 8:00-21:00) and to shop (many stores close Monday mornings).

Sleeping in Colmar (about 6F = US$1)

Weekends in June, September, and October get jammed. July and August are busy, but there are always rooms— somewhere. Try to call first, and stay near the *centre ville*. Consider a small-town private home (the TI has a list).

Hôtel Le Rapp (170-260F doubles plus 22F for an excellent breakfast, choose old, cheap, and funky or new rooms with a TV, 16 rue Berthe-Molly, tel. 89 41 62 10, from Switzerland call 00/33/89 41 62 10) has traded off some of its charm by adding forty new rooms, but the owner is still Saint Bernard to me. Bernard runs this hotel-restaurant, mixing class with warmth like no man I've met. Unless you're in a hurry, eat here for a taste of French elegance and impeccable service.

Hôtel Beau Sejour (250-300F doubles, 25 rue du Ladhof, a ten-minute walk from the charm of downtown, tel. 89 41 37 16) is a decent value with a new swimming pool.

Hôtel Turenne (250-320F doubles, 10 route du Bale, tel. 89 41 12 26) caters to the business traveler, so you can't avoid a TV and full bathroom. But it's still a fine hotel in a great location and often has rooms left when others are full. It's worth a little extra to get a room off the street.

La Chaumière (150-200F, a 3-minute walk toward the center from the train station at 74 ave. de la République, tel. 89 41 08 99) is Colmar's best one-star hotel.

Primo 99 (165F doubles, 5 rue des Ancêtres, tel. 89 24 22 24) is France's prefab hotel. A modern, efficient, bright, and nothing-but-the-plastic-and-concrete-basics place to sleep for those to whom ambience is a four-letter word and modernity is next to godliness.

Maison Jund (140-160F doubles, 12 rue de l'Ange, tel. 89 41 58 72), my favorite French bed and breakfast (without the breakfast), is in Colmar's old city. It's like a magnificent, half-timbered, medieval tree house, soaked in wine and festooned with flowers. The rooms are equipped with kitchenettes and full bathrooms but are available only when the students are gone—from June to mid-September. The Junds are proud owners of a vineyard and offer a very friendly wine tasting.

The best 35F dorm beds in Colmar are at the **Maison des Jeunes** (Camille-Schlumberger 17, past the station in a comfortable and fairly central location, 4- to 6-bed rooms, tel. 89 41 26 87). The desk is open from 14:00 to 23:00. The new **youth hostel**, open from March through October, has 8-bed dorms (2 rue Pasteur, a 15-minute walk from the station and town, tel. 89 80 57 39).

For a small-town alternative, consider these private homes in nearby Eguisheim: **Mr. Hertz-Meyer**, 3 rue du Reisling, tel. 89 23 67 74; **Mr. Stoeckle Müller**, 5 rue de Bruxelles, tel. 89 23 19 50; and **Mr. Stocky Gilbert**, 24 rue de Colmar, tel. 89 41 68 04.

Eating in Colmar

In Colmar, the **Hôtel Restaurant le Rapp** is my dress-up, high-cuisine splurge. I comb my hair, change my socks, and savor a slow, elegant meal served with grace and fine Alsatian wine. Bernard and Dominique won't let you or your taste buds down. (100-200F, closed Wednesday, see hotel listing above.) The air-conditioning is a relief on a hot summer evening.

Au Café du Colmar serves a good fixed-price menu. Excellent à la carte also (located above Matelas Herzog, at the intersection of rues Stanislas and Kleber, just off place Rapp).

Au Pave d'Alsace (moderate-expensive, 14 rue Étroite, just off rue Rapp in pedestrian zone) is owned by a very likable French couple who spent three years in the U.S.A. and miss it. Perfect English and very fine cuisine in a traditional Alsatian setting.

In the Tanners' Quarter and La Petite Venise, Colmar's most scenic dining locale, you'll find several reasonable restaurants and cafés. For crêpes with atmosphere, eat at **Crêperie Tom Pouce**, located right downtown (inexpensive, 10 rue des Tanneurs). Next door, the **Restaurant des Tanneurs Weinstub** is a bit more up-scale with fine Alsatian menus from 85F. For canalfront dining, head into La Petite Venise to the bridge on rue Turenne where you'll find a pizzeria, a weinstub-café (both cheap), and a fine canal-level restaurant, **Les Bateliers** (moderate).

Two good self-services dish up low-stress meals in sterile settings. **Flunch** (11:00-21:30), on place Rapp, is more pleasant but pricier than the **Monoprix cafeteria**. The best "self-serve" option is the Monoprix supermarket where you'll find sensational lunch and dinner picnic fixings at the fish and meat counters. Ask for a petite portion and a plastic fork, and find a French bench. If it's hot, get your lunch at Monoprix and join the locals in the park on place Rapp. Cool your ankles in the fountain.

Alsatian cuisine is a major tourist attraction itself. You can't miss the German influence—try the *choucroute* (sauerkraut and sausage), smelly Münster cheese, pretzels, and *Backenoffe* (potato, meat, and onion stew in white wine). The native *tarte à l'oignon* (like an onion quiche, but better), fresh trout, foie gras (fattened goose liver), and Alsatian cheesecake will bring you back to France. Alsatian wines, while less loved than Burgundy's, are good and much cheaper. The local specialties are whites: Riesling (drier than you're used to), Gerwürtztraminer (a spicy, before-dinner wine), Sylvaner (the cheapest), Tokay, and the tasty Cremant d'Alsace (champagne). You'll also see Eaux-de-Vie, a powerful, fruit-flavored brandy. Try the *framboise* (raspberry) flavor.

Itinerary Option—Burgundy

Profoundly French Burgundy nearly bumped Alsace from this 22-day plan. Alsace is another half-timbered, German-flavored stop, like several already included. And since this plan only has one stop other than Paris in

France, Burgundy would better round out this 22-day look at Europe. But I love Alsace, and after one last visit to each in rapid succession and a little gnashing of my teeth (to compare the croissants, escargots, cheese, and wine), I stuck with Alsace.

Ideally, you'll do both: Alps-Colmar-Beaune-Versailles-Paris would be great. (Colmar-Beaune is 4 hours by train, 10 trains a day.) Or if you're sick of half-timbered cuteness and want a full dose of high French cuisine, wine, and culture, go directly from the Alps to Beaune and on to Paris, via Versailles.

Here's Burgundy in a snail shell.

Beaune

You'll feel comfortable right away in this hardworking but fun-loving capital of one of the world's most serious wine regions. Beaune is a compact but thriving little city with a lace collar of vineyards. Life here centers around the production and consumption of the prestigious and expensive Côte d'Or wines.

Limit your Beaune (pronounced: "bone") ramblings to the town center, contained within its medieval walls and circled by a one-way ring road. The excellent TI has city maps, brochures on Beaune hotels and restaurants, a free room-finding service, and advice on winery tours and tastings, concerts, and events. (Open daily April-October 9:00-20:00, otherwise 9:00-19:00, tel. 80 22 24 51.)

Sightseeing Highlights—Beaune

▲▲**Hôtel Dieu**—A fascinating 500-year-old charity hospital offering a gory look at medieval medical instruments, a pharmacy with slug-slime cures for sore throats and cockroach powders for constipation, and Van der Weyden's dramatic Last Judgment altarpiece, all contained in a fine, flamboyant, Flemish building. (20F, open July to mid-September 9:00-18:30; off-season 9:00-11:40 and 14:00-18:00.)

Collegiale Nôtre-Dame—Built in the twelfth and thirteenth centuries, this church is a good example of

Clunyesque architecture with remarkable fifteenth-century tapestries and a variety of stained glass. (Open 9:00-12:00 and 14:00-18:00.)

Musée du Vin—This folk-wine museum shows how the history and culture of Burgundy and wine were fermented in the same bottle. You'll find antique wine presses, tools, costumes, scenes of Burgundian wine history but no wine tasting. (Open April-September 9:00-11:30 and 13:30-18:00; otherwise, 10:00-11:30 and 14:00-17:00, 9F.)

▲▲**Marché aux Vins (Wine Market)**—Beaune's wine smorgasbord is the best way to sample (and buy) its awesome array of Burgundy wines. Here you pay 50F for your *tastevin* (official tasting cup; 10F refunded if you return it) and have 45 minutes to sip Burgundy's best. Plunge into the labyrinth of candlelit caves dotted with 39 wine barrel tables, each home to a new bottle of wine to taste. Many serious tasters make good use of the spittoons and actually drink very little. But remember, the $70 reds are at the end, upstairs in the old chapel. (Hint: I taste better and longer by sneaking in some bread or crackers.) Grab a wine basket at the beginning and at least pretend you're going to buy some bottles so the occasional time checker will leave you alone. (Open 9:00-12:00, 14:30-18:20, near the TI.)

▲**Château La Rochepot**—This great mom-and-pop castle, a 20-minute drive out of town, is splendid inside and out. Serge Robin or his wife will greet you and take you "srou zee castle" (he learned his English at 65). Be ready for "zee grapplene ook" and "zee craws-a-bow." The kitchen will bowl you over. Sing chants in the resonant chapel and make ripples in the thirteenth-century well. Can you spit a bull's-eye at 72 meters? (Open June-August 9:00-11:30 and 14:30-18:00; shoulder season 10:00-11:30 and 14:00-17:30. Closed Tuesday and from November to Easter. Tel. 80 21 71 37, 15F.)

Burgundy Cuisine and Wine
Considered by many to be France's best, Burgundian cuisine is peasant cooking elevated to an art. Burgundy is

home to these classic dishes: *escargots Bourguignon* (snails served sizzling hot in garlic butter), *boeuf Bourguignon* (beef simmered for hours in red wine with onions and mushrooms), *coq au vin* (chicken stewed in red wine), and the famous Dijon mustards. Look also for *jambon persillé* (cold ham layered in a garlic-parsley gelatin), *pain d'épices* (spice bread), and *gougère* (light, puffy cheese pastries). Native cheeses are Époisses and Langres (both mushy and great) and my favorite, Montrachêt (a tasty goat cheese). Crème de Cassis (a black currant liqueur) is another Burgundian specialty. You'll find it in desserts and snazzy drinks (try a *kir*).

Along with Bordeaux, Burgundy is why France is famous for wine. You'll find it all here—great reds, whites, and rosés. The key grapes are Chardonnay (producing dry, white wines) and Pinot Noir (producing medium-bodied red wines). Every village produces its own, distinctive wine (usually named after the village—like Chablis and Meursault). Look for the *dégustation Gratuit* (free tasting) signs and prepare for a serious tasting and steep prices (if you buy).

For fine $20 meals near Beaune, try **Le Rélais de la Dilligence**. Come here to surround yourself with vineyards and taste the area's best budget Burgundian cuisine. (N-74 toward Chaginy, left at L'Hôpital Meursault on D-23; closed Tuesday evenings and Wednesday; call to reserve, tel. 80 21 21 32.) **Au Bon Accueil** is my favorite, on a hill overlooking Beaune. Take the Bligny sur Ouche turn off the ring road, follow signs to Sans Souci Disco, then signs to Au Bon Accueil; locals can direct you. Call to reserve (tel. 80 22 08 80, closed Tuesday). In Beaune, eat well for less at **Relais de la Madeleine** (44 place Madeleine).

Sleeping in Beaune (about 6F = U.S.$1)

The best budget hotels cluster around place Madeleine. For maximum value, efficiency, and comfort but less character, I stay in the big motelesque **Hotel au Grand St. Jean** (240F doubles, showers and W.C., 18 place

Madeleine, tel. 80 24 12 22, English spoken by Claude
Neaux and his father Claude Neaux, pronounced "no").
Auberge de Bourguignonne is petite, clean, and com-
fortable (250F doubles, unfortunately requires dinner, on
place Madeleine, tel. 80 22 23 53) and is also a good value.
Hôtel Rousseau is funky, with pet birds everywhere and
cheap, basic rooms (135-160F simple doubles, at 11 place
Madeleine, tel. 80 22 13 59).

Across town and also good: The **Beaun' Hôtel** (290F
doubles, 55 fbg. Bretonniere, tel. 80 22 11 01) and the better **Hostellerie de Bretonniere** (150-330F doubles
depending on plumbing, 43 fbg. Bretonniere, tel. 80 22
15 77). The newly remodeled **Hôtel de France** is across
from the station (180-240F doubles, 35 ave. du 8 Septembre, tel. 80 24 10 34). **Hôtel le Home** (270-330F doubles with shower and W.C., 38 route de Dijon, a half mile
out of town on the N-74 toward Dijon, tel. 80 22 16 43) is
Beaune's best two-star hotel.

For a very comfortable room in a private home (*chambre
d'hôte*), stay with the **Paulet family**, 7 miles away in the
village of Baubigny, just below the Rochepot castle (180F
doubles with breakfast, 21340 Nolay, tel. 85 47 32 18).

THE LONG DRIVE: COLMAR TO PARIS, VIA REIMS

Today's journey takes you halfway across France to Paris, with a stop for lunch, a champagne tour, and a visit to a great Gothic cathedral in Reims. You'll be in Paris in time for dinner, a subway lesson, and a city orientation tour.

Suggested Schedule

By Car:

7:00	Leave Colmar. Breakfast at rest stop en route.
12:00	Reims—picnic, tour cathedral and Champagne *cave*.
15:00	Autoroute back to Paris, turn in rental car.
18:00	Set up in Paris.

By Train:

7:00	Train to Strasbourg (40 min.).
8:00	Train from Strasbourg to Epernay (3.25 hrs.).
12:15	Train from Epernay to Reims (20 min.).
13:00	Visit Reims Cathedral and tour a Champagne *cave*.
16:00	Train from Reims to Paris (1.5 hrs.).
19:00	Set up in Paris.

Note: There's a night train option leaving Colmar at about 22:00 and arriving in Paris at about 7:00 the next morning (transfer in Strasbourg).

Transportation: Colmar to Paris (340 miles)

Driving, leave Colmar on the N-83 toward Strasbourg, which becomes the autoroute (A-4). Verdun is about a half hour after Metz on the autoroute. To visit the battlefield, take the Verdun exit, pass through the city onto the N-3 toward Etain, following signs to Champs de Bataille, *rive droite*. (The battlefield remains are split between two sides of the Meuse River—the rive droite, the right bank, is more interesting.) Follow signs to Fort Douamant.

(Note: from October to March, Verdun sights close from 12:00-14:00.)

From Verdun, return to the autoroute to Paris, passing miles of goofy modern Franco-freeway art. Take the Reims exit marked Cathedral, and you'll see your destination. Park near the church. Picnic in the park near its front (public W.C., dangerous grass, glorious setting). Back on the freeway, it's a straight shot into Paris.

If you're renting a car, consider turning it in at Reims and catching the train or bus into Paris.

If you're driving to your hotel and are in danger of going "in-Seine," hire a cab and follow your Parisian leader to your hotel.

If you think you're good behind the wheel, drive this welcome-to-Paris tour (any hotel you pass will have a rack of free maps at its reception): Follow the autoroute under the Périphérique (ring road) straight into the city along the Seine, cross over the Austerlitz Bridge to Luxembourg Gardens (via St. Marcel and Port Royal), down Boulevard St. Michel, past Notre-Dame on the island, left on the rue de Rivoli, up avenue des Champs-Élysées, around the Arc de Triomphe (6 or 8 giggly times), and to your hotel. (Confirm your hotel reservation earlier in the day by telephone.)

By train, there are good connections from Colmar to Reims and Reims to Paris (5 hours total). Or consider the overnight train option to Paris via Strasbourg (or from nearby Basel). The scenery between Colmar and Paris is rather dull, and the Gothic churches in Paris are nearly as good as Reims, so you're not missing much—well, except a night in a hotel. Verdun requires a car. Another way to streamline is to skip the Reims stop and do the champagne tour in Épernay, which is a stop anyway on the Colmar-Paris train. Upon arrival in Paris, make any departure plans you can.

Sightseeing Highlights—Between Alsace and Paris
▲▲ **Verdun**—Little remains in Europe to remind us of World War I. Verdun provides a fine tribute to the over

Alsace to Paris

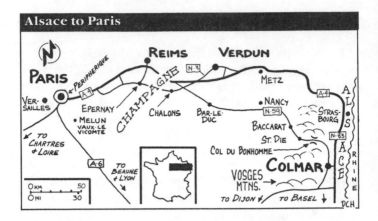

one million lives lost in the World War I battles here. You could spend several days exploring the battlefield monuments, but in two hours you can see the most impressive and appreciate the awesome scale of the battles that took place here.

Start with the Memorial-Musée de Fleury, where you'll see reconstructed scenes and models of the battles that raged here for over four years. (Open mid-March to mid-September 9:00-18:00; off-season 9:00-12:00 and 14:00-17:00, 18F.)

Next visit the bones of 130,000 French and Germans whose last home was the muddy trenches of Verdun at the strange monument of **L'Ossuaire** (open 9:00-18:30, sometimes with a noon-14:00 lunch break, 14F for the film). Look through the low windows for a gloomy memorial to those whose political and military leaders asked them to make the ultimate sacrifice to the hungry god of war. Inside this humbling and moving tribute, ponder a war that left half of all the men in France between the ages of 15 and 30 dead or wounded. Before leaving, walk to the cemetery and listen for the eerie silence of peace and the faint buzz of future wars. See the twenty-minute film in the basement—ask for the English version. (Verdun TI tel. 29 84 18 85.)

▲▲ **Reims**—The cathedral of Reims is a glorious example of Gothic architecture with the best west portal anywhere. The coronation place of 800 years of French kings and queens, it houses many old treasures, not to mention a lovely modern set of Marc Chagall stained glass windows. Take this opportunity to fall in love with Gothic, without the stifling crowds you'll find at Paris's Notre Dame. (Open 8:00-19:39 daily.) The TI is open 9:00-19:30 daily, tel. 26 47 25 69.

Reims is the capital of the Champagne region, and while the the best tours are in Épernay, the bubbly stuff's birthplace, drivers save over an hour of road time by touring a champagne *cave* right in Reims. Drive or walk (20 minutes) up rue de Barbatre from the cathedral to 9 place St. Nicaise (tel. 26 85 45 35) where for 15F, the Taittinger Company will do a great job trying to convince you they're the best. After seeing their movie (in very comfortable theater seats), follow your guide down into some of the three miles of chilly chalk caves, many dug by ancient Romans.

One block beyond Taittinger, on place des Droits de l'Homme, you'll find several other champagne firms. Most give free tours Monday through Saturday from 9:00 to 11:00 and 14:00 to 17:00. I'd recommend Piper Heidsieck with a free tour that includes a tacky train ride (51 blvd. Henry-Vasnier, tel. 26 85 01 94). Call to confirm tour times.

▲**Épernay**—This town is the actual birthplace of Champagne where, in the 1600s, Dom Perignon bubbled excitedly through the abbey, "Brothers, come quickly. I am drinking stars!" The best Champagne tours are given right downtown by Moet et Chandon (20 ave. de Champagne, tel. 26 54 71 11. Open daily with a break for lunch. Free 45-minute English tours plus tasting. Épernay TI tel. 26 55 33 00.)

Paris
See tomorrow.

DAY 22
PARIS

Only Paris could provide a fitting finale for this 22-day trip. Paris is sweeping boulevards, sleepy parks, staggering art galleries, friendly crêpe stands, Napoleon's body, sleek shopping malls, the Eiffel Tower, and people watching from an outdoor café. Some people fall in love with Paris. Many see the Mona Lisa and flee disappointed. Good travelers fall in love with Europe's capital city.

Suggested Schedule

8:00	Follow "First Day Paris Walk" through the Latin Quarter to Notre-Dame, Deportation Memorial, Sainte-Chapelle.
11:30	Lunch at 5th-floor Samaritaine department store cafeteria.
13:00	Tour the Louvre, hopefully with a guide.
16:00	Stroll through the Tuileries and up the Champs-Élysées to the Arc de Triomphe.
21:00	After-dinner river cruise, concert in Sainte-Chapelle or jazz club.

Suggested Schedule

Day 23 (only Paris could stretch a 22-day tour)

9:00	Shopping at les Halles.
10:30	Tour the Orsay Museum (in July and August, do Orsay first).
14:00	Free afternoon: cruise the Seine, visit museums, stroll.
19:00	Last evening and dinner in Montmartre. Think back over these 22 days. Plan next 22.

Paris Orientation

Paris is circled by a ring road freeway (the périphérique), split in half by the Seine River, and divided into 20 *arrondissements* (proud and independent governmental jurisdictions). You'll find Paris much easier to negotiate if you know which side of the river you're on, which arrondissement you're in, and which subway (*métro*) stop you're closest to. Remember, if you're above the river (look at a map), you're on the right bank (*rive droite*), and if you're below it, you're on the left bank (*rive gauche*). Arrondissements are numbered, starting at ground zero (Notre-Dame is 1ème) and moving in a clockwise spiral out to the ring road. The last two digits in a Parisian zip code are the arrondissement number, and the notation for the métro stop is "Mo." In Parisian jargon, Napoleon's tomb is on la rive gauche in the "7ème," zip code 75007, Métro: Invalides. Paris métro stops are a standard aid in giving directions.

Parisian train stations: Paris has six train stations (*gares*), all with métro connections. If you're coming from northern or central Europe, you'll land at the Gare de l'Est, Gare du Nord, or St. Lazare. From the south, you'll land at Gare de Lyon or Austerlitz. Pick up the RATP métro map and follow signs to the métro.

Parisian Public Transit

The Métro: Europe's best subway is divided into two systems; the métro covers the city, and the RER connects suburban destinations. You'll be using the métro for almost all your trips. In Paris, you're never more than a ten-minute walk from a métro station. One ticket takes you anywhere in the system with unlimited transfers. Save nearly 50 percent by buying a *carnet* (pronounced car-nay) of 10 tickets for about 35F at any métro station. Métro tickets work on city buses. If you're staying longer, the *Carte d'Orange* gives you free run of the métro and buses from Sunday through Saturday for 51F.

Before entering the station, find the "Mo." stop closest to your destination and which line(s) will get you there. The lines have numbers, but they're best known by their *direction* or end-of-the-line stop. (For example, the "Saint-Denis/Châtillon" line runs between Saint-Denis in the north and Châtillon in the south.)

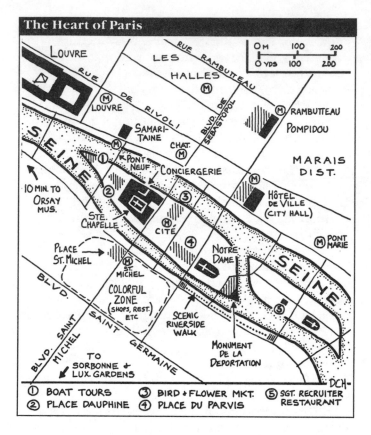

The Heart of Paris

LOUVRE

LES HALLES

RUE RAMBUTEAU

RUE DE RIVOLI

Ⓜ LOUVRE

SAMARI-TAINE

BLVD. DE SEBASTOPOL

Ⓜ

CHAT. Ⓜ

Ⓜ RAMBUTEAU

POMPIDOU

MARAIS DIST.

① PONT NEUF

CONCIERGERIE

SEINE

10 MIN. TO ORSAY MUS.

②

STE. CHAPELLE

③

Ⓜ CITÉ

④ NOTRE DAME

Ⓜ HÔTEL DE VILLE (CITY HALL)

Ⓜ PONT MARIE

PLACE ST. MICHEL →

Ⓜ ST. MICHEL

COLORFUL ZONE (SHOPS, REST. ETC)

SCENIC RIVERSIDE WALK

MONUMENT DE LA DEPORTATION

SEINE

⑤

BLVD. SAINT MICHEL

BLVD. SAINT GERMAINE

TO SORBONNE + LUX. GARDENS

0 M   100   200
0 YDS 100   200

DCH—

① BOAT TOURS   ③ BIRD + FLOWER MKT.   ⑤ SGT. RECRUITER RESTAURANT
② PLACE DAUPHINE   ④ PLACE DU PARVIS

Once in the métro station, you'll see signs directing you to the train going in your direction (e.g., "direction: Saint-Denis"). Insert your ticket in the automatic turnstile (brown stripe down), pass through the turnstile, reclaim and keep your ticket until you exit the system (toss it out when done so you don't confuse old and new tickets). Transfers are free and can be made wherever lines cross. When you transfer, look for the orange *correspondance* (connections) signs when you exit your first train, then follow the proper Direction or Destination sign.

Before you *sortie* (that's exit, not bomb), check the very helpful *plan du quartier* (map of the neighborhood) to get your bearings and decide which sortie you want. At stops with several sorties, you can save lots of walking by choosing the best exit. Remember your essential métro words: *direction* (direction), *correspondance* (connections), *sortie* (exit), *carnet* (cheap set of 10 tickets), and *"Donnez-moi mon porte-monnaie!"* (Give me back my wallet). Thieves thrive in the métro. Keep valuables in your money belt.

The RER suburban train system (thick lines on your map) works like the métro—but much speedier because it makes only a few stops within the city. One métro ticket is all you need for RER rides within Paris. To travel outside the city (to Versailles, for example), you'll need to buy another ticket at the station window. Save lots of time by using the RER whenever you can.

Public Buses: The trickier bus system is worth figuring out and using. The same yellow tickets are good on both bus and métro, though you can't use the same ticket to transfer between the two systems, and longer rides require more than one ticket. While the métro shuts down about 00:45, some buses continue much later. Schedules are posted at bus stops.

To ride the bus, study the big system maps at each stop to figure out which route(s) you need. Then look at the individual route diagrams, showing the exact route of the lines serving that stop to verify your route. Major stops are also painted on the side of each bus. Enter through the front doors. Punch your yellow métro ticket in the machine behind the driver, or pay the higher cash fare. Get off the bus using the rear door. Even if you're not certain you've figured it out, do some joyriding (outside of rush hour). Lines 24, 63, and 69 run Paris's most scenic routes and make a great introduction to this city.

Taxis: Parisian taxis are nearly reasonable. A ten-minute ride costs about 40F (versus 4F to get anywhere in town on the métro), and luggage will cost you more. You can try waving one down, but it's easier to ask for the nearest taxi stand ("oo-ay la tet de stah-see-oh"). Sunday and night rates are higher, and if you call one from your hotel, the meter starts as soon as the call's received. Taxis are tough to find on Friday and Saturday nights, especially after the métro closes.

Paris Information
Paris requires study and a good map. For an extended
stay, two fine guidebooks are the *Michelin Green Guide*
and the *Access Guide to Paris*. While it's easy to pick up
free maps of Paris once you've arrived (your hotel has
them), they don't show all the streets, and you may want
the huge Michelin #10 map of Paris. The *Pariscope*
weekly magazine (or one of its clones, 3F, at any news-
stand) lists museum hours, concerts and musical festivals,
plays, movies, nightclubs, and special art exhibits.

There are eleven English-language bookstores in Paris
where you can pick up guidebooks. Try Shakespeare and
Co. for used travel books (at 37 rue de la Boucherie,
across the river from Notre-Dame, 12:00-24:00) or W. H.
Smith's at 248 rue de Rivoli, or Brentanos at 47 avenue de
L'Opéra.

The American Church is a nerve center for the American émigré community and publishes a handy monthly
called the *Free Voice*. *France-USA Contacts*, an advertise-
ment paper, is full of useful information for those looking
for work or long-term housing.

Avoid the Paris TIs—long lines and short information.
This book, the *Pariscope* magazine, and a good map are
all you need for a short visit. If you need more information, visit the main TI (tel. 47 23 61 72, at 127 ave. des
Champs-Élysées, open 9:00-20:00), or ask your hotelier.
For recorded concert and special events information in
English, call 47 20 88 98. For a complete list of museum
hours and scheduled English museum tours, pick up the
free *Musées, Monuments Historiques, et Expositions*
booklet from any museum.

Helpful Hints
Most museums are closed on Tuesday, have reduced
entries on Sunday, and are least crowded very early, at
lunch, and very late. Carry small change for pay toilets, or
walk into any café with outdoor tables like you owned
the place and find the toilet in the back. Check price lists
before ordering at any café or restaurant. Rude surprises
await sloppy tourists. Remember, pedestrians don't have

the right of way—drivers do and they know it. Use your money belt, and never carry a wallet in your back pocket or a purse over your shoulder.

Don't try to see it all, pace yourself, enjoy the cafés between sightseeing and shopping. Assume you'll return. Useful telephone numbers: American Express, 42 66 09 99; American Hospital, 46 41 25 25; American Pharmacies at 47 42 49 40 (Opera) and 42 60 72 96 (Tuileries); Police, 17; U.S. Embassy, 42 96 12 02; Paris and France directory assistance, 12; AT&T operator 19 00 11; MCI operator 05 06 19 19.

▲▲▲First Day Paris Walk

Take a day to cover the core sights of Paris and get comfortable with the city in general. This walk laces together Day 22's suggested sights (see below for specific sights information).

Start by taking the métro to the St. Michel stop where you'll emerge in the heart of an uncharacteristically sleepy Latin Quarter. This place hops at night and uses mornings to recover. Walk down rue de la Huchette (past the popular jazz cellar at #5—check the schedule) and over the bridge to Notre-Dame cathedral. It took 200 years to build this church: tour it accordingly. Walk around to the impressive back side of the church (how about those buttresses). At the tip of the island, visit the moving memorial to the 200,000 French deported by Hitler in World War II. Across the bridge is the Île, or island, of St. Louis (tour it later). Walking back through the center of the island, Île de la Cité, you'll come to the Sainte-Chapelle church, a Gothic gem. After touring it, walk to the northeast tip of the island (lovely park, Seine boat tours depart from here) through the peaceful, triangular place Dauphine. Next, cross the oldest bridge in town, the Pont-Neuf (to the right, north) to the Right Bank. Drop into the Samaritaine department store. Have lunch on its fifth floor (cafeteria open 11:30-15:00, 15:30-18:30).

Then your time has come to tackle the Louvre (closed Tuesday). Europe's onetime grandest palace and biggest

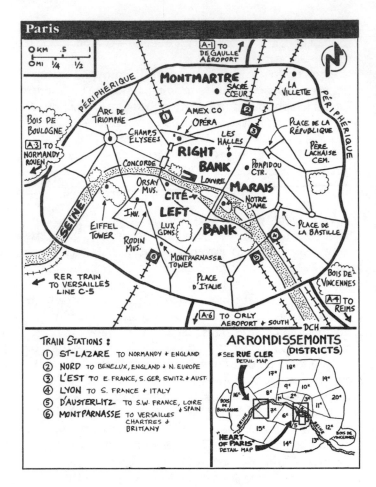

building houses its greatest—and most overwhelming—
museum. Enter the new Louvre entry, a grand modern
glass pyramid in the central courtyard.

For the rest of the afternoon, take a leisurely, people-
watching walk through the Tuileries Gardens (Monet's
Water Lilies glimmer in the Orangerie Museum at the far
end by the river) to the place de la Concorde, where over
1,300 heads rolled during the French Revolution. From
there, walk up the Champs-Élysées to the Arc de Triomphe (small museum on top with a great city view). Or,

you could métro to the Arc de Triomphe (Métro: Charles de Gaulle-Étoile) and walk downhill.

Sightseeing Highlights
(Reminder: Nearly all Parisian museums are closed on Tuesday. Those that aren't (e.g., Orsay, Rodin) normally close on Monday. Most have shorter hours on Sunday and from October through March. And many start closing down rooms 30 minutes before the actual closing time. Museum holidays are usually 1/1, 5/1, 5/8, 7/14, 11/1, 11/11, and 12/25. Those under age 26 and over age 60 get big discounts on most sights.)

▲▲ **Latin Quarter**—This area, which gets its name from the language used here when it was an exclusive medieval university district, lies between the Luxembourg Gardens and the Seine, centering around the Sorbonne University and boulevardes St. Germain and St. Michel. This is the core of the Left Bank—the artsy, liberal, hippy, Bohemian district of poets, philosophers, and winos. It's full of international eateries, far-out bookshops, street singers, pale girls in black berets, and jazz clubs. For colorful wandering and café-sitting, afternoons and evenings are best.

▲▲ **Notre-Dame Cathedral**—The cathedral is 700 years old and packed with history and tourists. Climb to the top (entrance on outside left, open 9:00-17:00, you get over 400 stairs for only 30F) for a great gargoyle's-eye view of the city. Study its sculpture (Notre-Dame's forte) and windows, take in a mass (or the free Sunday 17:15 recital on the 6,000-pipe organ, France's largest), eavesdrop on guides, walk all around the outside. (Open 8:00-19:00, treasury open 9:30-18:00, admission free. Ask about the free English tours, normally Tuesdays and Wednesdays in July and August at noon. Tel. 43 26 07 39. Clean 2.50F toilets are in front of the church near Charlemagne's statue.)

Back outside, the archaeological crypt offers a fascinating look at the remains of the earlier city and church (enter 100 yards in front of the church, daily 10:00-17:30). Drop into Hôtel Dieu, on the square opposite the river, for a pleasant courtyard and a look at a modern hospice, offering many a pleasant last stop before heaven.

▲▲**Deportation Memorial**—The architecture of this memorial to the French victims of the Nazi concentration camps is a powerful blend of water, sky, bars, confinement, concrete, eternal flame, the names of many concentration camps, and a crystal for each of the 200,000 victims. (Open at 10:00, east tip of the island near Île St. Louis, behind Notre-Dame, free.)

▲▲▲**Sainte-Chapelle**—The triumph of Gothic church architecture, a cathedral of glass, like none other. It was built in just five years to house the supposed Crown of Thorns (which cost the king more than the church). Downstairs was for commoners, upstairs for royal Christians. Hang out at the top of the spiral stairs and watch the room's beauty suck the breath from emerging tourists. There's a good little book with color photos on sale that explains the stained glass in English. There are concerts almost every summer evening (120F). Anything going on tonight? Even a beginning violin class would sound lovely here. (Open 9:30-18:00, 24F. Stop at the ticket booth outside the church, or call 43 54 30 09 for concert information. Handy free public toilets just outside.)

▲▲▲**The Louvre**—This is Europe's oldest, biggest, greatest, and maybe most crowded museum. Don't try to cover it thoroughly. The 90-minute English language tour is the best way to enjoy this huge museum (find Accueil des Groupes desk at entry, information tel. 40 20 50 50, normally nearly hourly, 24F). *Mona Winks* (buy in U.S.A.) includes a self-guided tour of the Louvre as well as of the Orsay, the Pompidou, and Versailles.

If you're unable to get a guide, a good do-it-yourself tour of the museum's highlights would include (in this order, starting in the Denon wing) Ancient Greek (Parthenon frieze, Venus de Milo, Nike of Samothrace); Apollo Gallery (jewels); French and Italian paintings in the Grande Galerie (a quarter-mile long and worth the hike); the Mona Lisa and her Italian Renaissance roommates; the nearby neoclassical collection (*Coronation of Napoleon*); and the romantic collection with works by Delacroix and

Gericault. (Open 9:00-18:00, Wednesday until 21:30, most of the collection on Monday until 21:30. Closed Tuesday. 30F, 15F for the young, the old, and those who visit on Sunday. Tel. 40 20 53 17 or 40 20 51 51 for recorded information. Métro: Palais-Royale/Musée du Louvre.)

▲▲▲**Orsay Museum**—This is Paris's long-awaited nineteenth-century art museum (actually, art from 1848-1914), including Europe's greatest collection of impressionist works (call for 25F English tour schedule).

Start on the ground floor. The conservative establishment "pretty" art is on the right, then cross left into the brutally truthful and, at the time, very shocking art of the realist rebels and Manet. Then go way up the escalator at the far end to the series of impressionist rooms (Monet, Renoir, Degas et al.) and van Gogh. Don't miss the art nouveau on the mezzanine level. The museum is housed in a former train station (Gare d'Orsay) across the river and 10 minutes downstream from the Louvre. (Open 9:00-17:30 in July and August and all Sundays, 10:00-17:30 other days, Thursday until 21:45, closed Monday, most crowded around 11:00 and 14:00. 30F, 15F for the young and the old, tel. 40 49 48 84.)

▲▲**Napoleon's Tomb and the Army Museum**—The emperor lies majestically dead under a grand dome—a goose-bumping pilgrimage for historians—surrounded by the tombs of other French war heroes and Europe's greatest military museum, in the Hotel des Invalides. (Open daily 10:00-18:00, 25F, tel. 45 55 37 70. Métro: La Tour Maubourg.)

▲▲**Rodin Museum**—This user-friendly museum is filled with surprisingly entertaining work by the greatest sculptor since Michelangelo. See *The Kiss, The Thinker*, and many more. Near Napoleon's Tomb. (Open 10:00-18:00, closed Monday; 20F, half-price on Sunday, tel. 47 05 01 34. Métro: Varennes, 75007. Cafeteria and great picnic spots in back garden.)

▲**Pompidou Center**—Europe's greatest collection of far-out modern art, the Musée National d'Art Moderne is housed in this colorfully exoskeletal building. After so

many Madonnas and Children, a piano smashed to bits
and glued to the wall is refreshing. It's a social center with
lots of people, street theater, and activity inside and
out—a perpetual street fair. Ride the escalator for a free
city view from the café terrace on top. (Open Monday-
Friday 12:00-22:00, Saturday, Sunday, and most holidays
10:00-22:00, closed Tuesday; 27F, free Sunday from
10:00-14:00; tel. 42 77 12 33, Métro: Rambuteau.)

▲**Beaubourg**—This was a separate village until the
twelfth century, and today it includes the area from the
Pompidou Center to the Forum des Halles shopping center. Most of Paris's hip renovation energy over the past 20
years seems to have been directed here—before then it
was a slum. Don't miss the new wave fountains (the *Hom-
age to Stravinsky*) on the river side of the Pompidou Center or the eerie clock you'll find through the Quartier
d'Horloge passage on the other side of the Pompidou
Center. A colorful stroll down rue Rambuteau takes you to
the space age Forum des Halles shopping center, on the
site of what was a wonderful outdoor food market. As
you tour this shopping mecca, peek into the huge 350-
year-old St. Eustache Church and admire the unusual
glass chandeliered altar. The striking round building at
the end of the esplanade is Paris's old Bourse, or Commercial Exchange. For an oasis of peace, continue to the
interior gardens of the Palais-Royal. (Métro: Les Halles or
Rambuteau.)

▲▲**Eiffel Tower**—Crowded and expensive but worth
the trouble. The higher you go, the more you pay. I think
the view from the 400-foot-high second level is plenty.
Pilier Nord (the north pillar) has the biggest elevator—
with the fastest-moving line. The Restaurant Belle France
serves decent 70F meals (first level). Don't miss the entertaining free movie on the history of the tower on the first
level. Heck of a view. (Open daily 9:00-23:00; 18F to the
first level, 34F to the second, 50F to go all the way for the
1,000-foot view. On a budget? You can climb the stairs to
the second level for only 9F. Tel. 45 50 34 56. Métro:
Trocadero. RER: Champs de Mars. Arrive early for less

crowds.) For a great view, especially at night, cross the river and enjoy the tower from Trocadero!

▲**Montparnasse Tower**—A 59-floor superscraper, cheaper and easier to get to the top than the Eiffel Tower. Possibly Paris's best view since the Eiffel Tower is in it. Buy the photo-guide to the city, go to the rooftop and orient yourself. This is a fine way to understand the lay of this magnificent land. It's a good place to be as the sun goes down on your first day in Paris. Find your hotel, retrace your day's steps, locate the famous buildings. (Open summer 9:30-23:00, off-season 10:00-22:00, 35F.)

▲**Samaritaine Department Store Viewpoint**—Go to the rooftop (ride the elevator from near the Pont Neuf entrance). Quiz yourself. Working counterclockwise, find the Eiffel Tower, Invalides/Napoleon's Tomb, Montparnasse Tower, Henry IV statue on the tip of the island, Sorbonne University, the dome of the Panthéon, Sainte-Chapelle, Hôtel de Ville (city hall), the wild and colorful Pompidou Center, Sacré-Coeur, Opéra, and the Louvre. Light meals on the breezy terrace and a good self-service restaurant on the 5th floor. (Rooftop view is free. Métro: Pont Neuf.)

▲▲**Sacré-Coeur and Montmartre**—This Byzantine-looking church is only 100 years old but very impressive. It was built as a praise-the-Lord-anyway gesture after the French were humiliated by the Germans in a brief war in 1871. The place du Tertre was the haunt of Toulouse-Lautrec and the original Bohemians. Today it's mobbed by tourists and unoriginal Bohemians—but still fun. Watch the artists, tip the street singers, have a dessert crêpe. The church is open daily and evenings. ("Plaster of Paris" comes from the gypsum found on this *mont. Place Blanche* is the white place nearby where they used to load it, sloppily.) Métro: Anvers or Abbesses.

Pigalle—Paris's red-light district, the infamous "Pig Alley," is at the foot of Butte Montmartre. Oo la la. More shocking than dangerous. Stick to the bigger streets, hang onto your wallet, and exercise good judgment. Can-can can cost a fortune as can con artists in topless bars. Métro: Pigalle.

Best Shopping—Forum des Halles is a grand new sub-
terranean center, a sight in itself. Fun, mod, colorful, and
very Parisian (Métro: Halles). The Lafayette Galleries
behind the Opera House is your best elegant, Old World,
one-stop, Parisian department store shopping center.
Also, visit the Printemps store and the historic Samaritaine department store near Pont Neuf.

Good browsing areas: rue Rambuteau from the Halles
to the Pompidou Center, the Marais/Jewish Quarter/place
des Vosges area, the Champs-Élysées, and the Latin Quarter. Window shop along the rue de Rivoli, which borders
the Louvre. The rue de Rivoli is also the city's souvenir
row, especially for fun T-shirts. Ritzy shops are around
the Ritz Hotel at place Vendôme (Métro: Tuileries).

▲▲▲**Place de la Concorde/Champs-Élysées/Arc de
Triomphe**—Here is Paris's backbone and greatest concentration of traffic. All of France seems to converge on
the **place de la Concorde**, Paris's largest square. It was
here that the guillotine made hundreds "a foot shorter at
the top"—including King Louis XVI. Back then it was
called the place de la Revolution.

Catherine de Medici wanted a place to drive her car-
riage, so she started draining the swamp that would
become the **Champs-Élysées.** Napoleon put on the
final touches, and ever since, it's been the place to be
seen. The Tour de France bicycle race ends here, as do all
French parades of any significance (Métro: FDR or
George V).

Napoleon had the magnificent Arc de Triomphe constructed to commemorate his victory at the Battle of
Austerlitz. There's no arch bigger in the world, and no
more crazy traffic circle. Eleven major boulevards feed
into the place Charles de Gaulle (Étoile) that surrounds
the arch. Watch the traffic tangle and pray you don't end
up here in a car. Take the underpass to visit the eternal
flame and tomb of the unknown soldier. There's a cute
museum of the arch (open daily 10:00-17:30, 25F) and a
great view from the top.

▲**Luxembourg Gardens**—Paris's most beautiful, interesting, and enjoyable garden-park-recreational area is a

great place to watch Parisians at rest and play. Check out the card players (near the tennis courts), find a free chair near the main pond, and take a breather. Notice any pigeons? A poor Ernest Hemingway used to hand-hunt (strangle) them here. The grand neoclassical domed Panthéon is a block away. (Park open until dusk, Métro: Odéon.)

▲ **Le Marais**—This once smelly swamp (*marais*) was drained in the twelfth century and soon became a fashionable place to live, at least until the Revolution. It's Paris at its medieval best. This is how much of the city looked until, in the mid-1800s, Napoleon III had Baron Haussmann blast through the boulevards (too big for revolutionary barricades, open and wide enough for the guns and marching ranks of the army), creating modern Paris. Here you'll find a tiny but thriving Jewish neighborhood, Paris's most striking and oldest square, place des Vosges, a monument to the revolutionary storming of the Bastille at place de la Bastille (nothing but memorial marks on the street is left of the actual Bastille prison), the new controversial Opera House, the largest collection of Picassos in the world, Paris's great history museum (see below), and endless interesting streets to wander. (Métro: St. Paul.)

Carnavalet (History of Paris) Museum—Inside this fine example of a Marais mansion, complete with classy courtyards and statues, are paintings of Parisian scenes, French Revolution paraphernalia, old Parisian store signs, a guillotine, a superb model of sixteenth-century Île de la Cité (notice the bridge houses), and rooms full of fifteenth-century Parisian furniture. (Open 10:00-17:30, closed Monday; 20 F, free on Sunday; 23 rue du Savigne, tel. 42 72 21 13. Métro: St. Paul.)

▲ **Picasso Museum (Hôtel de Sale)**—The largest collection in the world of Pablo Picasso's paintings, sculpture, sketches, and ceramics as well as his personal collection of impressionist art. It's well explained in English and worth * * * if you're a fan. (Open daily except Tuesday 9:00-17:00, and until 22:00 on Wednesday; 28 F; tel. 42 71 52 21. Métro: St. Paul or Rambuteau.)

▲**Père Lachaise Cemetery**—Littered with the tomb-
stones of many of the city's most illustrious dead, this is
your best one-stop look at the fascinating and romantic
world of the "permanent Parisians." The place is confusing, but maps (from the guardhouse or cemetery flower
shops) will direct you to the graves of Chopin, Moliére,
and even Jim Morrison. In section 92, a series of statues
memorializing the war makes the French war experience
a bit more real.

St.-Germain-des-Prés—A church has been here since
A.D. 452. The church you see today was constructed in
1163 and has been recently restored. The area around the
church hops at night, with fire eaters, mimes, and scads
of artists. (Métro: St.-Germain-des-Prés.)

Grande Arche, La Defense—Paris's newest attraction is
a modern architectural wonder and the pride of modern
Paris. Take the RER from Opéra or Étoile to La Defense,
then follow signs to Grande Arche. Great city views and a
huge shopping mall.

Side Trips from Paris

▲▲▲**Versailles**—Every king's dream (and many
tourists' nightmare), Versailles was the residence of the
French king and the cultural heartbeat of Europe for
about 100 years—until the Revolution of 1789 ended the
notion that God deputized some people to rule for Him
on earth. Louis XIV spent half a year's income of Europe's
richest country to build this palace fit for the ultimate
divine monarch. Europe's next best palaces are, to a certain degree, Versailles knock-offs.

Frankly, the place is a headache—crowded and user-
mean. Chantilly and Vaux-le-Vicomte are more likable
and easier to enjoy. But it's the sheer bulk of the place—
physically and historically—that makes Versailles almost
an obligation.

Versailles is 12 miles from downtown Paris. Subway to
an RER station (like Invalides or St. Michel) and follow the
RER signs to the train bound for "Versailles R.G." (26F
round-trip, 25 minutes each way; runs every 10 minutes,

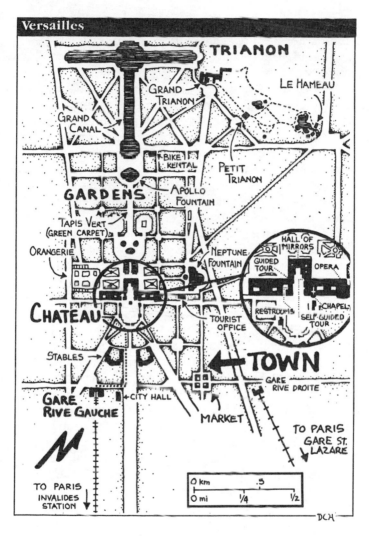

most but not all trains go to Versailles. Stops are listed on signs over the platform. The Versailles Station is a 10-minute walk to the palace).

Admission is 30F (15F for those 18-25 and over 60, and everybody else on Sunday). It's open Tuesday to Sunday 9:00-19:00, October-April from 9:45-17:30, last entry 16:00, closed Monday, information tel. 30 84 76 18 and 30

84 74 00. Tour groups pack the place from 9:00 to 15:00. Tuesdays and Sundays are most crowded. Arriving around 15:30 and doing the grounds after the palace closes works well.

To avoid most of the pandemonium and to have your own English-speaking art historian with a group of less than 30 for 90 minutes, take the private tour of the otherwise inaccessible King's Apartments and Opera. It leaves every 10 minutes from 9:30 to 15:30 from entrance 3 (small line on the left, opposite the long line, as you face the palace). Tours finish at the chapel, where those who suffer through the long regular admission line finally start. (Tours cost 24F, plus general admission.)

The main palace is a one-way free-for-all. The Hall of Mirrors is magnificent. Before going downstairs at the end, take a historic walk clockwise around the long room filled with the great battles of France murals. If you don't have *Mona Winks* (final plug, I promise), the guidebook called *The Châteaux, The Gardens, and Trianon* gives a room-by-room rundown.

Many enjoy the gardens as much if not more than the palace. The more intimate Petit Trianon is open from 11:30 to 18:00. Walk 45 minutes (or rent a bike in the park) to the Little Hamlet, where Marie Antoinette played peasant girl, tending her perfumed sheep and manicured garden, in her almost understandable retreat from reality. This is a divine picnic spot. Food is not allowed into the palace, but you can check your bag at the entrance. There's also a decent restaurant on the canal in the park.

The town of Versailles is quiet and pleasant. The central market is great for picnic stuff, and the cozy crêperie on rue de la Deux Portes has a crêpe selection that would impress Louis himself. (Some prefer to minimize the big-city headaches of Paris by turning in their car, sleeping in Versailles, and riding the commuter train into town. Hôtel Clagny, near the station, is good.)

▲▲**Chartres**—This is one of Europe's most important Gothic cathedrals. Malcolm Miller, or his equally impressive assistant, gives great "Appreciation of Gothic" tours

daily (except Sunday and off-season) at noon and 14:45.
Each tour is different and costs just a tip. Just show up at
the church. (Open 7:00-19:00, one-hour train trip,
hourly departures from Paris's Gare Montparnasse, 120F
round-trip, TI 37 21 50 00.)

▲▲**Château of Chantilly** (pronounced shan-tee-yee)—
One of France's best château (castle) experiences is just
30 minutes and 30 francs by train from Paris's Gare du
Nord station. Moat, drawbridge, sculpted gardens, little
hamlet (the prototype for the more famous *hameau* at
Versailles), lavish interior (rivals Versailles, with included
and required French language tour), world-class art collection (including two Raphaels), and reasonable crowds.
(Open daily except Tuesday, 10:00-18:00, fewer hours off-
season, 30 F.)

Horse lovers will enjoy the nearby stables (expensive)
literally built for a prince (who believed he'd be reincar-
nated as a horse). The quaint and impressively preserved
medieval town of Senlis is a 30-minute bus ride from the
Chantilly station.

▲**Giverny**—Monet's garden and home are very popular
with his fans. Open 10:00-18:00, April 1-October 31,
closed off-season and Monday; 30 F; no English-language
tours. Nice restaurant next door for pricey but good
lunches or picnic. Take the Rouen train from St. Lazare
Station to Vernon, a pleasant Normandy city. There is a
Vernon-Giverny bus in the summer. Otherwise, rent a
bike at the station, walk, hitch, or taxi the 4 km to
Monet's garden. Tel. 32 51 28 21.

▲▲**Vaux-le-Vicomte**—This château is considered the
prototype for Versailles. In fact, when its owner, Nicolas
Fouquet, gave a grand party, Louis XIV was so jealous that
he arrested the host and proceeded with the construction
of the bigger and costlier, but not necessarily more splendid, palace of Versailles. Vaux-le-Vicomte is a joy to tour,
elegantly furnished, and surrounded by royal gardens. It's
not crowded, but it's difficult to get to without a car.
(Near Fontainebleau, southeast of Paris. Train from Gare
de Lyon to Melun, southeast of Paris. Rent a bike or taxi

from there. Open daily 10:00-18:00. Special candle-lit hours: Saturday 20:30-23:00, May through September. 42F, tel. 60 66 97 09.)

Sleeping in Paris (about 6F = U.S.$1)

Paris is a huge city with a huge selection of hotels. To keep things manageable, I've focused on three safe, handy, and colorful neighborhoods, listing good hotels in each neighborhood to help make you a temporary resident. Good restaurants and cafés for each area are listed later under "Eating in Paris."

Choose your price range and your neighborhood. A hotel's star classification is indicated by an *. Old, characteristic, budget Parisian hotels have always been cramped. Now they've added elevators, W.C.s, and private showers and are even more cramped.

While you can save up to 100F by finding the increasingly rare room without a shower, these rooms are often smaller, and many places charge around 20F for each shower you take down the hall. Remember, baths and twin beds cost more than showers and double beds. A toilet in the room bumps the price up more. Breakfasts are usually optional and 20F to 30F (prices listed are without breakfast). You can save about 10F each by eating in a nearby café. Singles, unless the hotel has a few closet-type rooms that fit only one twin bed, are simply doubles inhabited by one person, only about 20 to 50F less than a double.

Assume Paris will be tight. Look early or have a reservation. Conventions clog the city in September (worst), October, May, and June. July and August are easier. Most hotels accept telephone reservations only for today or tomorrow until about midday. Most will have and hold a room for you if you call just after breakfast. Most require prepayment for a reservation far in advance (call first, and if they won't take a credit card number, follow up with a $50 traveler's check or a bank check in francs for the first night). Some, usually the very cheapest places, take no reservations at all.

Hotels in the Rue Cler Neighborhood—7th district, Métro: École Militaire, postal code 75007: Rue Cler, a villagelike pedestrian street, is safe and tidy and makes me feel like I must have been a poodle in a previous life. How such coziness lodged itself between the high-powered government-business district and the expensive Eiffel Tower and Invalides areas, I'll never know. This is the ideal place to call home in Paris. Living here ranks as one of the city's great experiences.

On rue Cler, you can step outside your hotel and eat and browse your way through a street full of tart shops, colorful outdoor produce stalls, cheeseries, and fish vendors. And you're within an easy walk of the Eiffel Tower, Les Invalides, and the Seine, as well as the Orsay and Rodin museums. (Métro: École Militaire.)

Hôtel Leveque (* 190F-300F, 29 rue Cler, tel. 47 05 49 15, fax 45 50 49 36 for reservation confirmations, English normally spoken, except by friendly Michele, who is very creative at communicating) is simple, clean, and well run, with a helpful staff, a singing maid, and, thanks to a warm spot in owner Francoise's heart, the cheapest breakfast (20F) on the block. Reserve by phone; leave Visa number. No elevator, right in the traffic-free rue Cler thick of things.

The **Hôtel du Centre** (* 300F doubles, all with TV and shower, five cheap 170F doubles, 28F breakfast, 24 rue Cler, tel. 47 05 52 33), across the street from the Leveque, has a few Eiffel Tower view rooms, is funkier, frumpier, and a bit less free-flowing than the Leveque. The Greze family accepts telephone reservations with a credit card.

The **Hôtel du Champs de Mars** (** 310F-340F doubles, all with shower or bath, 30F breakfast, 7 rue du Champs de Mars, tel. 45-51-52 30), with its fine rooms and a helpful English-speaking staff, is a top "normal hotel" rue Cler option.

Hôtel la Motte Piquet (** 310F-400F doubles, 30 ave. de la Motte Piquet, on the corner of rue Cler, tel. 47 05 09 57) with a plush lobby and basic comfortable rooms is high on gadgets and low on charm.

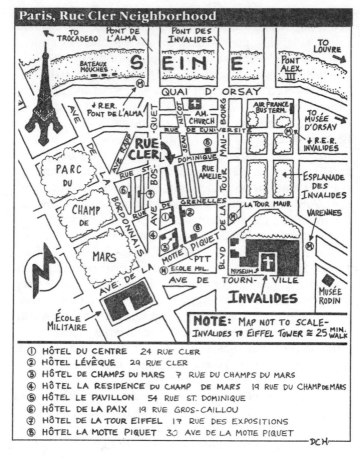

Paris, Rue Cler Neighborhood

① HÔTEL DU CENTRE   24 RUE CLER
② HÔTEL LÉVÊQUE   29 RUE CLER
③ HÔTEL DE CHAMPS DU MARS   7 RUE DU CHAMPS DU MARS
④ HÔTEL LA RESIDENCE DU CHAMP DE MARS   19 RUE DU CHAMP DE MARS
⑤ HÔTEL LE PAVILLON   54 RUE ST. DOMINIQUE
⑥ HÔTEL DE LA PAIX   19 RUE GROS-CAILLOU
⑦ HÔTEL DE LA TOUR EIFFEL   17 RUE DES EXPOSITIONS
⑧ HÔTEL LA MOTTE PIQUET   30 AVE DE LA MOTTE PIQUET

Hôtel Muguet (** 230F-340F doubles, 30F breakfast,
11 rue Chevert, tel. 47 05 05 93, fax 45 50 25 37) is a great
value on a quiet, bland street two blocks toward Les
Invalides from rue Cler. Most of its rooms are big, many
with extra sitting rooms. The upper floors offer balcon-
ettes with Eiffel views. It's a plain, antique-lamp-shades,
kittens-and-flowers kind of place, very French, with
worn carpets, sloping floors, an elevator, and homey public rooms.

Hôtel de la Paix (* 235F doubles all with shower,
385F triples, and four 130F singles without showers, 26F
breakfast, 19 rue Gros-Caillou, tel. 45 51 86 17) is a well-

worn, spartan place, run very agreeably by English-speaking Noël. If you want cheap twin beds, bright bed lights, and easy telephone reservations, this is a gem. No elevator, peeling plaster, saggy beds.

Hôtel de la Tour Eiffel (** 380F-450F doubles, 25F breakfast, 17 rue des Expositions, tel. 47 05 14 75), with petite but wicker-pleasant rooms, all with private facilities and TVs, is like a small salad with too much dressing.

Hôtel Eiffel Rive Gauche (** 340F-400F doubles, all with showers, TV, and phone, 6 rue de Gros Caillou, tel. 45 51 24 56, secure phone reservation with Visa number) is a decent value on a quiet street, with a tiny leafy court-yard that gives the place a little extra brightness.

Hôtel Malar Paris (* 260F doubles all with bath or shower, has a good 4-bed family room, 29 rue Malar, tel. 45 51 38 46) is cozy, quiet, and very French.

Résidence Latour Maubourg (** 400F-500F doubles with a few simple 210F doubles, 150 rue de Grenelle, tel. 45 51 75 28) is an Old World splurge with spacious rooms.

Rue Cler Helpful Hints: Become a local at a rue Cler café for breakfast, or join the afternoon crowd for *une bierre prossion* (a draft beer). Cute shops and bakeries line rue Cler, and there's a user friendly self-serve laundry at 16 rue Cler (easy and cheap) and another just off rue Cler on rue de la Grenelle. The métro station and a post office with phone booths are at the end of rue Cler, on avenue de la Motte Piquet. Your neighborhood TI is at the Tour Eiffel (open May-September 11:00-18:00, tel. 45 51 22 15).

At 65 quai d'Orsay, you'll find the **American Church and College**, the community center for Americans living in Paris. The interdenominational service at 11:00 on Sundays and coffee-fellowship and 40F lunch feast that follow are a great way to make some friends and get a taste of émigré life in Paris. Stop by on a weekday and pick up a copy of the *Free Voice* newspaper (tel. 47 05 07 99). There's a handy bulletin board for those in need of housing or work through the community of 30,000 Americans living in Paris.

Afternoon *boules* (lawn bowling) on the esplanade des Invalides is competitive and a relaxing spectator sport. Look for the dirt area to the upper right as you face the Invalides.

For a magical picnic dinner, assemble it in no less than six stops on rue Cler and lounge on the best grass in Paris (the police don't mind after dark) with the dogs, frisbees, a floodlit Eiffel Tower, and a cool breeze in the Parc du Champs de Mars. For an after-dinner cruise, it's just a short walk across the river (Pont d'Alma) to the Bâteaux Mouches.

Hotels in the Marais—4th district, Métro: St. Paul, postal code 75004: Those interested in a more Soho/Greenwich, gentrified, urban jungle locale would enjoy making the Marais-Jewish Quarter-St. Paul-Vosges area their Parisian home. The Marais is a cheaper and definitely more happening locale than rue Cler. Narrow medieval Paris at its finest, only 15 years ago it was a forgotten Parisian backwater. The Marais is now one of Paris's most popular residential areas. It's a very close walk to Notre-Dame, Île St. Louis, and the Latin Quarter. The subway stop St. Paul puts you right in the heart of the Marais.

Castex Hôtel (* 240F-280F doubles, all with showers, 25F breakfast, 5 rue Castex, just off place de la Bastille and rue Saint Antoine, Métro: Bastille, tel. 42 72 31 52, fax 42 72 57 91) is newly renovated, clean, cheery, quiet, and run by the very friendly Bouchand family (son Blaise speaks English; pronounced: blaze). This place is a great value, with the distinctly un-Parisian characteristic of seeming like it wants your business. Reserve by phone and leave your Visa number.

Hôtel de la place des Vosges (** 370F doubles all with shower, 33F breakfast, 12 rue de Biraque, just off the elegant place des Vosges, tel. 42 72 60 46, fax 42 72 02 64, English spoken, Visa accepted) is classy with a freshly made, antique feel, friendly, well run, with 14 rooms on a quiet street 50 yards from the elegant place des Vosges.

Grand Hôtel Jeanne d'Arc (** 360F doubles, 410F triples, 460F quads, 27F breakfast, 3 rue Jarente, 75004

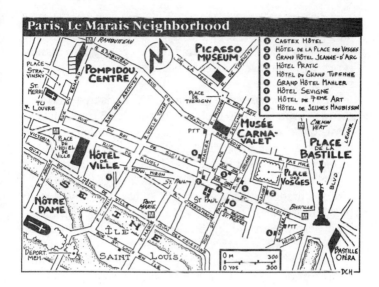

Paris, Le Marais Neighborhood

❶ Castex Hôtel
❷ Hôtel de la Place des Vosges
❸ Grand Hôtel Jeanne-d'Arc
❹ Hôtel Pratic
❺ Hôtel du Grand Tupenne
❻ Grand Hôtel Mahler
❼ Hôtel Sevigne
❽ Hôtel de 7ème Art
❾ Hôtel de Jeunes Maubisson

Paris, tel. 48 87 62 11), a plush place on a quiet street just off a cozy square, is the best normal hotel option in the Marais. Its 38 rooms all have shower or bath, TV, telephone, and W.C. Like the rest of the hotel, the breakfast room is elegant.

Hôtel Pratic (* 180-280F doubles, 9 rue d'Ormesson, 75004 Paris, tel. 48 87 80 47) has a slightly Arabic feel in its cramped lobby. The rooms are fine, and it's right on a great, people-friendly square.

Hôtel du Grand Turenne (** 450F doubles, 6 rue de Turenne, tel. 42 78 43 25, fax 42 78 50 66, English spoken) is being renovated but promises not to destroy its classy old atmosphere. All the comforts; excellent location

Grand Hôtel Mahler (* 160F-280F doubles, 5 rue Mahler, tel. 42 72 60 92, fax 42 72 25 37) should be "grand old" Hôtel Mahler. This very French place makes me nostalgic for all my old favorites that got renovated. There's no elevator, there are so many coats of paint that the molding is fading, and it's run by people who believe French is the only worthwhile language.

Hôtel Sevigne (* 250F-290F, required 16F breakfast, 2 rue Mahler, tel. 42 72 76 17) is likable only for its practicality, location, and price.

Hôtel de 7ème Art (** 360F doubles, all with shower, W.C., TV, 20 rue St. Paul, tel. 42 77 04 03, fax 42 77 69 10) is a Hollywood nostalgia place run by young, hip Marais types with a full service café/bar and Charlie Chaplin murals.

Hôtel de Jeunes Maubisson (70F beds in 4-bed rooms, noon to 16:00 lockout, 10 rue des Barres, Métro: Pont-Marie, tel. 42 72 72 09) is Paris's most elegant *foyer* (hostel), designed for travelers 18 to 35 years old and groups. It has a great location and comfortable atmosphere.

Marais Helpful Hints: Place des Vosges is Paris's oldest square, built for Henry IV. Victor Hugo lived at #6 (small museum). The nearby Musée Carnavalet offers your best look at the last 500 years of Parisian history. Rue des Rosiers is main-street Paris for the Orthodox Jewish community. The new opera house is just to the east, and a short wander to the west takes you into the hopping Beaubourg/Les Halles area. Paris's biggest and best budget department store is BHV, next to the Hôtel de Ville. Marais post offices are across from Hôtel Castex on rue Castex and on the corner of rue Pavée and Franc Bourgois.

Hotels in the Contrescarpe Neighborhood—5th district, 75005: This neighborhood is over the hill from the Latin Quarter, five minutes from the Panthéon and an easy walk to Notre-Dame, Île de la Cité, Île St. Louis, and blvds. St. Germain and St. Michel. Stay here if you like to be close to the action, which in the summer will be mostly tourist action. The rue Mouffetard and place Contrescarpe are the thriving heart and soul of the neighborhood, a market street by day and restaurant row by night. (Métro: Monge.) Listed here are one elegant, hard-to-get-into gem and three rock-bottom dives.

The **Hôtel des Grandes Ecoles** (** 300F-500F doubles, 30F breakfast, 75 rue de Cardinal Lemoine, tel. 43 26 79 23, fax 43 25 28 15) is a friendly and peaceful oasis with three buildings protecting its own garden courtyard. This place is very popular, so call far in advance or try your luck in the morning. Their cheapest rooms are nearly bad, but their top rooms are elegant.

Hôtel Central (* 200F doubles, all with showers, 6 rue Descartes, tel. 46 33 57 93) has a romantic location, steep and slippery, castlelike stairway, and stark rooms with saggy beds and meek showers. Nothing fancy but very Parisian.

The low-key and bare bones **Hôtel du Commerce** (no stars, 110F-140F doubles, no breakfast, 14 rue de La Montagne Sainte-Geneviève, Métro: Place Maubert, tel. 43 54 89 69, takes no reservations, call at 10:00 and he'll say *"oui"* or *"non"*) is run by Monsieur Mattuzzi, who must be a pirate gone good. He brags that the place is 300 years old. Judging by the vinyl in the halls, I believe him. It's a great rock-bottom deal and as safe as any dive next to the police station can be. In the morning, the landlady will knock and chirp *"Restez-vous?"* ("Are you staying for one more night?")

Y&H (young and happy) Hostel: Great location, easygoing, hip management, but depressing showers and generally crowded and filthy conditions. Four- to eight-bed rooms. Closed from 11:00-17:00. No reservations are taken, but call to see what's open (80F per bed plus 10F for sheets, 80 rue Mouffetard, tel. 45 35 09 53).

Contrescarpe Helpful Hints: The Contrescarpe neighborhood's PTT is between rue Mouffetard and rue Monge at 10 rue de l'Épée du Bois. Place Monge hosts a colorful outdoor market on Wednesdays, Fridays, and Sundays until 13:00. The street market at the bottom of the rue Mouffetard bustles daily, 8:00-12:00 and 15:30-19:00.

The Jardin des Plantes is close by and great for evening walks. But those in the know will head through the doorway at 49 rue Monge and into the surprising Roman Arena de Lutèce. Today, boules players occupy the stage while couples cuddle on the stone bleachers. Walk over to the Panthéon, and admire it from the outside. But go into the wildly beautiful St. Étienne-du-Mont church.

Eating in Paris

Everything goes here. Paris is France's wine and cuisine melting pot. While it lacks a distinctive style of its own, it draws from the best of all French provinces.

Paris could hold a gourmet Olympics—and import nothing. Picnic or go to snack bars for quick lunches and linger longer over dinner. You can eat very well, restaurant-style, for 120F. Ask your hotel to recommend a small restaurant nearby in the 80 to 100 franc range. Famous places are often overpriced, overcrowded, and overrated. Find a quiet neighborhood and wander, or follow a local recommendation.

Cafeterias and Picnics

Many Parisian department stores have top floor cafeterias offering not really cheap but low-risk, low-stress, what-you-see-is-what-you-get, quick budget meals. Try **Samaritaine** (Pont-Neuf near the Louvre, 5th floor) or **Mélodine** (Métro: Rambuteau, next to the Pompidou Center, open daily 11:00-22:00). The French word for self-service is *self-service*.

For picnics, you'll find handy little groceries all over town (but rarely near famous sights). Good picnic fixings include roasted chicken, half-liter boxes of demi-crème (2%) milk, drinkable yogurt, fresh bakery goods, melons, and exotic pâtés and cheeses. Great take-out deli-type foods like gourmet salads and quiches abound. While in the United States wine is taboo in public places, this is *pas de problem* in France. Most shops close from around 12:30 to 14:00.

The ultimate classy picnic shopping place is **Fauchon**—the famous "best gourmet grocery in France." It's fast and expensive but cheaper than a restaurant (26 place de la Madeleine, behind the Madeleine Church, Métro: Madeleine, open 9:30-19:00, closed Sunday). There's a stand-up bar in the bakery across the street. If you're hungry near Notre-Dame, the only grocery store on the Île de la Cité is tucked away on a small street running parallel to the church, one block north.

Good Picnic Spots: The pedestrian bridge, Pont des Arts, with unmatched views and plentiful benches is great. Bring your own dinner feast and watch the riverboats light up the city for you. The Palais Royal across the street from the Louvre is a good spot for a peaceful and

royal lunchtime picnic. Or try the little triangular Henry
IV Park on the west tip of the Île de la Cité, people watch-
ing at the Pompidou Center or in the elegant place des
Vosges, at the Rodin Museum, or after dark in the Eiffel
Tower park (Champs de Mars).

Restaurants (by Neighborhood)

Of course, the Parisian eating scene is kept at a rolling
boil, and entire books are written and lives are spent on
the subject. Here are a few places to consider, listed by
neighborhood, to work smoothly into your busy sightseeing strategy. If you'd like to visit a district specifically
to eat, consider the colorful, touristic but fun string of
eateries along rue Mouffetard behind the Panthéon;
Montmartre, which is very touristy around the place du
Tetre but hides some vampy values in the side streets; and
the well-worn Latin Quarter (see below).

   Rue Cler and Invalides: The rue Cler neighborhood
isn't famous for its restaurants. That's why I eat here. **Restaurant La Serne** (51 rue Cler) is friendly and reasonable. **Le Petit Niçois**, across from Hôtel Amelie at rue
Amelie, with the best moderately priced seafood in the
area, is where locals go for bouillabaise (fish stew). **Au
Café de Mars**, on the corner of rue Augerau and Gross
Caillou, is a contemporary Parisian café-restaurant with
sumptuous cuisine, fair prices, and an English-speaking
staff. **Le Petit Bosquet** (29 rue de l'Exposition) is
friendly and popular, serving Hungarian cuisine in simple
surroundings at reasonable prices. **L'Ami de Jean** (near
Hôtel Malar at 29 rue Malar) is a lively place to sample
Basque cuisine. Bring your own beret and rosy cheeks.
The **Ambassade du Sud-Ouest** is a locally popular
wine store cum restaurant specializing in southwestern
cuisine. Try the *daubes de canard* and toast your own
bread (46 ave. de la Bourdonnais, tel. 45 55 59 59). The
best and most traditional French brasserie in the area is
the dressy **Thoumieux** (79 rue St. Dominique, tel. 47 05
49 75). For a good intimate restaurant with a friendly,
English-speaking manager and a 100F menu, eat at **Restaurant Le Verdois** (19:30-22:15 for dinner, closed Sun-

day, 19 ave. de la Motte Picquet, just off rue Cler, tel. 45 55 40 38). For a quick sit-down or take-out meal, **Tarte Julie's** is just right (28 rue Cler).

The Marais: The candlelit windows of the Marais are filled with munching sophisticates. The epicenter of all this charm is the tiny square where rue Caron and rue d'Ormesson intersect, midway between the St. Paul métro stop and the place des Vosges. For more conspicuous elegance, a coffee or light lunch on the place des Vosges is good. Hobos with taste picnic on the place des Vosges itself, trying not to make the local mothers with children nervous (closed at night). For a memorable picnic dinner, ten minutes from the Marais, cross the river to Île St. Louis and find a river-level bench on the tip facing Île de la Cité. **Mexico Magico** (rue du Vielle du Temple and rue des Coutures St. Gervais) is small, fun Mariachi à la française. . . Paris's best Mexican restaurant. **Rélais de St. Paul** (31 rue François Miron) is cozy and classy, with a 110F four-course menu. **L'Énoteca** (across from Hôtel du 7ème Art at 20 rue St. Paul) has cheap, lively Italian cuisine in a relaxed, open setting. **Auberge de Jarente** (7 rue Jarente) is another popular, atmospheric, and reasonable eatery.

Latin Quarter: La Petite Bouclerie is a cozy place with classy family cooking (moderate, 33 rue de la Harpe, center of touristy Latin Quarter). Friendly Monsieur Millon runs **Restaurant Polidor**, an old turn-of-the-century-style place, with great *cuisine bourgeoise*, a vigorous local crowd, and historic toilet. Arrive at 19:00 to get a seat. . . in the restaurant, that is (moderate, 41 rue Monsieur le Prince, midway between Odéon and Luxembourg métro stops, tel. 43 26 95 34). **Atelier Maître Albert** fills with Left Bank types. The best value is its nightly fixed-price meal (dinner only, closed Sunday, 5 rue Maître Albert, Métro: Maubert Mutualité, tel. 46 33 13 78).

Île St. Louis: (Cruise the island's main street for a variety of good options.) For crazy (but touristy and expensive) cellar atmosphere and hearty fun food, feast at **La Taverne du Sergent Recruiter.** The "sergeant recruiter" used to get young Parisians drunk and stuffed here, then sign them into the army. It's all-you-can-eat, including wine and service, for 180F (41 rue St. Louis, in the center of Île St. Louis, 3 minutes from Notre-Dame, open Monday-Saturday from 19:00, tel. 43 54 75 42). There's a just-this-side-of-a-food-fight clone next door at **Nos Ancêtres Les Gaulois** (Our Ancestors the Gauls, 39 rue St. Louis-en-l'Île, tel. 46 33 66 07, open daily at 19:00).

Pompidou Center: The popular and very French **Café de la Cité** has long wooden tables and great lunch specials (inexpensive, 22 rue Rambuteau, Métro: Rambuteau, open daily except Sunday). The **Mélodine** self-service is right at the Rambuteau métro stop.

For an elegant splurge surrounded by lavish art nouveau decor, dine at **Julien** (250F meals with wine, 16 rue du Faubourg St. Denis, Métro: Strasbourg-St. Denis, tel. 47 70 12 06, make reservations).

Near Place de la Concorde: André Fauré serves basic, hearty, all-you-can-eat-and-drink, French farm-style meals for a very good price (40 rue du Mont Thabor, Métro: Concorde Madeleine, tel. 42 60 74 28, open Monday-Saturday 12:00-15:00, 19:00-22:30).

Near the Louvre: L'Incroyable serves *incroyable* meals at an equally *incroyable* price—cheap (26 rue de Richelieu, Métro: Palais-Royal, in a narrow passage between 23 rue de Montpensier and 26 rue de Richelieu, open Tuesday-Saturday 11:45-14:30, 18:30-20:30).

Near the Arc de Triomphe: L'Étoile Verte (The Green Star) is a great working-class favorite (inexpensive, 13 rue Brey, between Wagram and MacMahon, Métro: Étoile).

Three gourmet working-class fixtures in Paris are: **Le Chartier** (7 rue du Faubourge Montmartre, Métro: Montmartre), **Le Commerce** (51 rue du Commerce, Métro: Commerce), and **Le Drouot** (103 rue de Richelieu, Métro: Richelieu-Drouot). Each wrap very cheap and basic food in bustling, unpretentious atmosphere. That's my idea of the best 22 days Europe has to offer. Bon voyage!

TOURIST INFORMATION

Each of these countries has an excellent network of tourist information offices both locally and in the United States. Before your trip, send a letter to each country's National Tourist Office (listed below) telling them of your general plans and asking for information. They'll send you the general packet, and if you ask for specifics (calendars of local events, good hikes around Füssen, castle hotels along the Rhine, the wines of Austria), you'll get an impressive amount of help. If you have a specific problem, they are a good source of help.

During your trip, your first stop in each town should be the tourist office where you'll take your turn at the informational punching bag smiling behind the desk. This person is rushed and tends to be robotic. Prepare. Have a list of questions and a proposed plan to double check with him or her. They have a wealth of material that the average "Duh, do you have a map?" tourist never taps. I have listed phone numbers throughout, and if you'll be arriving late, call ahead.

National Tourist Offices in the U.S.A.

Netherlands National Tourist Office, 355 Lexington Avenue, 21st Floor, New York, NY 10017, (212) 370-7367

German National Tourist Office, 747 Third Avenue, New York, NY 10017, (212) 308-3300; 444 South Flower Street #2230, Los Angeles, CA 90010, (213) 688-7332

Austrian National Tourist Office, 500 Fifth Avenue, Suite 2009, New York, NY 10110, (212) 944-6880; 11601 Wilshire Boulevard 2480, Los Angeles, CA 90025-1703, (213) 477-3332

Italian Government Tourist Office, 630 Fifth Avenue 1565, New York, NY 10020, (212) 245-4822; 360 Post Street, Suite 801, San Francisco, CA 94108 (415) 392-6206

Swiss National Tourist Office, 608 Fifth Avenue, New York, NY 10020, (212) 757-5944; 260 Stockton Street, San Francisco, CA 94108, (415) 362-2260

French Tourist Office, 628 Fifth Avenue, New York, NY 10020, (212) 757-1125

TELEPHONE DIRECTORY

Smart travelers use the telephone every day. Hotel reservations by phone the morning of the day you plan to arrive are a snap. If there's a language problem, ask someone at your hotel to talk to your next hotel for you.

The key to dialing long distance is understanding area codes and having a local phone card. Hotel room phones are reasonable for local calls but a terrible rip-off for long distance calls. Never call home from your hotel room (unless you are putting the call on your credit card).

For calls to other European countries, dial the international access code, followed by the country code, followed by the area code without its zero, and finally the local number (four to seven digits). When dialing long distance within a country, start with the area code (including its zero), then the local number. France has no area codes (see text for long-distance instructions). Phone booths normally have a toll-free English-speaking long-distance information number posted. Phone information in English is often in the first pages of the telephone directory. Post offices have fair metered long-distance booths.

Most countries now have phone cards (worth from $4 to $10; buy at post offices, TIs, and tobacco shops), which are much easier than coins for long-distance calls. Buy one on your first day in each country to force you to find smart reasons to use the local phones. Blow the last of your card with a call home before leaving each country. The old vandal-plagued coin-op phones, which are getting more and more difficult to find, work if you have the necessary pile of coins.

Telephoning the United States from a pay phone is easy if you have a local phone card or an AT&T or MCI credit card or can call with a coin ($1 for 20 seconds) to have the other person call you back at a specified time at your hotel. From the United States, they'd dial 011-country code-area code (without zero)-local number. Europe-to-United States calls are twice as expensive as direct calls from the United States. Midnight in California is breakfast time in Europe.

If you plan to call home often, get an ATT or MCI card. Each card company has a toll-free number in each European country which puts you in touch with an American operator who takes your card number and the number you want to call, puts you through, and bills your home telephone number for the call (at the cheap U.S.A. rate of about a dollar a minute plus a $2.50 service charge). If you talk for 3 minutes, you save more than enough in the rates to cover the $2.50 service charge. MCI and ATT numbers are listed below.

City: Area Code/Tourist Information Number
Amsterdam: 020/626-6444
Haarlem: 023/319059
St. Goar (Rhine): 06741/383
Bacharach: 06743/1297
Rothenburg: 09861/40492
Munich: 089/23911
Füssen: 08362/7077
Reutte (Tirol): 05672/2336
Innsbruck: 0512/5356
Venice: 041/522-6356
Florence: 055/282893
Orvieto: 0763/43884
Vatican: 06/6984466
Rome: 06/488-3748
La Spezia (Cinque Terre): 0187/36000
Monterosso (Cinque Terre): 0187/817506
Interlaken (Jungfrau): 036/22.21.21
Grindelwald: 036/53.12.12
Lauterbrunnen: 036/55.19.55
Bern: 031/227676
Colmar (Alsace): 89-41-02-29
Beaune: 80-22-24-51
Reims: 26-47-25-69
Paris: 01/47-20-88-98 (taped), 47-23-61-72
London: 071/730-3488
Schiphol Airport (Amsterdam) Flight Information: charters—5110666, regular flights—5110432, Paris train information, north and to Britain—42-80-03-03

International Access Codes
USA: 011
Germany: 00
Austria: 050
Italy: 00
Switzerland: 00
France: 19

Country Prefix Codes
Austria: 43
Belgium: 32
Canada: 1
Denmark: 45
England: 44
France: 33
Germany: 49
Greece: 30
Italy: 39
Netherlands: 31
Norway: 47
Portugal: 351
Spain: 34
Sweden: 46
Switzerland: 41
United States: 1

USA Direct Toll-free Credit Card Operators

Country	AT&T	MCI
Netherlands	06-tone-022-9111	06-tone-022-9122
Germany	0130-0010	0130-0012
Austria	022-903-011	022-903-012
Italy	172-1011	172-1022
Switzerland	046-05-011	155-02-22
France	19-tone-00-11	19-tonc-00-19

European Currency Exchange Rates (as of October 1991)

Netherlands—Guilder (f) US$.50
Germany—Deutsch mark (DM) US$.55
Austria—Schilling (S or AS) US$.08
Italy—Lira (L) 1,300 L US$1
Switzerland—Swiss franc (SF or F) US$.65
France—Franc (F) US$.16

Metric Conversions (approximate)

1 inch = 25 millimeters
1 foot = 0.3 meter
36-24-36 = 90-60-90
1 yard = 0.9 meter
1 mile = 1.6 kilometers
1 square yard = 0.8 square meter
1 acre = 0.4 hectare
1 quart = 0.95 liter
1 ounce = 28 grams
32 degrees F = 0 degrees C
82 degrees F = about 28 degrees C
1 kilogram = 2.2 pounds
1 kilometer = .62 mile
1 centimeter = 0.4 inch
1 meter = 39.4 inches

22 DAYS IN EUROPE BY TRAIN

While this itinerary is designed for car travel, it can be adapted for train and bus. The trains take you effortlessly from city to city but can be frustrating in a few rural sections. This itinerary would make a three-week first-class Eurailpass ($550, available from your travel agent or by mail from Europe Through the Back Door—see catalog page) worthwhile, especially for a single traveler. You could use the $450 nine out of twenty-one day Flexipass (see itinerary), but the small fares necessary on the off-days would eat up most of the savings.

Eurailers should know what extras are included on their pass—like any German buses marked "bahn" (run by the train company), boats on the Rhine, Mosel, and Danube rivers and the Swiss lakes, and the Romantic Road bus tour.

A train/bus version of this trip requires some tailoring to avoid areas that are difficult without your own wheels and to take advantage of certain bonuses that train travel offers. Trains in this region are punctual and well organized. Below is an efficient plan and a simple chart of applicable train trips. If you are Eurailing and did not receive a small train schedule, send a request (with your Eurail serial number) to Eurail, Box 10383, Stamford, CT 06904-2383, for your free schedule.

Revised 22 Day Schedule for Train Travelers	
Day	**Sleep in**
1 Arrive in Haarlem	Haarlem
2 Haarlem, sightsee Amsterdam	Haarlem
3* Amsterdam—Arnhem—Koblenz— St. Goar	St.Goar
4 Cruise St. Goar—Bacharach	Bacharach
5* Train—Frankfurt, Romantic Road to Rothenburg	Rothenburg
6* Rothenburg, Romantic Road to Munich	Munich
7 Side trip into Bavaria, castles	Munich
8 Munich	Night train
9* Venice	Venice
10* Venice—Florence	Florence
11 Florence—Orvieto— Bagnoregio/Città	Bagnoregio
12 Bagnoregio—Orvieto—Rome	Rome
13 Rome	Rome
14 Rome	Night train
15* Cinque Terre beaches	Vernazza
16 More Italian Riviera	Night train
17* Bern and Alps	Gimmelwald
18 Hike in Alps	Gimmelwald
19* Interlaken—Bern—Basel—Colmar	Colmar
20 Colmar, Alsace Villages	Night train
21* Paris	Paris
22 Paris	Paris
*travel day if you get a 9 out of 21 day Flexipass	

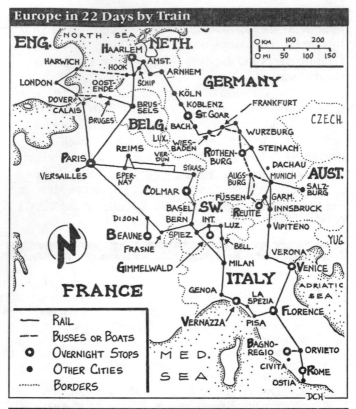

Europe in 22 Days by Train

—	Rail
– –	Busses or Boats
⊙	Overnight Stops
•	Other Cities
....	Borders

Sample Train Schedule

From	To	Approx. Length (hrs.:min.)	Trips per Day
Amsterdam	Paris	6:00	7
Amsterdam	London	7:30	6
Amsterdam	Koblenz	3:45	8
Amsterdam	Frankfurt	6:00	7
Frankfurt	Amsterdam	6:00	11
Frankfurt	München	4:00	17
Frankfurt	Koblenz	1:45	19
Frankfurt	Berlin	8:00	7
München	Amsterdam	8:30	5
München	Innsbruck	1:45	7
München	Frankfurt	3:30	15

Sample Train Schedule cont.

From	To	Approx. Length (hrs.:min.)	Trips per Day
München	Salzburg	2:00	12
München	Venezia	9:00	2
München	Zurich	4:30	5
Innsbruck	München	2:15	8
Innsbruck	Venezia	8:00	2
Venezia	Firenze	3:00	12
Venezia	München	9:00	4
Venezia	Milano	2:30	13
Venezia	Roma	6:00	12
Firenze	Bern	8:00	5
Firenze	Venezia	2:30	6
Firenze	Roma	2:00	13
Roma	Bern	10:00	4
Roma	Genova	5:00	10
Roma	Firenze	2:00	14
Roma	Paris	12:00	6
Genova	Bern	6:30	5
Genova	Nice	3:30	5
Genova	Paris	10:00	6

(Genova is near the Cinque Terre)

From	To	Approx. Length	Trips per Day
Bern	Amsterdam	9:00	5
Bern	Paris	4:30	5
Bern	Genova	6:30	8
Bern	Strasbourg	3:00	7

(Bern is near Interlaken)

From	To	Approx. Length	Trips per Day
Strasbourg	Amsterdam	8:00	3
Strasbourg	Bern	3:00	5
Strasbourg	Paris	3:30	9

(Strasbourg is near Colmar)

From	To	Approx. Length	Trips per Day
Paris	Amsterdam	6:00	9
Paris	London	6:00	9
Paris	Madrid	14:00	5
London	Amsterdam	11:00	8
London	Oostende	5:00	8
London	Paris	7:00	9

Use this information only for planning. The times are approximate. Some *rapido* trains will be shorter trips, just as some milk runs will be longer.

YOUTH HOSTELS

Youth hosteling is the cheapest way to travel. Europe's 2,000 hostels, charging $4 to $10 per night, provide kitchens for self-cooked meals. They have curfews (generally 23:00) and midday lock-ups (usually 9:00-17:00); require sheets (you can rent one) and membership cards ($20 per year from your local U.S. office); and, except for southern Germany, are open to "youths" from 8 to 80. (For a complete listing of Europe's 2,000 hostels, see the *International Youth Hostel Handbook*, vol. 1.) Here are the hostels lying along our 22-day route:

Netherlands: *Amsterdam*—Stadsdoelen, Kloveniers-burgwal 97, 1011 KB Amsterdam; 184 beds; Metro: Niewmarkt; bus 4, 9, 16, 24, 25; tel. 020/624 6832. Vondelpark, Zandpad 5, 1054 GA Amsterdam; 300 beds; bus 1, 2, 5; tel. 020/683 1744. *Haarlem*—Jan Gijzenpad 3, 2024 CL Haarlem-Noord; 108 beds; 3km bus 2, 6; tel. 023/37 37 93.

Germany: *Bacharach*—Jugendburg Stahleck, 6533 Bacharach/Rhein; 207 beds; tel. 06743/1266; wonderful castle hostel, 15 minutes above town, view of Rhine. *Bingen-Bingerbruck*—Herter Str. 51, 6530 Bingen, Bingerbruck/Rhein; 194 beds; tel. 06721/32163. *Oberammergau*—Malensteinweg 10, 8103 Oberammergau; 130 beds; tel. 08822/4114. *Oberwesel*—Jugendgästeus, Auf dem Schönberg, 6532 Oberwesel; 179 beds; tel. 06744/7046. St. Goar—Bismarckweg 17, 5401 St. Goar; 150 beds; tel. 06741/388. *Rothenburg/Tauber*—Rossmühle Muhlacker 1, 8803 Rothenburg/Tauber; 96 beds; tel. 09861/4510. Spitalhof, Postfach 1206, 8803 Rothenburg/Tauber; 90 beds; tel. 09861/4510. *Creglingen*—Erdbacherstr. 30, 6993 Creglingen; 100 beds; tel. 07933/336. *Dinkelsbuhl*—Koppengasse 10, 8804 Dinkelsbuhl; Open March 1-Oct 31; 148 beds; tel. 09851/6509. *München*—Wendl-Dietrich Str. 20, 8000 München 19; trolley 21, 1 Rotkreuzplatz; tel. 089/13 11 56. Jugendgästehaus, Miesingstr. 4, 8000 München 70;

trolley 16, 26, Boschetsrieder Str.; 344 beds; tel. 089/723 6550. *Pullach*—Munich, Burg Schwaneck, Burgweg 4-6, 8023 Pullach; 130 beds; tel. 089/793 0643; a renovated castle. *Füssen*—Mariahilferstr. 5, 8958 Füssen; 150 beds; tel. 08362/7754. *Garmisch-Partenkirchen*—Jochstr. 10, 8100 Garmisch-Partenkirchen; 290 beds; tel. 08821/2980.
Austria: *Reutte*—6600 Reutte, Prof. Dengel-Strasse 20, Tirol; 28 beds; tel. 05672/3039. *Reutte-Hofen*—6600 Reutte, Jugengästehaus am Graben, Postfach 3, Tirol; 38 beds; tel. 05672/264-445. *Innsbruck*—6020 Innsbruck, Reichenauerstr. 147, Tirol; 190 beds; tel. 05222/46179. Studentenheim, 6020 Innsbruck, Reichenauerstr. 147; 112 beds; tel. 0512/46179. 6020 Innsbruck, Rennweg 17b, Tirol; 75 beds; tel. 0512/25814. 6020 Innsbruck, Volkshaus, Radetzkystr. 47; 52 beds; tel. 0512/46 66 82.
Italy: *Venezia*—Fondamenta Zitelle 86, Isola della Giudecca, 30123 Venezia; 320 beds; tel. 041/5238211. *Cortona*—Via Maffei 57, 52044 Cortona; 80 beds; tel. 0575/60 13 92. *Firenze*—Viale Augusto Righi 2-4, 50137 Firenze; 400 beds; tel. 055/60 14 51. Ostello Santa Monaca, via Santa Monaca 6, Firenze; tel. 055/26 83 38; unofficial, no card required. *Lucca*—"Il Serchio," Via del Brennero (Salicchi), 55100 Lucca; 90 beds; tel. 0583/34 18 11. *Roma*—"Aldo Franco Pessina," Viale delle Olimpiadi 61 (Foro Italico), 00194 Roma; 350 beds; tel. 06/396 4709.
Switzerland: *Gimmelwald-Murren*—Mountain Hostel, 3826 Gimmelwald; 44 beds; tel. 036/55 17 04. *Grindelwald*—Terrassenweg, 3818 Grindelwald; 133 beds; tel. 036/53 10 09. *Interlaken-Bonigen*—Aareweg 21, am See, 3806 Bonigen; 200 beds; tel. 036/22 43 53.
France: *Colmar*—2 rue Pasteur, 68000 Colmar (Haut-Rhin); 100 beds; tel. 89 80 57 39. *Paris*—8 boulevard Jules Ferry, 75011 Paris; 99 beds; tel. 1/43 57 55 60. Auberge de Jeunesse Le D'Artagnan, 80 rue Vitruve, 75020 Paris, 400 beds, Métro: Porte de Bagnelet, tel. 1/43 61 08 75.

EUROPEAN FESTIVALS

Each country has an "independence day" celebration. A visit to a country during its national holiday can only make your stay more enjoyable. They are as follows: Austria, October 26; France, July 14; Italy, June 2; Netherlands, April 30; Switzerland, August 1.

Netherlands

Kaasmarkt: Fridays only from late April to late September, colorful cheese market with members of 350-year-old Cheese Carriers' Guild, Alkmaar, 15 miles north of Amsterdam.

North Sea Jazz Festival: Weekend of third Sunday in July, world's greatest jazz weekend, 100 concerts with 500-plus musicians, Den Haag.

Germany

Der Meistertrunk: Saturday before Whit Monday, music, dancing, beer, sausage in Rothenberg ob der Tauber.

Kinderzeche: Weekend before third Monday in July to weekend after, festival honoring children who saved the town in 1640s, Dinkelsbuhl.

Trier Weinfest: Saturday to first Monday in August, Trier.

Der Rhein in Flammen: Second Saturday in August, dancing, wine and beer festivals, bonfires, Koblenz to Braubach.

Moselfest: Last weekend in August or first in September, Mosel wine festival in Winningen.

Backfischfest: Last Saturday in August for 15 days, largest wine and folk festival on the Rhine, in Worms.

Wurstmarkt: Second Saturday in September through following Tuesday, and third Friday through following Monday, world's largest wine festival, in Bad Durkheim, 25 miles west of Heidelberg.

Oktoberfest: Starting third-to-last Saturday in September through first Sunday in October, world's most famous beer festival, Munich.

Austria
Salzburg Festival: late July through August. Greatest music festival, focus on Mozart.

Italy
Sagra del Pesche: Second Sunday in May, one of Italy's great popular events, huge feast of freshly caught fish, fried in world's largest pans, Camogli, ten miles south of Genoa.

Festa de Ceri: May 15, one of the world's most famous folklore events, colorful pageant, giant feast afterward, Gubbio, in hill country 25 miles northeast of Perugia.

Palio of the Archers: Last Sunday in May, reenactment of medieval crossbow contest with arms and costumes, Gubbio, 130 miles northeast of Rome.

Palio: July 2 and August 16, horse race is Italy's most spectacular folklore event, medieval procession before-hand, 35,000 spectators, Siena, 40 miles southwest of Florence.

Joust of the Saracen: First Sunday in September, costumed equestrian tournament dating from thirteenth-century crusades against the Muslim Saracens, Arezzo, 40 miles southeast of Florence.

Historical Regatta: First Sunday in September, gala procession of decorated boats followed by double-oared gondola race, Venice.

Human Chess Game: First or second weekend in September in even-numbered years, medieval pageantry and splendor accompany reenactment of human chess game in 1454, Basso Castle in Marostica, 40 miles northwest of Venice.

Switzerland
Landsgemeinde: First Sunday in May, largest open-air parliamentary session, Glarus, 40 miles southeast of Zurich.

Montreux International Jazz Festival: First through third weekends in July, comprehensive annual musical events featuring top artists, Montreux.

William Tell Plays: Second Thursday in July through first

Sunday in September, dramatic presentations retelling the story of William Tell, open-air theater, Interlaken.

Swiss National Day: August 1, festive national holiday, parades, concerts, bell ringing, fireworks, yodeling, boat rides, nationwide.

France

Tour de France: First three weeks of July, 2,000-mile bike race around France ending in Paris.

Bastille Day: July 13 and 14, great national holiday all over France, Paris has biggest festivities.

Alsace Wine Fair: Second and third weekends in August, Colmar.

Festival of Minstrels: First Sunday in September, wine, music, folklore, etc., Ribeauville, 35 miles south of Strasbourg.

Fête d'Humanite: Second or third Saturday and Sunday in September, huge communist fair, colorful festivities—not all red, Paris.

WEATHER CHART

Here is a list of average temperatures and days of no rain. This can be helpful in planning your itinerary, but I have never found European weather to be particularly predictable.

(1st line, average daily low; 2nd line, avg. daily high; 3rd line, days of no rain)

	J	F	M	A	M	J	J	A	S	O	N	D
France	32°	34°	36°	41°	47°	52°	55°	55°	50°	44°	38°	33°
Paris	42°	45°	52°	60°	67°	73°	76°	75°	69°	59°	49°	43°
	16	15	16	16	18	19	19	19	19	17	15	14
Germany	29°	31°	35°	41°	48°	53°	56°	55°	51°	43°	36°	31°
Frankfurt	37°	42°	49°	58°	67°	72°	75°	74°	67°	56°	45°	39°
	22	19	22	21	22	21	21	21	21	22	21	20
Great Britain	35°	35°	37°	40°	45°	51°	55°	54°	51°	44°	39°	36°
London	44°	45°	51°	56°	63°	69°	73°	72°	67°	58°	49°	45°
	14	15	20	16	18°	19°	18	18	17	17	14	15
Italy	39°	39°	42°	46°	55°	60°	64°	64°	61°	53°	46°	41°
Rome	54°	56°	62°	68°	74°	82°	88°	88°	83°	73°	63°	56°
	23	17	26	24	25	28	29	28	24	22	22	22
Netherlands	34°	34°	37°	43°	50°	55°	59°	59°	56°	48°	41°	35°
Amsterdam	40°	41°	46°	52°	60°	65°	69°	68°	64°	56°	47°	41°
	12	13	18	16	19	18	17	17	15	13	11	12
Switzerland	29°	30°	35°	41°	48°	55°	58°	57°	52°	44°	37°	31°
Geneva	39°	43°	51°	58°	66°	73°	77°	76°	69°	58°	47°	40°
	20	19	21	19	19	19	22	21	20	20	19	21

INDEX

Rick Steves' BACK DOOR CATALOG

*All items field tested, highly recommended, completely guaran-
teed, discounted below retail and ideal for independent, mobile
travelers. Prices include tax (if applicable), handling, and postage.*

The Back Door Suitcase / Rucksack $70.00

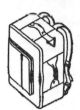

At 9"x22"x14" this specially designed, sturdy functional
bag is maximum carry-on-the-plane size (fits under the
seat) and your key to foot-loose and fancy-free travel.
Made of rugged water resistant Cordura nylon, it converts
easily from a smart-looking suitcase to a handy rucksack.
It has hide-away padded shoulder straps, top and side
handles and a detachable shoulder strap (for toting as a
suitcase). Lockable perimeter zippers allow easy access to
the roomy (2,700 cubic inches) central compartment. Two
large outside pockets are perfect for frequently used
items. Also included is one nylon stuff bag. Over 40,000 Back Door
travelers have used these bags around the world. Rick Steves helped design
and lives out of this bag for 3 months at a time. Comparable bags cost much
more. Available in navy blue, black, or grey.

Moneybelt $8.00

This required, ultra-light, sturdy, under-the-pants, nylon
pouch just big enough to carry the essentials (passport, airline ticket, travelers checks, and so on) comfortably. I'll
never travel without one and I hope you won't either. Beige,
nylon zipper, one size fits nearly all, with "manual."

Catalog FREE

For a complete listing of all the books, travel videos,
products and services Rick Steves and Europe Through the
Back Door offer you, ask us for our 64-page catalog.

Eurailpasses . . .

...cost the same everywhere. We carefully examine each
order and include for no extra charge a 90-minute Rick
Steves VHS video Train User's Guide, helpful itinerary
advice, Eurail train schedule booklet and map, plus a free
22 Days book of your choice! Send us a check for the cost
of the pass(es) you want along with your legal name (as it
appears on your passport), a proposed itinerary (including
dates and places of entry and exit if known), choice of 22 Days book
(Europe, Brit, Spain/Port, Scand, France, or Germ/Switz/Aust) and a list of
questions. Within 2 weeks of receiving your order we'll send you your
pass(es) and any other information pertinent to your trip. Due to this unique service Rick Steves sells more passes than anyone on the West Coast
and you'll have an efficient and expertly-organized Eurail trip.

Back Door Tours

We encourage independent travel, but for those who want
a tour in the Back Door style, we do offer a 22-day "Best of
Europe" tour. For complete details, send for our free 64
page tour booklet/catalog.

*All orders will be processed within 2 weeks and include tax (where applicable),
shipping and a one year's subscription to our Back Door Travel newsletter.
Prices good through 1993. Rush orders add $5. Sorry, no credit cards. Send
checks to:*

**Europe Through The Back Door ● 120 Fourth Ave. N.
Box C-2009 ● Edmonds, WA 98020 ● (206) 771-8303**

Other Books from John Muir Publications

Adventure Vacations: From Trekking in New Guinea to Swimming in Siberia, Bangs 256 pp. $17.95

Asia Through the Back Door, 3rd ed., Steves and Gottberg 326 pp. $15.95

Belize: A Natural Destination, Mahler, Wotkyns, Schafer 304 pp $16.95

Buddhist America: Centers, Retreats, Practices, Morreale 400 pp. $12.95

Bus Touring: Charter Vacations, U.S.A., Warren with Bloch 168 pp. $9.95

California Public Gardens: A Visitor's Guide, Sigg 304 pp. $16.95

Catholic America: Self-Renewal Centers and Retreats, Christian-Meyer 325 pp. $13.95

Costa Rica: A Natural Destination, Sheck 280 pp. $15.95 (**2nd ed.** available 3/92 $16.95)

Elderhostels: The Students' Choice, 2nd ed., Hyman 312 pp. $15.95

Environmental Vacations: Volunteer Projects to Save the Planet, Ocko 240 pp. $15.95 (**2nd ed.** available 2/92 $16.95)

Europe 101: History & Art for the Traveler, 4th ed., Steves and Openshaw 372 pp. $15.95

Europe Through the Back Door, 9th ed., Steves 432 pp. $16.95 (**10th ed.** available 1/92 $16.95)

Floating Vacations: River, Lake, and Ocean Adventures, White 256 pp. $17.95

Great Cities of Eastern Europe, Rapoport 240 pp. $16.95

Gypsying After 40: A Guide to Adventure and Self-Discovery, Harris 264 pp. $14.95

The Heart of Jerusalem, Nellhaus 336 pp. $12.95

Indian America: A Traveler's Companion, 2nd ed., Eagle/Walking Turtle 448 pp. $17.95

Mona Winks: Self-Guided Tours of Europe's Top Museums, Steves and Openshaw 456 pp. $14.95

Opera! The Guide to Western Europe's Great Houses, Zietz 296 pp. $18.95

Paintbrushes and Pistols: How the Taos Artists Sold the West, Taggett and Schwarz 280 pp. $17.95

The People's Guide to Mexico, 8th ed., Franz 608 pp. $17.95

The People's Guide to RV Camping in Mexico, Franz with Rogers 320 pp. $13.95

Ranch Vacations: The Complete Guide to Guest and Resort, Fly-Fishing, and Cross-Country Skiing Ranches, 2nd ed., Kilgore 396 pp. $18.95

The Shopper's Guide to Art and Crafts in the Hawaiian Islands, Schuchter 272 pp. $13.95

The Shopper's Guide to Mexico, Rogers and Rosa 224 pp. $9.95

Ski Tech's Guide to Equipment, Skiwear, and Accessories, ed. Tanler 144 pp. $11.95

Ski Tech's Guide to Maintenance and Repair, ed. Tanler 160 pp. $11.95

A Traveler's Guide to Asian Culture, Chambers 224 pp. $13.95

Traveler's Guide to Healing Centers and Retreats in North America, Rudee and Blease 240 pp. $11.95

Understanding Europeans, Miller 272 pp. $14.95

Undiscovered Islands of the Caribbean, 2nd ed., Willes 232 pp. $14.95

Undiscovered Islands of the Mediterranean, Moyer and Willes 232 pp. $14.95

Undiscovered Islands of the U.S. and Canadian West Coast, Moyer and Willes 208 pp. $12.95

A Viewer's Guide to Art: A Glossary of Gods, People, and Creatures, Shaw and Warren 144 pp. $10.95

2 to 22 Days Series

Each title offers 22 flexible daily itineraries that can be used to get the most out of vacations of any length. Included are not only "must see" attractions but also little-known villages and hidden "jewels" as well as valuable general information.

22 Days Around the World, 1992 ed., Rapoport and Willes 256 pp. $12.95
2 to 22 Days Around the Great Lakes, 1992 ed., Schuchter 192 pp. $9.95
22 Days in Alaska, Lanier 128 pp. $7.95
2 to 22 Days in the American Southwest, 1992 ed., Harris 176 pp. $9.95
2 to 22 Days in Asia, 1992 ed., Rapoport and Willes 176 pp. $9.95
2 to 22 Days in Australia, 1992 ed., Gottberg 192 pp. $9.95
22 Days in California, 2nd ed., Rapoport 176 pp. $9.95
22 Days in China, Duke and Victor 144 pp. $7.95
2 to 22 Days in Europe, 1992 ed., Steves 276 pp. $12.95
2 to 22 Days in Florida, 1992 ed., Harris 192 pp. $9.95
2 to 22 Days in France, 1992 ed., Steves 192 pp. $9.95
2 to 22 Days in Germany, Austria, & Switzerland, 1992 ed., Steves 224 pp. $9.95
2 to 22 Days in Great Britain, 1992 ed., Steves 192 pp. $9.95
2 to 22 Days in Hawaii, 1992 ed., Schuchter 176 pp. $9.95
22 Days in India, Mathur 136 pp. $7.95
22 Days in Japan, Old 136 pp. $7.95
22 Days in Mexico, 2nd ed., Rogers and Rosa 128 pp. $7.95
2 to 22 Days in New England, 1992 ed., Wright 192 pp. $9.95
2 to 22 Days in New Zealand, 1991 ed., Schuchter 176 pp. $9.95
2 to 22 Days in Norway, Sweden, & Denmark, 1992 ed., Steves 192 pp. $9.95
2 to 22 Days in the Pacific Northwest, 1992 ed. Harris 192 pp. $9.95
2 to 22 Days in the Rockies, 1992 ed. Rapoport 192 pp. $9.95
2 to 22 Days in Spain & Portugal, 1992 ed., Steves 192 pp. $9.95
22 Days in Texas, Harris 176 pp. $9.95
22 Days in Thailand, Richardson 176 pp. $9.95
22 Days in the West Indies, Morreale and Morreale 136 pp. $7.95

Parenting Series

Being a Father: Family, Work, and Self, *Mothering* Magazine
176 pp. $12.95

**Preconception: A Woman's Guide to Preparing for Pregnancy
and Parenthood,** Aikey-Keller 232 pp. $14.95

Schooling at Home: Parents, Kids, and Learning, *Mothering*
Magazine 264 pp. $14.95

Teens: A Fresh Look, *Mothering* Magazine 240 pp. $14.95

"Kidding Around" Travel Guides for Young Readers
Written for kids eight years of age and older.

Kidding Around Atlanta, Pedersen 64 pp. $9.95
Kidding Around Boston, Byers 64 pp. $9.95
Kidding Around Chicago, Davis 64 pp. $9.95
Kidding Around the Hawaiian Islands, Lovett 64 pp. $9.95
Kidding Around London, Lovett 64 pp. $9.95
Kidding Around Los Angeles, Cash 64 pp. $9.95
Kidding Around the National Parks of the Southwest, Lovett
108 pp. $12.95
Kidding Around New York City, Lovett 64 pp. $9.95
Kidding Around Paris, Clay 64 pp. $9.95
Kidding Around Philadelphia, Clay 64 pp. $9.95
Kidding Around San Diego, Luhrs 64 pp. $9.95
Kidding Around San Francisco, Zibart 64 pp. $9.95
Kidding Around Santa Fe, York 64 pp. $9.95
Kidding Around Seattle, Steves 64 pp. $9.95
Kidding Around Spain, Biggs 108 pp. $12.95
Kidding Around Washington, D.C., Pedersen 64 pp. $9.95

Environmental Books for Young Readers
Written for kids eight years of age and older.

The Indian Way: Learning to Communicate with Mother Earth,
McLain 114 pp. $9.95

The Kids' Environment Book: What's Awry and Why, Pedersen
192 pp. $13.95

**Rads, Ergs, and Cheeseburgers: The Kids' Guide to Energy and
the Environment,** Yanda 108 pp. $12.95

"Extremely Weird" Series for Young Readers
Written for kids eight years of age and older.

Extremely Weird Bats, Lovett 48 pp. $9.95
Extremely Weird Frogs, Lovett 48 pp. $9.95
Extremely Weird Primates, Lovett 48 pp. $9.95
Extremely Weird Reptiles, Lovett 48 pp. $9.95
Extremely Weird Spiders, Lovett 48 pp. $9.95

Quill Hedgehog Adventures Series
Written for kids eight years of age and older. Our new series of
green fiction for kids follows the adventures of Quill Hedgehog and
his Animalfolk friends.

Quill's Adventures in the Great Beyond, Waddington-Feather
96 pp. $5.95

Quill's Adventures in Wasteland, Waddington-Feather 132 pp.
$5.95
Quill's Adventures in Grozzieland, Waddington-Feather 132 pp.
$5.95

Other Young Readers Titles
Kids Explore America's Hispanic Heritage, edited by Cozzens
112 pp. $7.95 (avail. 2/92)

Automotive Repair Manuals
How to Keep Your VW Alive, 14th ed., 440 pp. $21.95
How to Keep Your Subaru Alive 480 pp. $21.95
How to Keep Your Toyota Pickup Alive 392 pp. $21.95
How to Keep Your Datsun/Nissan Alive 544 pp. $21.95

Other Automotive Books
**The Greaseless Guide to Car Care Confidence: Take the Terror
Out of Talking to Your Mechanic,** Jackson 224 pp. $14.95
Off-Road Emergency Repair & Survival, Ristow 160 pp. $9.95

Ordering Information
If you cannot find our books in your local bookstore, you can order
directly from us. Please check the "Available" date above. If you
send us money for a book not yet available, we will hold your money
until we can ship you the book. Your books will be sent to you via
UPS (for U.S. destinations). UPS will not deliver to a P.O. Box;
please give us a street address. Include $3.25 for the first item
ordered and $.50 for each additional item to cover shipping and
handling costs. For airmail within the U.S., enclose $4.00. All foreign
orders will be shipped surface rate; please enclose $3.00 for the
first item and $1.00 for each additional item. Please inquire about
foreign airmail rates.

Method of Payment
Your order may be paid by check, money order, or credit card. We
cannot be responsible for cash sent through the mail. All payments
must be made in U.S. dollars drawn on a U.S. bank. Canadian
postal money orders in U.S. dollars are acceptable. For VISA,
MasterCard, or American Express orders, include your card number, expiration date, and your signature, or call (800) 888-7504.
Books ordered on American Express cards can be shipped only to
the billing address of the cardholder. Sorry, no C.O.D.'s. Residents
of sunny New Mexico, add 5.875% tax to the total.

Address all orders and inquiries to:
    John Muir Publications
    P.O. Box 613
    Santa Fe, NM 87504
    (505) 982-4078
    (800) 888-7504